THE SECRET
VYSOČANY CONGRESS

Proceedings and Documents of the
Extraordinary Fourteenth Congress of the
Communist Party of Czechoslovakia,
22 August 1968

*

EDITED AND WITH AN
INTRODUCTION BY JIŘÍ PELIKÁN

*Translated from the Czech by
George Theiner and
Deryck Viney*

ALLEN LANE THE PENGUIN PRESS

JN 2229
A5 K6
1968a

105374

Printed in Great Britain by
Latimer Trend & Co. Ltd, Plymouth
Set in Monotype Times New Roman

Contents

Contents

An international proletarian movement is only possible amongst independent nations. . . . They had to learn, and must go on learning, from daily experience that international co-operation is possible only among equals *and that even a* primus inter pares *can only enjoy this role for short-term purposes.*

Friedrich Engels, from a letter to Karl Kautsky, 1882

We must distinguish between the nationalism of an oppressor nation and the nationalism of an oppressed nation, the nationalism of a great nation and the nationalism of a small one.

As regards the second sort of nationalism we, as members of a big nation, have almost always in historical practice been found guilty of an endless chain of oppression, and what is more we still commit acts of oppression and behave offensively without realizing it ourselves . . .

That is why the internationalism of an oppressor, or if you like 'great', nation (sometimes great only in the extent of its oppression like a 'great tyrant') must consist not only in the maintenance of a formal equality of nations, but also in such a degree of inequality as will allow the big, oppressor, nation to compensate for the inequality created in practice. Anyone who fails to understand this has failed properly to understand the proletarian standpoint on the question of nationalities; he has to all intents and purposes retained a petit-bourgeois standpoint and is therefore bound at any moment to go over to the bourgeois standpoint.

V. I. Lenin, *Collected Works*, vol. 36, p. 585*

* All references in this book to Lenin's *Collected Works* are to the Czech edition, published by Svoboda Publishing House, Prague.

I

Introduction

The protocols and documents emanating from the congresses of political parties interest as a rule only those who are themselves politicians or political theorists and commentators. The material in this book forms an exception. It is no exaggeration to say that it is one of the most extraordinary documents of contemporary history.

It has never happened before that the congress of a communist party in power in a socialist country had to meet illegally because that country was occupied by the armies of other socialist lands.

It has never happened before that the results of that congress, properly convened and held in accordance with the constitution of the party concerned, could not be published in that country.

It has never happened before that the leading representatives of a ruling communist party were prevented from taking part in their party's congress; they were first of all surrounded by the tanks of other socialist countries while attending a meeting in the building of their party's central committee, and then arrested and brutally abducted to another socialist country, where, under duress, they were made to 'annul' the results achieved by the congress of their own party.

All this took place in August 1968 in Czechoslovakia, a socialist country in the centre of Europe, where the Extraordinary Fourteenth Congress of the Communist Party of Czechoslovakia met under the conditions described above.

The following is a brief summary of the events leading up to the Congress:

The plenary session of the Central Committee of the KSČ* on 1 June 1968 unanimously approved a resolution which stated that, in accordance with Article 24 of the Party's constitution, the Extraordinary Fourteenth Congress would convene on 9 September 1968. The Congress was referred to as 'extraordinary' because the 'ordinary' Fourteenth Congress was not due until 1970, four years after

* *Komunistická strana Československa*: Communist Party of Czechoslovakia.

1

the Thirteenth Congress of 1966. Giving the reasons for this, the resolution said:

> The Central Committee of the KSČ, having duly reviewed the situation within the Party, has taken this decision because it finds it necessary to settle the Party's political line for the months to come and to elect a new Central Committee which will enjoy absolute confidence and have the necessary authority to ensure concerted action by the whole Party.

This was a logical consequence of the new political situation created after the Central Committee's plenary session in January 1968, when it was decided to abolish the practice of combining the office of the First Secretary of the Party with that of the President of the Republic, both of which had hitherto been in the hands of Antonín Novotný, and when the first steps were taken to ensure the growth of socialist democracy and to initiate the reformist movement which came to be known as the 'Prague Spring' or as 'socialism with a human face'.

Preparations for the Extraordinary Fourteenth Congress of the KSČ were made with the unprecedented co-operation of all communists and of the public as a whole, the entire nation showing itself in favour of the post-January policies and lending its support to the Party leadership headed by Alexander Dubček. Delegates to the Fourteenth Congress were elected at local, district and regional Party conferences held during June and July 1968. Committees whose task it was to prepare the Congress material also sat at this time, while the published draft of the new Party constitution was discussed in the press. There can be no doubt – as will be borne out by the Party documents, many of which appear at the end of this book – that the Extraordinary Fourteenth Congress of the KSČ would have meant the complete victory of the post-January policies, that it would have increased the Party's authority and strengthened its leading role in the endeavour to bring about a rebirth of socialism, and thereby would also have led to a general stabilization of the political situation in Czechoslovakia.

This is exactly what the military intervention of the five Warsaw Pact countries on the night of 20 August 1968 was intended to prevent. The representatives of the bureaucratic police-state concept of socialism had waited, although the military occupation of Czechoslovakia had been prepared long before, in the hope that disagreements within the Party would topple the KSČ leadership. Their efforts to bring this about culminated in the so-called Letter of the Five (i.e. the Communist Parties of the USSR, Poland, East Germany, Hungary and Bulgaria), drafted in Warsaw on 15 July 1968. In this letter the representatives of these five parties directly urged the hard-liners in Czechoslovakia to rise in opposition to their own Party leadership, which had the support of the overwhelming majority of communists and of the nation as a whole. However, they achieved exactly the opposite. The Party and the people of Czechoslovakia became even more united than before, in a way that has no parallel in the post-war history of Czechoslovakia.

As the date of the Fourteenth Congress approached it became increasingly clear that the hopes of overthrowing the KSČ leadership were in vain. As a result, half a million soldiers armed to the teeth and equipped with planes, tanks and rockets had to be sent to occupy Czechoslovakia and thus prevent the Extraordinary Fourteenth Congress from being held.

Yet even in this case their calculations failed. The Presidium of the Central Committee of the KSČ, which happened to be in session on the night of the invasion, discussing preparations for the Congress, condemned the armed intervention of the five Warsaw Pact powers. The entire Party supported this condemnation. Neither the arrest of Alexander Dubček, Josef Smrkovský, František Kriegel, Oldřich Černík and other leading KSČ representatives, nor the attempt made by the hard-liners to set up a so-called revolutionary government of the workers and peasants under Alois Indra, succeeded in breaking the unity of the communists. A broadcast appeal brought Congress delegates flocking to Prague by train and by car, by bicycle and on foot. Since it was essential to keep the location of the Congress secret, the delegates were told to report at several of the largest Prague factories, from which workers took them to the meeting place. Taking into account the atmosphere prevailing in the country during the first few days of the occupation, the transport and communication facilities, the patrols carried out by the occupying forces, and the fact that the delegates came from all over the country, the presence after so short a time of 1,290 delegates (i.e. more than two-thirds of all those elected to the Congress) in the Prague industrial district of Vysočany bears witness to the high political maturity and the courage and enthusiasm of the delegates, as well as to the way in which, at that time, the Party expressed the feelings and wishes of the majority of Czechoslovakia's inhabitants. This account of the 'Vysočany Riot', as Leonid Brezhnev called it, will undoubtedly go down in history as one of the most glorious in the annals of the Communist Party of Czechoslovakia.

All this has to be borne in mind when one reads the unique protocol of the first session of the Extraordinary Fourteenth Congress of the K S Č, here published* for the first time. Owing to the dramatic circumstances attending the Congress, it is easy to understand why this protocol was made not on the basis of shorthand notes, but instead from a tape recording. Since the only microphone was on the speaker's rostrum, it was impossible to record some of the proceedings, in particular those speeches made by delegates from their seats during the discussion periods. For the same reason the names of the speakers are not always on record, and it has not been possible to identify those who presided at the individual sessions, a function undertaken in turn by the various members of the Congress Presidium. All the speeches were extempore. No texts had been prepared beforehand, and the proceedings were frequently interrupted by warnings of troop movements in the vicinity of the Congress building and announcements about the situation in Prague and in Czechoslovakia as a whole. Nevertheless, the editors have refrained from making any alterations to the record except for linguistic corrections, adhering strictly to the principle that only grammatical errors should be corrected, either in the speeches or in the other material. Some parts of the proceedings were lost when tapes were changed, others are almost inaudible owing to the difficult conditions under which the Congress had to meet. A factory hall had to be hurriedly adapted for a conference with 1,300 delegates and there was none of the usual amplifying and recording equipment. None of the committee meetings could be taped at all. Once normal conditions are restored in Czechoslovakia, it will doubtless become possible, by collating the various existing records and enlisting the help of a sizable number of participants, to compile an accurate protocol of this Congress which, despite the attendant difficulties, was in every respect the most democratic of all K S Č Congresses. It was the first one since the war which, because it was not carefully staged down to

* The reference is to the German translation, published in 1969 by Europa Verlag. The present book is the first English translation.

the last technical detail as had usually been the case, gave everyone a genuine opportunity to make his opinions felt. Hardly anything had been decided beforehand. It was a working Congress in the real sense of the word, in total contrast to the old bombastic, ritual Congresses at which bureaucrats arranged to have themselves praised in Byzantine fashion by the rank-and-file and repeatedly 'voted' into the highest offices, being themselves their own nominees. The 1968 Congress was destined to be the last act of the post-January reforms, but it was a dignified, independent and sovereign ending, in keeping with the best democratic traditions of Czechs and Slovaks. Thus will it go down in the history of our times.

Apart from the actual Congress proceedings, the reader can also acquaint himself in the following pages with the work of several groups of experts, totalling some hundred historians, economists, philosophers, political theorists, sociologists and professional politicians, all of them members of the KSČ. The authors of these texts drafted for the purposes of the Congress have never belonged, and do not belong today, to either of the extreme, radical wings; they are not 'right-wingers' and still less are they 'left-wingers' in the sense of current official terminology. Their views and attitudes place them somewhere in the centre, perhaps even the moderate centre. This 'centre' is sober in its thinking, showed considerable tolerance and tried to take into account as many internal and international political factors as possible. It also wished to avoid designing any utopias or going too far in anticipating future developments, being well aware that the very nature of the documents that were to form the Congress programme made it impossible for them to be conceived on an exclusively scientific basis. It was responsible for three of the documents published in this book:

1. The draft 'theses' of the Party's programme which, after being discussed at the Extraordinary Fourteenth Congress, were to provide the basis for a 'definitive' political programme, to be approved at the next, Fifteenth, Congress of the KSČ (pp. 100–124);
2. The draft of a new Party constitution, which had already been the subject of discussion when published in the daily press (pp. 128–85);
3. The main report for the Extraordinary Fourteenth Congress of

the KSČ, which was at the same time to form the gist of the main speech by the First Secretary and provide subjects for discussion by the delegates (pp. 187–253).

The careful reader will not fail to notice one thing which all the documents have in common: they show the urgent need for fundamental reforms in the entire socialist system in Czechoslovakia, from the necessity of formulating anew both its short- and long-term aims, through a far-reaching reform of the economy and the political system, right down to a reform of the mechanism of the ruling Communist Party itself.

The need for some of these reforms had made itself felt in Czechoslovakia long before January 1968. The general outlines of certain economic reforms had already been approved during the reign of Antonín Novotný, and even the preparatory efforts of a scientific team set up to consider the reform of the Czechoslovak political system were tolerated. The dividing line between the progressives and the 'conservatives' did not run between the supporters and opponents of reform, but rather between those who were in favour of fundamental and general reform, including reform of the political system of socialism, and those who did not wish to go so far, recommending instead a limited programme of partial reforms dealing primarily with the economy, and even then only in the sense of 'improving' the existing system.

It is here that we must seek the true *casus belli*, which culminated in outright confrontation. Had this been merely a confrontation of domestic forces, the outcome would never have been in doubt and would most probably not have necessitated the use of any means other than political ones.

The draft programme was thus compiled with a view to the need for essential economic, political and Party reforms, having regard to the indivisible unity of democracy and socialism, as well as to the differing interests of the individual, various groups and society as a whole on the one hand, and on the other their compatibility and their complementary character in a socialist community. In all its previous political programmes, in so far as the KSČ had drafted them on its own over the past few decades, it had invariably been content mechanically to adopt Soviet programmes, or else had declared uncritical devotion to them. In these programmes socialism

6

was taken to mean a society with socialized means of production and with a planned economy, a society without an exploiting class; and its further development was seen in the continued rise of material prosperity and improved living conditions, the yardstick in this respect being, somewhat paradoxically, the much-maligned capitalist world. How else can one explain the famous slogan, no longer heard these days, about 'catching up with and outstripping' capitalism?

In contrast to this earlier concept of the Party's programme, the 'Draft Theses' did not see in the socialization of the means of production or in the planned economy an end in itself but merely *a starting point and method for the gradual and endless process of liberating man from various kinds of oppression*, including the division of labour, production relations, coercive manipulation by uncontrollable forces and even the role of the State itself.

The process of regeneration that took place in Czechoslovakia in 1968 and was known abroad as the 'Prague Spring' contained yet one more striking feature which set it apart from similar movements in other socialist countries. All these movements – *mutatis mutandis* – had demanded a certain liberalization of public life and greater control of State power. The Czechoslovak debate on this subject was markedly different in that it laid the main emphasis on the creation of actual guarantees to enable democracy to work in practice. Czechoslovakia was concerned with the practical safeguarding of the autonomous position of the various components of the political system and with the creation of conditions under which public opinion could really make itself felt, so that the ruling élite could no longer interfere with the fundamental civic rights of the individual, much less with the rights of whole groups of people or nations. Democracy was thus to pass from the sphere of verbal promises into legally codified practice for which the necessary structure was to have been created.

In this connection the reader may find the draft of the new Party Statutes interesting, for it was conceived as the practical application of the spirit of the Czechoslovak process of regeneration to the everyday activity of the Party. This document was aimed at giving wider rights to the individual Party members *vis-à-vis* Party institutions. The same applied to the primary organizations, who would also have greater autonomy in their dealings with higher Party organs, and minority opinion was to be respected even when outvoted by the majority, thus leaving open the possibility – to quote a Chinese communist saying of more than a decade ago – 'that today's minority might become the majority of tomorrow'.

The new draft Party Statutes therefore presupposed not only far greater autonomy among the individual Party organizations but also the creation of horizontal connections between the various organizations, to which the Party bureaucrats had been strongly opposed, quite rightly fearing the diminution of their hitherto unchallenged power.

A note on pp. 128–9 draws attention to some of the passages of the revised Draft Statutes which compare most strikingly with the preliminary version printed on the facing pages. A watchful reader will note the zeal with which senior bureaucrats amended the original text, drafted by a group of Party experts, and infer which passages they found most disturbing.

Another document included in this book is the 'analysis' prepared by a group of specialists in the history of modern Czechoslovakia, which was to provide material for the opening address by the First Secretary, Alexander Dubček, as well as for the general discussion with which the Congress was to begin. This report reviews developments from the Thirteenth Congress of the Party in June 1966 up to the Extraordinary Fourteenth Congress which was to take place in September 1968, analysing the causes of the Czechoslovak crisis and the circumstances under which that crisis came to a head in January 1968. As the report sums up the events of the past two years, it necessarily repeats some of the basic ideas and theses contained in the other two documents, but it provides a great deal of important information for anyone not intimately acquainted with the problems involved.

In this spirit we lay these documents before the world public as a contribution by Czechoslovak communists to the debate on the further development of socialism and modern society. However modest, this contribution is all the more significant when one recalls the tragic price that was paid for it.

II

Excerpts from Documents on the
Preparation of the Extraordinary Fourteenth
Congress of the Czechoslovak
Communist Party*

Alexander Dubček's Report to the Plenary Session of the Party's Central Committee, 29 May 1968 (excerpts):

. . What, then, are the main tasks confronting us today?

We must, first and foremost, decisively dissociate ourselves – our whole Party – from the deformations of the past. We must, in particular, dissociate ourselves from the crimes of the fifties, for which certain groups in the Party leadership were responsible, groups which ceased to be controlled by the Party, placing themselves above the Party and its members, as well as above society and the laws of the land; they abandoned and discredited the communist ideals of our Party, as well as the democratic and socialist ideals of our whole society . . .

Communists demand that the Party dissociate itself, clearly and unequivocally, from all the deformations of the past, and that it part company with those who bear the chief responsibility for these deformations. They demand that the Party provide clear and convincing guarantees that there will be no return to the old, bureaucratic methods of administration, and especially no return to the deformations which so tragically marked the fifties.

Have we given such guarantees? In some respects we undoubtedly have. During the past four months the Party leadership has quite unmistakably dissociated itself from the methods that were typical of conditions prevailing before January . . . . We have fundamentally altered the composition of the Central Committee's organs and its leading personnel, yet both communists and people outside the Party

* All the excerpts from official documents in this chapter are quoted from *The Year 1968 in the Resolutions and Documents of the Central Committee of the Czechoslovak Communist Party*, Svoboda Publishing House, Prague, 1969, pp. 183–297.

9

complain that the highest Party organ still contains certain comrades who have lost the confidence of Party members as well as of the public at large . . .

How are we to discard the errors of the past? How are we to provide everyone with guarantees that our road will lead neither to the conditions before January of this year, nor to the conditions before February 1948, much less to the conditions that existed before 1938; that our road leads only forward, to a higher phase of socialist development? . . .

Our most urgent task is to put the Party as a whole in the forefront of our social development, to enable it to fulfil its leading role under changed conditions.

In view of certain new circumstances, a thorough reform of the Party requires that the Extraordinary Fourteenth Party Congress be called as soon as possible. Without it we cannot create within the Party definitive guarantees that the new policy will be consistently implemented. We therefore propose to convoke the Congress on 9 September 1968.

We are convinced that the Congress will endorse the line we adopted last January and will create the necessary conditions for the formation of a new political line. We must assess the political developments in our country since the Thirteenth Party Congress and since the January session of the Central Committee, and we must decide on the political and tactical action our Party is to take in the immediate future . . . . It will also be up to the Congress to approve the Party's new statutes and to elect a new Central Committee which will have full authority to improve and defend the unity and efficiency of the Party, which will stand in the forefront of the Party's united and organized action in implementing the resolutions of the Congress . . .

Resolution on the Current Situation and Further Party Action, Passed by the Central Committee Plenum on 1 June 1968 (excerpt):

. . . The Central Committee of the Czechoslovak Communist Party is convinced that a thorough reform of the Party necessitates the convocation of an Extraordinary Fourteenth Congress at the beginning of September 1968, for without such a Congress, the Party cannot fully solve the problem of creating all the guarantees of a consistent implementation of the new policy. The Party Congress agenda will be as follows. It will:

(a) discuss developments since the Thirteenth Party Congress, and in particular since the January plenum of the Central Committee; evaluate the basic trends in the development of our society and Party; on the strength of this evaluation determine the Party's political line in the coming period . . .

(b) discuss the progress made in rehabilitating wrongly persecuted comrades and apportioning the responsibility the former Party leadership must bear for the illegalities of the past;

(c) adopt new Party Statutes, which will give detailed expression to the principles of Party democracy and of its working methods;

(d) elect a new Central Committee and a Central Control and Audit Commission.

The Central Committee considers it essential to carry out preparations for the Extraordinary Fourteenth Congress of the Party as speedily and responsibly as possible. It believes that it is necessary to organize all this preparatory work and the election of the delegates in such a way as to enable the Congress to be held at the beginning of September, so that . . . the Communist Party of Czechoslovakia may emerge as the leading political force in the country . . .

The Central Committee's Resolution on the Convocation of an Extraordinary Fourteenth Congress, Passed by the Central Committee Plenum on 1 June 1968 (excerpts):

In accordance with Article 24 of the Party Statutes, the plenary session of the Central Committee of the Czechoslovak Communist Party held between 29 May and 1 June 1968 decided to hold the Extraordinary Fourteenth Party Congress in Prague, beginning on 9 September 1968. This decision was taken by the Central Committee after it had reviewed the situation within the Party, which requires that it adopt a political programme for the immediate future and elect a new Central Committee which will enjoy full confidence and have the necessary authority to ensure that the Party is united in its action . . .

Delegates to the Congress will be elected in accordance with the Party Statutes at extraordinary regional conferences and at extraordinary municipal conferences in Prague and in Bratislava. One delegate with the right to vote is to be elected for each 1,100 Party members. The plenary session of the Central Committee also made the following decisions:

Meetings of the basic organizations are to be held between 10 and 23 June 1968 to elect delegates to Extraordinary district conferences.

Extraordinary district conferences are to be held on 29 and 30 June 1968, electing delegates to Extraordinary regional conferences.

The Extraordinary regional conferences and the Extraordinary municipal conferences in Prague and Bratislava are to be held on 6 and 7 July or on 13 and 14 July 1968, and will elect delegates to an Extraordinary Fourteenth Congress of the Czechoslovak Communist Party. Such delegates will also be elected at these conferences by members of Party organizations in the army and security forces.

Resolution on Preparations for the Extraordinary Fourteenth Congress, Passed by the Central Committee Plenum on 1 June 1968 (excerpts):

The Central Committee of the K S Č has discussed the demand for a speedy convocation of the Extraordinary Fourteenth Congress as voiced at various Party meetings, as well as at district and regional conferences. It agrees with the view that a number of new fundamental circumstances have arisen in the last few weeks, concerning the process initiated by the January session of the Central Committee, which urgently require an answer by the Party's supreme organ – Congress . . .

Having taken all the circumstances into consideration, and with a view to the urgent need of electing a new Central Committee which will enjoy the full confidence of the Party so that it can direct the Party's work in the present complex and exacting period with full authority according to the principles of democratic centralism, the Central Committee has decided to call an Extraordinary Fourteenth Congress for 9 September 1968 in Prague . . .

For the exceptionally difficult task of preparing the Extraordinary Fourteenth Congress of the K S Č, the plenary session of the Central Committee directs that:

1. The basic material and documents be drawn up in time in the spirit of the fundamental mission and programme of the Congress. The work to be organized so that communists from both the theoretical and practical spheres shall participate and so that every communist and every Party organization and organ can express its views on them in discussion . . .

The cadre preparation of the elections to the Central Committee and the Central Control and Audit Commission will require that new members be chosen in a way consonant with Party democracy, a way that reflects the social composition of the Party and makes it possible to select the most capable representatives who stand high in the esteem of Party members as well as of non-Party people, enjoying their absolute confidence . . .

The Central Committee of the KSČ expects that as many communists and non-communists as possible will take an active part in the preparations for the Congress, thus helping to bring about the best type of socialist development in Czechoslovakia . . .

Report on the Meeting of the Central Committee Presidium on 11 June 1968 (excerpts):

. . . The Presidium of the Central Committee has approved the draft plan for the preparation of the Extraordinary Fourteenth Congress and the formation of working groups . . . to prepare the basic documents for the Congress. It has instructed the working groups to begin work at once on matters relating to the Congress; by 7 July to lay before the Political Commission for Congress Preparations, and the Central Committee Presidium, the basic theses and a draft of new Party Statutes; and by the end of July to prepare the basic texts of the reports to be delivered at the Congress, together with draft resolutions and documents for the individual points on the Congress agenda. The working groups are immediately to enter into consultation with the *aktif* of communist experts and with the lower Party organs . . .

The Central Committee Presidium has placed Comrade Alexander Dubček at the head of the working group charged with analysing the Party's work and its development since the Thirteenth Congress and with defining its chief aims in the immediate future. This group will set up seven working committees.

Report of a Meeting of the Central Committee Presidium on 25 June 1968 (excerpt):

. . . On the basis of past experience, the majority of the delegates for the Extraordinary district conferences were elected by secret ballot. The nomination and election of delegates was carried out in a democratic way, i.e. from below. They were carefully chosen, especially from among communists who are open to new ideas and have a critical and circumspect approach to things.

At their June meetings the Party organizations discussed the conclusions reached by the May plenum of the Central Committee. Communists everywhere expressed agreement with these conclusions and welcomed the cadre decisions made by the plenum. The decision to call an Extraordinary Congress of the Party on 9 September 1968 has been welcomed . . .

Report of a Meeting of the Central Committee Presidium on 3 July 1968 (excerpts):

. . . The Presidium has discussed the preliminary report on the Extraordinary district conferences . . . . The district conferences were held in a democratic spirit, which made possible a useful exchange of views and a careful selection of candidates. The conferences did their work openly and in a critical manner. A significant factor was the large number of delegates from primary organizations [97 per cent], their discipline and their interest in decisive political problems.

The discussions carried out by the district conferences and the resolutions passed by them show that an absolute majority of Party members support the policy outlined in the Action Programme of the KSČ. In the debate delegates expressed full confidence in the progressive forces within the Central Committee of the Party . . .

The extraordinary district and regional conferences of the Party have fulfilled their aims. They serve as yet another proof that the Party's unity of action and ideas at a higher level is gradually being formed in a dialogue which brings to the fore the best and most progressive forces, minds and suggestions . . .

*Report of a Meeting of the Central Committee Presidium
on 25 July 1968 (excerpt):*

. . . The Presidium . . . also evaluated the Extraordinary district, regional and municipal Party conferences. It stated that these Extraordinary conferences had brought to an end one important stage in the preparations for the Extraordinary Fourteenth Party Congress. Roughly within thirty days of the decision, taken by the plenum of the Central Committee in May 1968, to hold the Extraordinary Fourteenth Congress, meetings were held in the primary organizations, as were 125 district conferences attended by 47,231 delegates and 12 regional and municipal conferences attended by 5,750 delegates. Communists, Party organs and organizations showed themselves to be very active, and by their creative thinking and critical approach endeavoured to give the Congress the best possible conditions. They elected 1,539 delegates and recommended 935 candidates for the new Central Committee and Central Control and Audit Commission, the proposals to be laid before the Electoral Commission of the Congress.

*Report of a Meeting of the Central Committee Presidium
on 6 August 1968 (excerpts):*

. . . The Presidium of the Central Committee of the KSČ discussed . . . the draft Statutes of the Communist Party of Czechoslovakia. This draft will be published in *Rudé právo*, *Pravda* [the organ of the Slovak Communist Party, published in Bratislava], and *Új Szó* [the Hungarian-language Party paper in Slovakia] on Saturday 10 August, so that the entire Party can read it and comment on it . . .

*Proclamation by the Central Committee Presidium
on 21 August 1968:*

TO ALL THE PEOPLE OF THE CZECHOSLOVAK SOCIALIST REPUBLIC!

Last night, 20 August 1968, at about 23.00 hours, the armed forces of the Soviet Union, the Polish People's Republic, the German

Democratic Republic, the Hungarian People's Republic and the Bulgarian People's Republic crossed the frontiers of the Czechoslovak Socialist Republic. They did so without the knowledge of the President of the Republic, of the Speaker of the National Assembly, the Prime Minister or the First Secretary of the Central Committee of the KSČ, or of any of these bodies.

The Presidium of the Central Committee was in session at the time, debating the preparations for the Fourteenth Party Congress. The Presidium appeals to every citizen of our Republic to keep calm and to offer no resistance to the advancing armies. For the same reason neither our army, nor our security forces, nor the People's Militia have received orders to defend the country.

The Presidium of the KSČ Central Committee considers this act to be not only a violation of all the principles underlying the relations between socialist States, but also a negation of the basic norms of international law.

All the leading officials of the government, the Communist Party and the National Front remain in their posts, to which they were elected as representatives of the people and members of their organizations in accordance with the valid laws of the Czechoslovak Socialist Republic.

The constitutional authorities are immediately calling into session the National Assembly and the government of the Republic; the Presidium of the Central Committee is convening the Central Committee plenum to discuss the situation that has arisen.

Presidium of the KSČ Central Committee

[From a special edition of *Rudé právo*, published on 21 August 1968.]

III

Transcript of a Tape Recording of the Proceedings of the Extraordinary Fourteenth Congress on 22 August 1968

[*The Congress opens: 10 a.m.*]

THE CHAIRMAN: Dear Comrades, in view of the irregular situation created through the invasion by the armed forces of the five Warsaw Pact powers, a large number of our regional organizations and many of the delegates elected to the Fourteenth Congress have demanded that the Congress be held at once. For this reason a group of delegates from Prague have asked the municipal committee of the Party, which is working normally and has organizational facilities, to use all means at its disposal to call together the elected delegates and enable them to meet and decide what is to be done under the circumstances.

Despite the difficult conditions some 1,000 delegates have met here, which is far more than the necessary majority, and the Congress is therefore able to take place. Since, however, there is a difference of opinion on the subject, and delegates are still arriving, we recommend that this assembly be considered a conference of the delegates, which can then decide by a majority vote whether we are to open the Fourteenth Congress. [*Enthusiastic applause, several delegates speak from their places in the auditorium and cannot be heard.*]

Comrade Kabrna, a member of the KSČ Central Committee, takes the chair.

KABRNA: The Preparatory Committee puts forward the following agenda:

1. Opening of the delegates' conference;
2. Election of a Working Presidium;
3. Report on the discussions held by members of the Central Committee on the previous day;
4. Adoption of a political statement;

17

5. Election of the preparatory committees of the Congress.
Please raise your hands if you approve the proposed agenda . . .*
Thank you. Is anyone against the agenda? . . No. Does anyone
abstain? . . No. The conference agenda is thus approved.

We shall now propose a Working Presidium. We would like to
suggest that you vote for its members *en bloc*. I shall then ask each
region to elect two of its own members to supplement the Working
Presidium.

We propose the following members:

Dubček, Svoboda, Černík, Smrkovský [*tumultuous applause and
cheers*], Kriegel, Špaček, Císař, Šimon, Vodsloň, Martin
Vaculík, Colotka, Husák, Ťažký, Zrak, Koscelanský, Hejzlar,
Goldstücker, Pelikán, Litera, Starý, Kabrna, Hrdinová, Machá-
čová, Šilhan, Miková, Linhart, Devera, Krček, Morkes,
Kadlec and Borůvka.

Now I would ask the individual delegations to suggest two
candidates each to supplement this list of candidates.

Prague region – any proposals, please? . . Comrade Tomsa,
Prague 2, Milan Hübl, he isn't here, Comrade Helge. Comrades,
please don't put forward too many names, or these procedural
matters will take more time than we have at our disposal.

If there are no serious reasons why we should have any one particular comrade, please withdraw your proposal. I shall now name
the delegations, starting with Prague.

Central Bohemia – any suggestions? – yes? Comrade Bejček,
    Comrade Zoubek.

South Bohemia – Comrade Šimeček, Comrade Vališ.

West Bohemia – Comrade Kopřiva, Comrade Metlička.

North Bohemia – Comrade Kreperát, Comrade Raiman.

East Bohemia – Comrade Štěpán and Comrade Václav Polák.

West Moravia – Comrade Šimek and Comrade Stavárek.

South Moravia – Comrade Kožich and Comrade Šabata.

Slovak regions are not adequately represented at the moment;
we'll wait until the comrades arrive before we elect their members
to the Working Presidium since we have had reports that they are
trying to get to Prague.

---

* An ellipsis of three points (. . .) within this tape recording indicates indecipherable passages; an ellipsis of two points (. .) indicates the speaker's hesitation.

Comrades, may I now ask you to approve this list *en bloc*. All those in favour? .`.

Thank you.

Is anyone against? . . No.

Does anyone abstain? . . No one.

The Working Presidium is approved.

Will the elected comrades please come forward. I now hand over to Comrade Morkes, who will chair the first part of our discussion.

MORKES: Comrades, let us continue our conference. Before I ask Comrade Vaculík to speak on the present situation, allow me to make a technical comment. The organizers wish to point out that should it become necessary to leave, there are two emergency exits by which you can reach the dining-room and kitchen and then scatter in the factory.

Comrade Vaculík has something to say on the present situation.

[*Applause.*]

VACULÍK: Comrades, Delegates, I have been delegated to contact the Party's municipal committee which has called together this conference of delegates to the Extraordinary Fourteenth Congress. I can only pass on the information we received yesterday, which was discussed at yesterday's meeting of the Central Committee of our Party, about a third of whose members were present. In my view there are two main points about the present situation.

The first is the occupation of the country by the Warsaw Pact allies, without – according to the last legal document of the Central Committee Presidium – without the knowledge of the President of the Republic, the government, the National Assembly or the Central Committee of our Party. Nevertheless it remains a fact which we must take into account, doing everything we can not to exacerbate the situation here any further, for that would only exacerbate the situation on the other side, too. That is the reason for the appeals for calm, for work, for the resumption of normal everyday life, for the avoidance of any provocation which might lead to reprisals or be used as a pretext for the introduction of an occupation regime.

The second fact is the absolutely unanimous reaction of our people to the occupation of our country by the allied armies, a totally unjustified occupation, since even at yesterday's meeting of the Central Committee not one member of the Presidium could

19

confirm that any of our official representatives, be they leading officials of our Party, of the government or of the National Assembly, had asked for protection by the allied armed forces. This unanimous reaction by our people, this unanimous opposition to the occupation of Czechoslovakia by the allied armies is, I think, the single decisive guideline for the attitude which our Party ought to adopt towards this fact. I think our attitude must be that we cannot reconcile ourselves to this reality, that we cannot accept it, that we must speak out unanimously against it. [*Prolonged and tumultuous applause.*]

If we wish to speak the language of our people, of our nations, we cannot speak any other way.

This is what took place at the Central Committee session during the night:

On Tuesday afternoon the Presidium had started to discuss the preparations for the Extraordinary Fourteenth Congress, and the discussion lasted well into the night. A few minutes after twelve Comrade Černík, the Prime Minister, received a telephone message to the effect that the first allied units were crossing our border.

The Party Presidium immediately debated the situation, the result being the well-known Proclamation by the Presidium of the Central Committee.

Then, after adopting this Proclamation, the Presidium discussed the letter sent by the Central Committee of the Soviet Communist Party to the Central Committee of the KSČ.

I can only reproduce it roughly, Comrades, so please don't take this to be the literal wording. What I heard was a Czech translation of the Russian original, and I can only tell you what I remember of it.

The Soviet Party wrote to our Central Committee complaining that our Party was not adhering to the agreements made at Čierná nad Tisou and Bratislava. We don't know exactly what was agreed there, for the Central Committee was not informed about the assurances given by the Party Presidium at Čierná nad Tisou and the agreements it had entered into. But I understood from the letter that the Presidium of our Party had undertaken, in concert with the communist and workers' parties of the other socialist countries, to abstain from polemics.

In their letter the Soviet comrades expressed the view not only that we had not done so, but that in the last few days we had in-

20

tensified our polemics. This was borne out – according to them – by the attacks made by certain groups against the Central Committee after their return from Čierná nad Tisou, when various incidents took place: the stones which were thrown, the petitions against the People's Militia, certain acts by leading representatives such as Comrade Prchlík and Comrade Císař and other similar facts are set out by the Soviet comrades in this letter to our Central Committee. Comrade Dubček is said to have received it on Monday, and on Tuesday he acquainted the Presidium of our Party with its contents. This means that it was in fact only after the first report of allied troops crossing our frontier that this letter was discussed in the Party Presidium.

Part of the Party Presidium remained in the Central Committee building, i.e. Comrades Dubček, Smrkovský, Kriegel, Špaček, while some of the others left to take a short rest. They simply left the building and could not again contact the group of Comrades Dubček, Smrkovský, Kriegel and Špaček, being either isolated when they were about to return to the Central Committee or prevented from entering the building.

Together with Comrades Vodsloň, Krček and Rákosník from Kladno I tried several times in the course of yesterday to contact our Party leadership; in the morning we even sent a delegation of Central Committee members to the army commandant with a request that we should be permitted to contact the Central Committee of our Party or its Presidium. Our request was refused and we were not allowed inside the Central Committee building.

For this reason we started to gather those members of the Central Committee who were available at the Praha Hotel. We contacted a number of comrades; right at the beginning when there were twenty-two members of the Central Committee present we adopted a short resolution in support of the Presidium of our Central Committee and in support of Comrade Dubček. We demanded the release of our leading representatives so that our properly elected Party and State organs could meet to discuss the situation and try to seek a solution. Then, in the afternoon, roughly a third of the members of the Central Committee of our Party got together and decided to remain in permanent session and bring in further members of the Central Committee. Out of this late session came the following communiqué:

21

In answer to the appeal of the KSČ Central Committee, issued early on Wednesday 21 August 1968, those members and candidates of the KSČ Central Committee and of the Central Control and Audit Commission who were able to come, met to affirm their responsibility and express their views on the present situation. The members and candidates of the Central Committee of our Party and of the Central Control and Audit Commission fully support the proclamation issued by the Central Committee on 21 August concerning the occupation of Czechoslovakia by forces of the five Warsaw Pact countries. In the spirit of this proclamation the assembled members of the Central Committee appeal to all communists and citizens of the Czechoslovak Socialist Republic under all circumstances to keep calm and behave sensibly and responsibly, not allowing themselves to be provoked by anyone or anything to hasty, ill-considered action, thus respecting the harsh reality in which we find ourselves and which cannot be altered overnight.

Aware of their responsibility to the Party and our nation, the members and candidates of the Central Committee and Central Control and Audit Commission appeal urgently to all to co-operate with State bodies and National Committees in preventing panic and provocation, in averting the disorganization of industry and transport, thus avoiding irreplaceable losses; we appeal to them to ensure regular supplies of food and to preserve law and order in factories and offices, in towns and villages.

We appeal to all communists and to all honest people in this country, hoping that they will realize the gravity of the hour and do their best to achieve stabilization and normalization of conditions throughout the land. This alone will help us to find a way out of the present very difficult situation. The Central Committee is determined not to permit a return to pre-January conditions. The Action Programme of the KSČ Central Committee remains the cornerstone of our policy. The assembled members of the KSČ Central Committee have decided to meet in permanent session and to work for the earliest convening of the plenary session of the KSČ Central Committee, which is to be attended by all the members of the Presidium and all the members of the Central Committee, and to renew the regular activities of all Party organs and the Party press.

The delegated members of the Presidium of the KSČ Central Committee are establishing contact with the command of the armies of the five Warsaw Pact countries with a view to bringing about a speedy normalization. It is imperative that discipline, law and order be maintained at this time and essential supplies provided. We appeal to the district and regional Party committees to heed only the instructions issued by the Central Committee and its organs, and to act on them.

This resolution was adopted. By some mistake, instead of the resolution, the radio broadcast the text of a telex message intended for the individual regional committees. That was the cause of all the confusion about the convening of delegates for the Extraordinary Fourteenth Party Congress. The delegation sent to negotiate with the army commanders had not reported by the time I left the Central Committee headquarters, so we don't know how those negotiations went or what decisions they reached.

We have as yet no contact with Comrade Dubček, Comrade Smrkovský, Comrade Kriegel and Comrade Špaček. Last night we received news that Comrade Dubček was at the castle with Comrade Svoboda. I don't know whether this report was confirmed or not. The negotiations with the army representatives included, in addition to such things as the regularization of conditions, the resumption of normal transport and food supplies, etc., an unequivocal demand for the release of our leaders so that they could not only take part in the meeting of the Central Committee, but also in the conference of the delegates to the Fourteenth Congress. About an hour ago we, together with the Party's municipal committee, informed the members of the Central Committee who are working, who are in the Central Committee building, of your conference, and I again repeated this information so that the comrades would know that you were here, that you had met.

I asked the comrades, not only those in the Presidium but also the other members of the Central Committee, to come to your conference if they could.

That, Comrades, is all I can tell you at the present moment, for I don't know any more myself, and I don't want to make things up, I don't want to make forecasts or jump to any conclusions. In my opinion there are enough brains gathered here for us to be able to decide in a clear-headed fashion what is to be done in this terribly complicated, I might say tragic, situation. I think we should try and avoid pressing things too far and causing situations in which further valuable lives of our people would be put at risk, and on the other hand we should resolutely maintain the position adopted by our Presidium as regards the illegal and unjustified occupation of our land by the allied forces. That's all, Comrades.

THE CHAIRMAN: I thank Comrade Vaculík, but before he leaves the rostrum I'd like to ask him a question on behalf of the Working Presidium of our conference. If the rest of you agree, we would

23

like to have him explain what standpoint was adopted by the individual members of the Central Committee Presidium with regard to the proclamation of the 20–21 August session. [*Applause.*]

I also have some fresh information for you. First of all, a good piece of news:

It has been ascertained that of the total number of 1,500 delegates, 935 are present here at this moment, as well as 22 guests. [*Enthusiastic applause.*] And now, Comrades, a less pleasant piece of news. The Slovak delegates have evidently been detained by Soviet troops near Břeclav. [*Voices from the hall:* Shame!] And now would Comrade Vaculík please answer the question. Those of you who agree with the proposal, kindly raise your hands. . Thank you, that shows you are fully in favour.

VACULÍK: Comrades, may I recommend that you put this question to the first member of the Presidium to come to your conference. I should hate to distort the standpoint adopted by the various members of the Presidium and thus perhaps throw doubt on them. [*Protests from the hall.*] Look, Comrades, I was not there, at the Presidium meeting, so I don't want on the basis of the limited information I have to the effect that certain disagreements took place and that a very heated vote was taken, I simply don't want to cast doubt on certain comrades because I just don't have all the facts. [*Applause.*]

THE CHAIRMAN: One more item of information. A large number of members of the legal government have sought the protection of this assembly. They are here in the factory [*enthusiastic applause*], in the Vysočany works, and at the disposal of the conference. [*Applause.*]

One more thing in this connection. The comrades I have mentioned are consulting together and no doubt we'll make it possible for them to come and join us here as soon as they have finished. Yes?

A DELEGATE: May I put a differently phrased question to Comrade Vaculík? How did the members of the Central Committee Presidium behave at the meeting which he attended yesterday?

THE CHAIRMAN: Comrade Šimeček wishes to say something about this.

ŠIMEČEK: Comrades, I was one of the few provincial candidates of the Central Committee to attend yesterday's session. I went there alone, on the initiative of our comrades – [*An interruption.*]

THE CHAIRMAN: Comrades, Comrade Šimeček – some of the members of our government have arrived at our conference. [*Enthusiastic applause.*] The Working Presidium recommends that they should be co-opted into that body. [*Applause.*] They have heard your enthusiastic response and will come up to the platform as soon as they can. And now Comrade Šimeček.

ŠIMEČEK: I merely wish to convey to you some of my impressions of yesterday's Central Committee session. I came late, Comrades, at half-past nine, and without knowing when the meeting had started. I listened very attentively, watching with horror those faces and the activity of some of the members of the Presidium and of the Central Committee who were present. Altogether there were some fifty comrades. I was absolutely staggered by the position adopted by Comrade Jakeš, Chairman of the Central Control and Audit Commission, I was surprised by the activity of Comrades Pastyřík, Pavlovský and Městek, who were displaying a great deal more verve than I had seen them show at any meeting since January. Yesterday they were suddenly claiming that the Soviet Union had probably been justified in taking the action it had taken, criticizing the fact that the [Soviet] letter had not been discussed in the Presidium, and so on and so forth. I listened for about half an hour and then I put forward my view, which I would like to put to you briefly now. I said I was very surprised to hear the things that were being said and that I didn't consider that particular assembly to be a plenum of the Central Committee capable of taking decisions, and that I only wanted to sit in a plenum that had all its members present and with a complete Presidium. Should that plenum adopt the standpoint taken by those comrades, then I would have to ask to be excused, for I had no intention of returning in disgrace to the factory in which I work. [*Applause.*]

Thereupon Comrade Piller, who was in the chair, asked me what standpoint I had in mind. I said that from what I had heard of their discussions I surmised that we were supposed to go and tell people, 'Yes, it's right that the Soviet comrades have occupied us, we have to bow nicely and thank them for coming to our aid.' That was something I would never do, being aware of my responsibility and of the gravity of the hour. That is why I welcomed this conference, that is why I am so glad to see decent faces here. It's high time, Comrades. And may I say that we are now paying the price for Comrade Dubček's refusal to act on our advice, far-sighted as he otherwise was, because those comrades I have mentioned should have been dismissed long ago. But I think that today we'll save the situation. Thank you. [*Applause.*]

THE CHAIRMAN: Thank you, Comrade Šimeček. Comrade Vaculík will now answer the question that was put to him. [*A delegate in the hall protests that there isn't time, that it is necessary to discuss what steps are to be taken and to open the Fourteenth Congress without delay.*]

THE CHAIRMAN: The Working Presidium wanted to ask you to make this very suggestion. Since we are working in extraordinary conditions and under considerable pressure of time, we can only answer the most fundamental questions and then discuss the draft declaration, or rather the drafts of all the documents we intend to discuss at the Congress, once the conference of delegates is over. Do you all agree that Comrade Vaculík's reply should be the last item in this part of our meeting?

. . . [*Indecipherable reply from the hall.*] . . .

THE CHAIRMAN: This depends largely on Comrade Vaculík's reply and I therefore ask him to speak.

VACULÍK: Comrades, I'm going to try to inform you as objectively as I can about the Central Committee meeting. As I have told you already, some twenty-two members of the Central Committee met yesterday morning, when we issued a quite unambiguous and clear proclamation signed by all the members present, and this was then made public over the radio and television. We expressed our unanimous support for the Presidium, the Party leadership headed by Comrade Dubček. We demanded their release so that they could come and discuss things with us, or that we should be given the opportunity of making contact with them.

Then at a second meeting in the afternoon, attended by roughly a third of the Central Committee, I think the basic difference of opinion that arose was that between comrades who recognized only one reality, i.e. that we had been occupied by Soviet troops, and not the other reality, the way our people reacted to the occupation.

The fact is with us, but the reaction of our people is another thing. And if our Party wishes to save its face, it cannot ignore this, it cannot identify itself with the occupation or condone it. It must state categorically that it does not agree with it. Some of the comrades wanted to turn it into a toothless compromise, advising us not to provoke the occupation forces unnecessarily and saying, as for instance Comrade Pavlovský did, that higher interests, higher strategic forces were at stake, that when he had earlier had talks with Comrade Brezhnev, the latter had emphasized that Czechoslovakia was not Romania or Yugoslavia, that they would not let Czechoslovakia go. That, quite simply, was his argument.

Comrade Městek used similar arguments, whereas Comrades Kolder, Piller and Bil'ak asked why we had to call an Extraordinary Congress at all. Why call the delegates together, what kind of initiative was the Party's municipal committee showing in calling the delegates of the Extraordinary Congress to Prague?

Comrade Indra even doubted whether the Central Committee ought to be meeting today, whether it would not be sufficient to have a meeting of the Central Committee tomorrow or the day after.

There was discussion on this subject. As someone has already pointed out here, a number of comrades, for instance Academician Macek, Comrade Hrdinová, Comrade Kabrna, and others, said quite clearly: 'Are we some kind of illegal organization, then, or are we going to speak up on behalf of our legal Party? If so, then we must speak the same language as our people. Otherwise we can issue a hundred proclamations imploring the people to keep calm, but if we do not speak their language there will not be calm in this country.' [*Applause.*]

That, in a nutshell, is what the arguments were about. We, those twenty-two members, based our standpoint on a simple fact. The Party's municipal committee had issued an appeal to the delegates of the Extraordinary Congress asking them to meet in Prague, and so when Comrade Rattinger of the municipal committee contacted us in the morning and told us about it, we said to ourselves, when the delegates meet surely we can't go and tell them, 'Well, dear Comrades, just go back home again and keep calm'. What would the delegates think of a Central Committee that acted in such a way? We therefore agreed that we would take whatever steps were necessary in the light of the existing situation. If only some of the delegates met, they would confer as a group of delegates. If a majority met, they could then hold the Congress. That they were fully entitled to do. [*Applause.*]

That was what the discussion in the Central Committee was about – whether it was right to call the delegates together. Some comrades suggested that we should split the delegates up on a regional basis, explain the situation to them and send them home to calm people down. That was the content of the speeches by those comrades who advised coming to terms with the occupation forces and trying to return to a normal life. Other comrades said we must make it quite clear that we had no intention of coming to terms with the occupation forces, that of course we wanted to return to a normal life and to keep the peace, but that this presupposed adopting an unequivocal standpoint on what had happened, which I personally consider a terrible tragedy, Comrades, a tragedy from which the international working-class movement will not recover for many years. Nor shall we, Comrades, and there can be no question for years to come of any friendship with the Soviet Union. That is the terrible fact we cannot possibly ignore . . . If any more comrades come up to speak, then let them give their own opinion on this. [*Applause*.]

THE CHAIRMAN: Will the secretaries of the district committees go upstairs for a short conference? Someone over there's asking to speak . . . please give your name, this is being recorded . . .

RUML, DELEGATE FOR THE PRAGUE REGION: I have no question, Comrades. I'd like to state my view, that is why I came here. I consider yesterday's conclusion, as reported by Comrade Martin Vaculík, to be a deception. A deception because there was a division at that very meeting. Some of the comrades came there under the protection of tanks and others under the threat of tanks. As far as we know, Comrades Bil'ak, Barbírek, Kolder and Indra came protected by the Soviet tanks – I may be wrong, there may have been others, I don't know.

As far as the mistake Comrade Vaculík spoke of is concerned, where one proclamation was adopted and something else was sent by telex from the Central Committee, I consider that too to have been a trick. A public announcement is made and conflicting instructions are sent internally to the regional secretariats. I think, on the contrary, that it was quite right for our radio stations to broadcast, which they did under dreadful conditions – you can't imagine, Comrades, we have been working since yesterday like outlaws in this country [*applause*], we have to change our locations from one

28

hour to the next in order to be able to tell the nation the truth. And on the other side there exists the so-called legal, yet quite illegal, broadcasting station calling itself Vltava, which has the full support of those traitors. You see, I think it is important that the text of that telex message was broadcast, since it was clear from the way it was phrased that it was an appeal for collaboration and not a straightforward demand for the withdrawal of Soviet and other occupation troops. I see in it an attempt to establish a puppet government, a collaborationist Party leadership and other bodies. That is why these so-called comrades were so scared of the Fourteenth Congress. [*Applause.*]

... [*The ensuing exchange is unintelligible.*] ...

THE CHAIRMAN: Thank you.... Another question. Yes?... [*Passage unintelligible.*] ... Comrade Litera wishes to say something.

LITERA: Comrades, when we in the municipal committee last night and in the early hours of this morning discussed the obvious alternative, that we should meet like this, and when we held consultations about it with the individual regions, with the individual secretaries, we, that is the Prague muncipal committee, realized that they had the same idea in every region, both in Bohemia and in Moravia. But, believe me, not even in our most optimistic moments did we imagine that we would meet in such numbers. This attendance is all the more significant in view of the debate we had last night with a representative of the Soviet Army, which now runs the Central Committee, or rather which has occupied both the Central Committee and the municipal committee buildings, as well as the Central Bohemian and regional committees. He told us he could not give us a reply to our question as to whether the delegates from the country would be able to reach Prague for the Congress. As representatives of the Prague Party organizations, and I'm sure Olda Matějka will forgive me if I say also of the organization in Prague 9, we are therefore glad that we have met like this. And now I would ask you to be as brief as possible. I think we mustn't waste time with a lot of proposals on relatively unimportant issues. I think the major question is this – before we continue our debate we should carefully consider the suggestion put forward by the comrade who spoke before me. That means whether, in view of the fact that the Slovak delegates have been detained, we should immediately set up a working group to decide if this conference should be turned into a congress of Czech communists, or into the Extraordinary Fourteenth Congress of the Czechoslovak Communist Party, or into the inaugural conference of Czech communists. There are many circumstances which make this very urgent indeed:

1. the fact that Comrade Indra – well, at a time when Comrade Dubček is inaccessible, when he is interned and when there are reports, brought to us by some comrades who have come from the Ministry of Transport, that Comrade Černík was also seen being taken away in a certain manner from Ruzyně Airport, when there are rumours which indicate that the legal government may be deposed and another put in its place;
2. at a time when the announcement made this morning over the radio that the National Assembly would be given the necessary conditions for its work has been proved worthless and the building is encircled by tanks;
3. at a time when Comrade Indra has again sent us a message demanding that the secretaries of the regional committees go to the Central Committee, where talks are to be held with the intention of preventing this assembly of ours; and at a time when the Soviet commandant of the Central Bohemian region, who is also the Soviet commandant for Prague, is supposed to have sent orders – let the comrades tell us if this is really so – to some country districts to the effect that no public assemblies are to be allowed . . . [*Unintelligible voices from the hall.*] . . .

Well, there you are, we can show that these are facts. I would therefore ask you to adopt this proposal: that every regional delegation send or nominate to this assembly one comrade to form a group which will in the shortest possible time put forward a proposal on what kind of conference or congress this is to be. I think we should not dwell too much on formalities. I nominate the following comrades to this group, which I suggest be called the Provisional Organizational Committee: Comrade Pokštefl representing the Prague municipal committee; Comrade Míla Havlíček, whom you know as the chairman of the original working group dealing with the draft Statutes; Comrade Vojtěch Mencl, commandant of the Military Political Academy; Comrade Miloš Hájek, who is deputy director of the Institute for the History of Socialism. I would urge that, if they agree, the individual delegations empower their leading members, that is the regional secretaries or their deputies, to put such a proposal before this assembly. I think it is high time this was done. [*Applause.*]

. . . [*An unintelligible question from the hall.*] . . .

THE CHAIRMAN: I'm sorry, Comrades, would you mind . . . yes, you are right, let us deal with all this already as a Congress, let the comrades get to work.

. . . [*Unintelligible questions from the hall.*] . . .

THE CHAIRMAN: There will be many more questions and suggestions on this point. I believe the proposals were put quite accurately. There was, first of all, the requirement that this assembly, which is meeting under difficult conditions, adopt a standpoint on the present situation. That is Number One. And secondly, that a group should prepare a proposal as to whether this working conference of delegates should constitute itself a Congress. There will be many different views and proposals. I think it would be right to take a vote on the proposals put forward – Yes? . . I'm sorry, Comrades, but we really are in an unusual situation and time is short. For this reason we can't very well adhere to certain democratic principles in selecting contributions to the debate. Once again I ask your pardon, these are extraordinary conditions . . and there's no time to be lost. The next to speak is . . . [*unintelligible*] . . . who will put forward an alternative proposal.

DELEGATE: . . . Comrades, we have considered the situation and have come to the conclusion that at this moment practically two-thirds of the delegates of the whole Communist Party are present at this assembly, so that according to the valid Statutes there is nothing to prevent it from constituting itself as the Extraordinary Congress. [*Enthusiastic applause.*] We therefore suggest that the Working Presidium put the matter to the vote and, if the result is favourable, open the Extraordinary Congress as planned.

THE CHAIRMAN: . . . Well, Comrades, as I said before, there will be many different opinions, but we must hurry. Express your views by voting as the Comrade suggests.

A proposal has been put forward – [*Voice from the floor:* 'We've come to a Congress!'] A proposal has been put forward recommending that this working conference be transformed into the

31

Extraordinary Fourteenth Congress, as the condition which says that a majority of properly elected delegates must be present has been fulfilled – [*Voices from the floor:* 'Take a vote!'] Yes, Comrades, that's exactly what I have in mind. I think it would be as well if we adopted this resolution with a rider that the Slovak delegates when they arrive will have an opportunity of expressing their views on the subject, since the majority aren't in fact here at the moment and we want them to take part in the Congress as delegates with equal rights with the rest of us. There exists a political agreement between our parties to the effect that we will not use our numerical superiority against the Slovak minority, either at the Congress or anywhere else. I therefore ask you to adopt this with the rider that the Slovak delegates can later express their views on it. Would those Slovak delegates who *are* here say what they think on the subject?

A SLOVAK DELEGATE: Comrades, there are four of us who have come to the Congress off our own bat – five? . . right, so there are five of us here – if the fifth comrade has any objections, let him say so, I haven't been able to consult him yet. I can therefore only speak for a proportion of the delegates.* We agree that this Congress, the Extraordinary Fourteenth Congress of the Communist Party of Czechoslovakia, be declared open. [*Applause.*] . . . We are speaking for ourselves. We believe it is true that our delegates have been detained near Břeclav, and we can only think that they were on their way to Prague because they wanted the Extraordinary Fourteenth Congress to be held. [*Applause.*] . . . [*Voice from the hall.*] . . . The comrade says that a delegation of Communists of Žilina has left to take part in the Congress. We consider not only that this is an Extraordinary Congress, but that it is also being held under extraordinary circumstances. Naturally it will not discuss everything, there isn't time to discuss everything that was intended and covered in the original preparations for the Extraordinary Fourteenth Congress.

* *Editor's Note:* While the Congress was in session, over fifty more Slovak delegates arrived. On 24 and 25 August the overwhelming majority of the Slovak delegates who were unable to attend the Prague Congress expressed their agreement, by letter and cable, with the results of the Extraordinary Fourteenth Congress in Prague, thus acknowledging its validity also for the Communist Party of Slovakia.

THE CHAIRMAN: I thank the Slovak comrades, and I repeat that everything we decide will later be discussed with the Slovak delegates when a majority of them is present.

Now I suggest we take a vote on the Commission's motion to turn this assembly of delegates to the Fourteenth Congress, who were properly elected at district and regional conferences and a majority of whom have met here today, into the Extraordinary Fourteenth Congress of the KSČ. [*Enthusiastic applause.*] Who supports this motion? . . An absolute majority – Yes? . . There are two abstentions.

On the basis of this decision I suggest that we elect a working committee to put before the delegates to the Fourteenth Congress a draft agenda and a draft of the principles on which the Congress is to be conducted . . . [*The leaders of the individual delegations put up candidates for the committee . . the names cannot be heard.*] . . . I think that this is a very correct proposal, seeing how the delegates were elected to the Congress. Mencl, Štika, Mácl, Mára – are there any more suggestions? No, there aren't. I therefore put it to the vote. Who supports the proposal? . . Thank you. Who is against? . . Nobody. Did anyone abstain? . . No, no abstentions.

Thank you. Now will the elected comrades go to this exit over here and then to the first floor, to the verandah. There they will be met by the comrades who are organizing the Congress and they will take them to the committee rooms . . . And now, Comrades, I recommend that we have a short intermission which we can make use of for an important organizational matter, by which I mean that the individual delegations, which are at the moment split up, should group themselves together so that they are able to make quick decisions on important questions.

[*Interval*]

[*After the interval the Chairman opens the Extraordinary Fourteenth Congress and reads out the proposals made by its Working Presidium*]:

THE CHAIRMAN: . . . First point: On no account should we dissolve the Congress of our own accord. [*Applause.*] We shall be in session for as long as is necessary to fulfil our task. We can only be dispersed by force.

Second point: Having regard to the circumstances, which are becoming more dramatic all the time, the Congress is obliged to approve documents which will make it clear to the public at large that the Congress has met and has adopted a standpoint on the present situation. [*Applause.*] That means that it is our first duty to adopt the necessary resolutions. I would therefore ask the committees to work as quickly as possible. The problems are quite clear to all of us.

Third point: This Congress is fully entitled to elect the Party organs and it will elect them. [*Applause.*] In order to do so, however, it must follow the usual procedure. It will be necessary to choose an Electoral Commission and also a Credentials Commission. Will the leaders of the delegations consult their members and put forward two of them from each delegation for these two Commissions. We take it that your delegations have long ago decided whom to present as candidates for the Party's Central Committee. I think I ought to explain something at this stage. The Congress ought to elect these organs even if there is some danger that it may make certain minor errors. These organs need not exist for ever. They may possibly survive only for a short time, perhaps no longer than will be needed to normalize the situation. There is no reason why the Congress could not meet again in three or four months' time and finish its job in this respect. [*Applause.*]

Comrades, the foregoing were three brief conclusions reached by the Presidium. Do you agree that we should adjust our proceedings accordingly? [*Expressions of assent from the hall.*]

Good. Oh, I beg your pardon, I ought really to take a vote and see who agrees with these conclusions. Who agrees with them? . . Thank you. Who does not agree? . . Any abstentions? . . Sorry, would those who disagree raise their hands once more so I can count them. Ten . . Abstentions? . . . [*Unintelligible voices from the hall.*] . . . Yes, I am coming to that, don't interrupt. Well, this means the vote has been taken on our further programme. And now let me pass to the second point on our agenda, which is the election of the individual Commissions.

Let us start with the Credentials Commission . . I see that one member from each delegation would suffice for this Commission . . Now, Comrades, approximately in the same order as we voted last time:

Prague municipal committee – Comrade Pavlištík.
Central Bohemian Region – Comrade Mejzlík.
North Bohemia – Comrade Holub.
West Bohemia – Comrade Černý.
South Bohemia – Comrade Kratochvíl.
East Bohemia – Comrade Ladislav Jirků.
North Moravia – Comrade Vítězslav Frank.
South Moravia – Comrade Chmelová.

Are all these comrades present? . . Do they agree to being nominated? . . Now will you please vote *en bloc* on these suggestions. .
We have no one from the Slovak regions. . Perhaps our Slovak comrades can tell us whether they wish to be represented on the Credentials Commission from the beginning? . . . [*Voices from the hall.*] . . .
The comrades from Slovakia say that it isn't necessary for them to
be members of the Commission for the time being. They will
nominate their representatives when we have more delegates here
from Slovakia.

Comrades, let us vote on this *en bloc*. Those in favour kindly
raise their hands. Who is against? . . Any abstentions? . . No.
Approved unanimously. Will the members of the Credentials
Commission now go to the organizational bureau and start work
in accordance with the usual procedure, electing their chairman
and preparing the necessary document for the Working Presidium.

. . . And now to the second point on our election agenda. This
is extremely important, for it concerns the Electoral Commission
which is to lay before our Congress a proposal for the new
Central Committee until the next Congress. I repeat that there
will be sufficient places left in the Committee for the Slovak delegates who will be nominated later. This Electoral Commission
will consider or take action on the views expressed about the
individual candidates by the various delegations.

. . . Before we take the vote there are several comrades who wish
to say something. Yes, what is it? You want to put forward your
nominations already? I wouldn't do that, not yet. Are there any
more questions on this problem? . . . [*Unintelligible query from the
hall.*] . . . I'm sorry, Comrade, but we have already taken a contrary
decision on this. We decided on the strength of a democratic vote
that the Congress is to go on indefinitely unless it is interrupted by
force, and that it is to fulfil its task as an Extraordinary Congress,

including the election of the highest Party organ between two Congresses, that is, the Central Committee of the Party. [*Applause.*] Unless the majority decides otherwise, we will have no more discussion on this point, since it has been settled . . . Comrade Pelikán wishes to say something. Go ahead.

PELIKÁN: Comrades, I do not wish to hold up the proceedings, but perhaps I may ask you for a few moments' attention because Comrade Vodsloň and I have just come from the parliament, from the city, and we have some information for you. I think we must consider the present situation. We are of the opinion that with things as they are in Prague and in the country as a whole, once this Congress disperses it will not meet again. Why should this be so? For one thing you already know that at a meeting of some of the members of the Central Committee yesterday it was said that Comrade Dubček was perhaps able to conduct talks after all, and so on and so forth. At today's meeting of the National Assembly Comrade Nový asserted that Comrade Dubček was not interned, but the Vice-chairman of our parliament, Comrade Való, contacted President Svoboda, who confirmed that Comrades Dubček, Černík, Kriegel, Smrkovský, and perhaps also Šimon and Špaček, had been taken away to an unknown destination in armoured cars and that as a result he had no means of communication with them.

In other words, all the reports being circulated by certain members of the Central Committee or of the former Party Presidium to the effect that these comrades are somewhere at the castle negotiating an agreement have no foundation in truth, as has been confirmed by the President himself.

Comrade Svoboda has asked the Soviet Ambassador to come and see him this afternoon, and he will resolutely demand the release of our representatives.

Secondly, the National Assembly met in spite of obstacles – the building was surrounded by tanks and the soldiers on guard at the doors would not let the Deputies inside – with more than half its members present. That means that the National Assembly is in fact the only legal organ capable of taking decisions and, after a discussion, a resolution was passed by an overwhelming majority of votes, condemning the occupation of our country. The resolution demands the immediate liberation of our representatives, the implementation of the Constitution, and the normal functioning of our elected bodies. That is one side of the picture, the positive side. Of course on the other hand several comrades claimed that the Central Committee was in session and that it alone had the right to do anything, even though it was pointed out to them that many of its members were absent.

Apart from this, even some of the comrades who took part in yesterday's meeting of the incomplete Central Committee declared that they only agreed with certain decisions because they had received false reports about Comrade Dubček not being interned and so on.

There is here an evident attempt to create chaos and to declare a minority of the Central Committee and Presidium members to be the leading representatives of the Party, while the real leading representatives cannot be present at the meeting.

Also there are in Prague and elsewhere various demonstrations and there is a danger – one such demonstration took place in the centre of Prague only a little while ago – that there will be shooting and that the consequences will be very grave indeed. I think we are in duty bound to do two things. To announce that the Party Congress is in session and is the legal representative of the Party, and to adopt a short resolution on the present situation: an appeal for calm and at the same time for steadfastness and unity.

I also believe that in a situation like this people are waiting to see who is their spokesman. At a time when both the government and the President are powerless to act, I think this Congress must elect a Central Committee whose composition will correspond as much as possible to the present opinions of the majority of the Party members or delegates.

You see, I am convinced that it is the Party's representatives who must negotiate a solution to this extraordinary situation. And for this we must have representatives who have the right to negotiate on behalf of the Party. On the one hand there is the President, the government and parliament, but also, since some of the Central Committee members are saying that this is an ideological Party matter, there must be representatives of the Party in a position to act. If we leave here without having first elected this new Central Committee, we will find we are being represented by comrades whose actions we cannot really predict and by others who, we are convinced, will not do the right thing. In my view,

37

Comrades, our only hope of finding a way out of this tragic situation is to maintain the broadest possible unity of Party members on the one hand and of the people on the other.

It will then be impossible to form any kind of shadow government or shadow Central Committee – and we have heard already that feverish preparations are being made for this. We have, for example, been informed that the regional Party secretariats were occupied today, that new people are being co-opted into the apparatus of the Central Committee. We have no idea how long our parliament will be able to continue in session, and therefore I think that in this situation it is necessary to maintain the greatest possible unity. And I would like to appeal to you, Comrades – even though I know that we may have different views on various problems and on various people – to forget everything we have had cause to disagree about in these past few weeks and months. Let us not pin labels on anyone, let us take as the only yardstick according to which we judge people – as communists – their present attitude in these decisive and historic days. Let us today elect a Central Committee in which it will not matter whether a man said this or that in the past, a Central Committee capable of action, and competent to elect its Presidium.

Of course, if we succeed in doing this and normal, legal conditions return, the Congress can continue and nothing will prevent it from going back to the ballot and supplementing this Central Committee or even electing a new one on the basis of normal conditions.

But on the strength of the information we have, both from this country and from abroad, I can tell you that once this gathering, which derives its strength from the fact that we are all here together, once it disperses it is almost 100 per cent certain it will never meet again in the same circumstances.

It was, after all, the chief purpose of the invasion to prevent our Congress from taking place. Let us be quite clear about this. They did it because they knew that the Congress expresses the opinion of the majority of communists and of the whole nation and that it would mean final victory for the post-January policies, leaving the way open for the further development of our socialist society.

Comrade delegates, we have been elected at properly convened district and regional conferences and are therefore today the only

truly representative spokesmen of the Party. I believe it is our
historic task to elect a new Central Committee and its Presidium,
which can then conduct negotiations with the representatives of
those five countries and with other communist and workers'
Parties on how to resolve the situation that has arisen, on the basis
of respect for our sovereignty and of the joint interests of the
international workers' movement. [*Enthusiastic applause.*]

THE CHAIRMAN: Perhaps we can have a discussion on this point.
On the other hand I don't think we can afford the luxury of having
as extensive an exchange of opinions as we would like to have. I'll
therefore invite the first few comrades who have asked to speak to
give us their views – Yes? . . . [*A delegate speaks from the hall, but
his words are inaudible.*] . . .*

. . .

DELEGATE: . . . We have been told that we ought to go up to the
microphone, for, as it is, most of those present cannot hear
properly. There should be someone here at the table noting who
wants to speak in the discussion, so that the delegates are called
upon to speak in the order in which they have applied.

I agree that we have constituted ourselves as the Fourteenth
Congress without too many formalities. That is as it should be.
And now we must try and keep calm because a cool head is the
only asset we have at the moment. I wanted to say something
about the strike. Look, we – [*Hubbub in the hall.*]

THE CHAIRMAN: Wait a moment, Comrade, we'll come to the
question of the strike and other action when we deal with the draft
resolutions. [*Applause.*] Comrades, we have made it a rule that
everyone should come up to the microphone and now you have
the opportunity. Kindly come up here and introduce yourselves. .
Yes, Comrade. .

KOLT: Kolt, Znojmo, South Moravian region, Czechoslovak Road
Transport. Forgive me, but I must take this opportunity, I have
been looking forward to this and have been asked to represent
12,000 of my comrades. I am surprised at one thing and I agree
with the last but one comrade. I am gaining some experience as a
functionary but it is not good experience. What is happening is
common knowledge and we have all seen it, but I think that since

* *Editor's Note:* This part of the proceedings was not recorded owing to a
technical hitch, and is therefore missing from the record.

we have met at this Congress we need not fear that anyone will disperse us or anything of that sort and I would therefore like to appeal for calm so that we can proceed with due care. Then we shall not have to revoke anything in the future. As we drove to Prague from Znojmo and people recognized us, for there was a convoy of four cars, they waved to us in encouragement, showing us that they trusted us to act on their behalf. When I return from the Congress I am to visit some twenty or twenty-five villages and tell the people what we have discussed and decided. That is why I wish to ask you to proceed strictly according to the proposal we adopted at the outset.

THE CHAIRMAN: Thank you. Next please.

ŠTIKA: Štika, representing Prague 5 and the army. In my view, Comrades, the nervous atmosphere at the Congress is due to the circumstances under which we have met. It is difficult to hold discussions when the guns of tanks are pointing at you. The whole Party has been waiting for this Congress and it may be a long time before it gets a Congress that is in every way as it should originally have been. It is my opinion that above all we need a new representative Party organ. [*Applause.*] Nevertheless, we ought not to elect this organ hurriedly and without due consideration. There is nothing to prevent us adopting the provisional documents, which were prepared for the Congress. On the other hand we should of course not deprive hundreds of thousands of our Party members, whom we represent here, of their right to have account taken of all their comments on the new Party Statutes and on the work of the Party as a whole, which they sent in in preparation for the Congress. These we should debate later when the situation is calmer and we can give due time to them. However, there is one decision we can take right now: we can add to the Statutes a paragraph saying that under exceptional circumstances, and after all we have the right to change the Party Statutes, we can elect a provisional Central Committee which need not be definitive. We can provisionally approve the Congress agenda, we can approve provisional Statutes. And in the second half of the Congress we will then already have a representative organ capable of taking steps to set up or supplement the State organs we need for negotiations with the military authorities and the State organs of the Soviet Union, Hungary, Poland, etc.

40

The military aggression that has taken place is not solely a matter for the Party, it is a State matter. We need to put all these Party organs in order and give them instructions as a new representative organ, even if only a provisional one.

THE CHAIRMAN: Thank you. . the next comrade.

KÁBELE: Kábele, Liberec, North Bohemian region. Let us be quite clear about the responsibility of the Electoral Commission for the quality of the comrades whose names are put forward for the central authorities. We are of the opinion that as far as the rank-and-file members put forward by democratic methods from the ranks of the basic Party organizations are concerned, none of the delegates of this Congress can have any doubts as to their suitability for the functions into which they will be voted. [*Applause.*]

The only problem is that the Electoral Commission should show this Congress that it can choose suitable comrades from among those already serving on the Central Committee. [*Applause.*] Thank you.

THE CHAIRMAN: Next please, but can we have only views that have not already been expressed here.

ŠÁLEK: Šálek, East Bohemian region. Whatever else we do, we must today agree on the next steps to be taken by our Party. The way I look at it is this: we can sit here as long as we like, we can talk and argue, but I think that the important thing, as some of the others have said before me, is that the entire nation should know that here is a properly constituted organ, in this case our Congress or perhaps the Central Committee, and that they can put their trust in it. For this they must know our views. We have on the whole expressed these views in our resolutions, but I don't think that is enough. It really is not enough because the next few days may bring quite unexpected developments –

THE CHAIRMAN: Comrades, would you please be as brief as you can and make your meaning quite clear so that we don't get any repetitions.

ŠÁLEK [*continuing*]: . . I think that as far as the election of the new Central Committee is concerned it is right to accept the election of those comrades who were put forward by the primary organizations, and the Electoral Commission should include them in the list. [*Applause.*]

THE CHAIRMAN: Thank you. Should we go on with the discussion? I'll put it to the vote. Who thinks that we should discontinue the discussion on this point?.. I'm afraid this is going to be rather more complicated.. At least from where I am sitting it is impossible to see.. Comrades, the question was: are we to discontinue the discussion on the election of a new Central Committee? And should we instead deal with the list of candidates for the Electoral Commission?.. I'll put it to the vote. Shall we interrupt, or rather stop the discussion on this question? Who agrees with this proposal?.. [*Counting the vote.*].. Thank you. Who is against?.. Thank you. Who abstained?.. Comrades, I cannot count all the votes, but the Working Presidium can judge the ratio of votes, which was obviously in favour of discontinuing the discussion. We shall therefore not discuss this point any more.

Now if you will allow me, just a minor organizational matter. Will Comrades Mejzlík, Bartůněk, Frank and Chmelová, elected to the Credentials Commission, go to the appointed place so that they can join in its work.

Let us now pass on to the election of the Electoral Commission. Would the representatives of the individual delegations, beginning with the delegation of the Prague Municipal Party Organization, put forward two members each for the Electoral Commission...

NĚMČANSKÝ: Němčanský, Prague 1. On behalf of the Prague 1 delegation and after consultations with the leader of the delegation from Prague 9, I recommend Comrade Ludvík Pacovský and Comrade Jan Ketner from Prague 9.

THE CHAIRMAN: Thank you.. now the Central Bohemian delegation... [*Voices from the hall.*]...

DELEGATE: I do not wish to be a delegate at a Congress which acts hurriedly, without thinking. We must act with deliberation and in order to do so everyone must have the opportunity to express his opinion. It is impossible, whatever the circumstances, to take a vote on whether or not there is to be a discussion. Each of us represents eleven hundred communists who elected us and sent us here and they expect something of us. We simply cannot afford to make mistakes by being in too much of a hurry. According to the valid Statutes, once the Congress is in session it becomes the sole organ of the Party. Should we wish to elect the Central Committee during the course of the day we would succeed only in creating an unpleasant situation. I am convinced that the Congress can last longer, that it can perhaps be interrupted, but the only organ of power in the Party should be the Congress, its elected Presidium and its delegates. We should give careful thought to the election of the Central Committee and beware of the luxury of recommending someone in a hurry. And we must not forget those members of the Central Committee whom we trust but about whom we know nothing.

THE CHAIRMAN: Comrade, if you please, I think this can be left to the discretion of the Electoral Commission. It is not my intention to rush the Congress into any decision . . . [*Voices from the hall.*] . . . No one wants to suppress discussion. We have acted in a way I believe to be democratic. The Congress must act like a Congress and discharge the tasks of a Congress. This task is one of the most important and no one can absolve us of it. Otherwise we shall just be a lot of people having similar views and adopting certain weighty resolutions without giving them an institutional character. In doing so we would deprive this Congress of its driving force, crippling it and taking away its importance. [*Applause.*]

A VOICE FROM THE HALL: Let me ask you something. Who are the 'we' you keep talking about? I could also stand up and say I'm speaking for 'us'. We are all of us delegates to this Congress and we must achieve unanimity, otherwise we cannot take any action . . . [*A hubbub of voices.*]

THE CHAIRMAN: Quiet, Comrades, please, or we'll not be able to keep order. We must abide by certain rules. Those rules which we have accepted must be respected by everyone, that too is democracy. If we don't, then as soon as one or two comrades don't agree with any particular issue the discussion will just drag on and the Congress will get bogged down. I appreciate the danger that lies in rash and ill-considered action and as Chairman of this Congress, I am doing my best to avoid it. Try and help me to do so, that is all I ask. Yes, Comrade . . . [*An inaudible voice from the hall.*] . . . After we have elected the Electoral Commission I'll give you the latest news we have on the situation. Now let us get on with the election for the Electoral Commission. Prague, I repeat – Pacovský, Ketner. The Central Bohemian region did not finish its nomination. Oh, sorry, Zelenková was the first if I remember rightly . . who else? . . . [*Voices from the hall.*] . . . just a moment, please. Let us go on while the delegation from Central Bohemia decides whom to propose.

North Bohemia – Kratochvílová and Mrázek . . . I repeat, the North Bohemian delegation nominates Kratochvílová and Mrázek . . . oh, all right, let's start again . . . Comrades, before the interval I asked that all the members of one delegation should get together so that they could easily discuss their nominations. It seems to me that not all of them have really done so. Once again then . . the North Bohemian region . . one of those nominated . . one of those nominated is Comrade Kreperát, who is the chief secretary and also leader of the North Bohemian delegation . . but you have also elected him to serve on the Credentials Commission . . . [*Voices from the hall.*] . . . Comrades, we shan't get anywhere like this. Why don't you make one nomination and try to agree on it. Kratochvílová has been put forward . . . [*Voices can be heard debating.*] . . . make a note of it, Kratochvílová, Mrázek.

West Bohemian region . . . [*Voices heard debating.*] . . . right – Veselovský, Bartůněk. South Bohemia – Jakeš, Hrubý. East Bohemia – Makovský, Rejl. North Moravia – Čejka, Tržil. Central Bohemia – Zelenková, Holer.

As regards the Slovak regions, of course, our original decision holds good. So that is all. Yes, what is it? . . . [*A question from the hall.*] . . . Sorry, yes, we'll make a note of it . . . Devera, Pavlus . . . a change?

Comrades, here is a suggestion that the Electoral Commission should include one delegate representing the security forces, the Ministry of the Interior. Let us take a vote on it so that we can continue with our agenda. Who agrees with this suggestion? . . . [*Voices debating.*] . . . Well, the proposal has been put forward. Who agrees? . . Who is against the proposal that a representative of communists in the Ministry of the Interior should serve on the Electoral Commission? . . I ask you again, who is against? . . The delegates nominated for the armed forces are – They were elected as representatives of the armed forces in general and not specifically for the security forces – I'm sorry, Comrades, we have to be quite clear about this. We mustn't make any bloomers here. This delegate says that at the Prague municipal conference delegates of the security forces were elected separately. Of the communists in the security forces, that is. Sorry, this is a little confused. In the minutes of the municipal conference the delegates of the security forces and the army were bracketed together under the heading of the armed forces. Perhaps it would be best if the army delegates would substitute a delegate from the security forces for one of their own. You agree? Excellent. Then we don't have to take a vote on it. The two bodies concerned have agreed it between them. Now can we have your nominations. Comrade Štefan Šarik. So we have Devera and Šarik representing the armed forces.

A VOICE FROM THE HALL: May I say something, Comrades?... We have already had the nominations of Devera and Pavlus . . . Devera was put down and – yes, also for the army. Of course under these circumstances it is impossible to nominate for the army. We must all sit together, most of us are sitting at the back here, it can't be done like this . .

THE CHAIRMAN: Perhaps the delegates of the armed forces could go over there together and agree on a joint nomination . . if you don't mind –

A VOICE FROM THE HALL: We have a small change in the nomination for the Prague municipal organization. We would like to nominate Comrade Jiří Kučera for Prague 9 in place of Comrade Ketner, that's me.

A MEMBER OF THE WORKING PRESIDIUM: Pardon?... Yes, that's right, I think we can accept that all the Slovak delegates present here, all of them I would say, owing to their small number, have a right to serve on the Electoral Commission. They are aware of their responsibility. We have already agreed that the whole Slovak delegation is to nominate members for the future Central Committee. They can of course now sit on the Electoral Commission while reserving the right later to nominate their delegates for the Central Committee. Now allow me to repeat all the names . .

For the East Bohemian region Kovaříček and Václav Šolc. Is that correct? Yes, it is. So I repeat, according to my notes: Prague – Pacovský, Kučera, Central Bohemia – Zelenková, Holer. North Bohemia – Kratochvílová, Mrázek. West Bohemia – Veselovský, Bartůněk. South Bohemia – Jakeš, Hrubý. East Bohemia – Kovaříček, Šolc. North Moravia – Makovský, Frank – I'm sorry – Frank, Hrubý. South Moravia – Čejka, Tržil.

THE CHAIRMAN: Now we are only waiting for the nominations from the armed forces. Before we get them, let me read you a proposal put forward by a comrade whose signature I cannot read. It is, I think, Comrade Hrubý or Hladký . . This is what he

suggests: let each regional delegation vote on the nominations because they have not met yet and even here there is neither the time nor
the place for such a meeting . . . Comrades, personally I think it is
possible for the delegations to vote among themselves, but that we
should then vote on their nominations with confidence in the proposed candidates. But we must vote as a Congress. I'm now only
waiting for the nominations of the armed forces before I put it to
the vote.

In the meantime let me give you some information. I have received a report from the municipal secretary Kotrč. The radio has
announced that the military authorities have issued an ultimatum
to the remaining members of the Central Committee Presidium,
demanding that they form a new Presidium. The occupation
authorities themselves nominate Bil'ak, Barbírek and Indra, who
are to form a new government, and all this by tonight, otherwise
they will appoint their own Soviet occupation organs . . . [*Uproar
in the hall, expressions of disagreement.*] . . . Quiet, Comrades, that
is the news I have received.

Another piece of information: some of the secretaries, for instance Lenárt, Kolder, Indra, and others, are working in the
Central Committee building. They have called a plenary meeting
of the Central Committee for four o'clock this afternoon in the
Praha Hotel. They say they do not wish to talk to the Congress
delegates.

We'll discuss these questions after we have elected the new
organs, which will then draft the necessary proposals. It will be
necessary first of all to verify these reports and then decide what
course of action our Congress is to take in order to implement its
right to be the supreme organ of the Party – which it has gained
by the very fact that it has met. While the Congress is in session, all
the members of the former Central Committee come under its juris-
diction, relinquishing their seats on the Committee the moment it
is convened. We must look at this question very carefully and
decide how to force these comrades from the Central Committee
to respect Party discipline – [*Cries of 'Hear, Hear!', applause, expressions of approval from the whole Congress.*]

THE CHAIRMAN [*continuing*]: The Organizational Committee has
made progress and is handing out papers for those who wish to take
part in the debate. The first three have been handed to me. So that

we can finish the voting on the Electoral Commission, may I have the nominations by the armed forces ... once again, please, we can't hear ... Škrob? ... excellent, so it is Škrob and Šarik. The armed forces put forward these two names. I should now like to take the vote – Yes, what is it you want to say? ... [*A voice from the hall.*] ... Comrades, I consider this proposal to be a very sensible one ... [*Voices.*] ... It is a proposal that the Working Presidium of the Congress should nominate two or three of its members who have already taken part in earlier discussions on the election of a new Central Committee and who may perhaps know the intentions of Comrade Dubček or other members of the Party Presidium. We can then consider their proposals and thoroughly discuss them. I believe this is a sensible suggestion ... [*Voices debating in the hall.*] ... With your permission, I would make my own nominations. Comrade Vodsloň and Comrade Martin Vaculík ... [*Voices from the hall.*] ... All right, there are three nominees, anything else? ... We can nominate three delegates to the Electoral Committee ... [*Someone nominates Pelikán.*] ... Comrade Pelikán tells me that as he is a member of the Press Commission he can't be elected to the Electoral Commission .. That leaves the original nominations – Comrades Vodsloň and Martin Vaculík.

... Someone has put forward Comrade Litera ... and Comrade Šimeček. We have four nominations.

Comrades, I learn that Comrade Vodsloň is not a delegate to the Congress, he is here in a purely advisory capacity and therefore cannot sit on the Electoral Commission. That reduces the number of candidates to three again. I think we can leave it at that – Comrade Vaculík is also not a delegate – So the nomination for the Electoral Commission is Comrade Šimeček and Comrade Litera. And now let us take a vote on it. Does anyone else want to say something? All right, Comrade ... [*A voice from the hall.*] ... I can't give a satisfactory answer to that, Comrades. Whether they are standing as candidates or not.

A DELEGATE: Sorry to be butting in like this, but I sent in my question a long time ago and the Chairman has simply overlooked it so that others are having their say and I am not. I'd like to draw your attention to the following, Comrades. We as delegates ought to bear in mind that as far as the world at large is concerned, the Party is still being represented by the members of the old Central

Committee. The nation expects our Congress to adopt a standpoint on this. And that is why I propose, as I have already done from where I was sitting, that we should vote the Working Presidium of the Congress to be the Party Presidium, with the Congress plenum playing the role of the Central Committee plenum, even if for only a short time, perhaps a matter of hours, until the Electoral Commission decides what is to be done. Thank you for listening to me.

THE CHAIRMAN: This proposal was already put forward this morning and was rejected. But we can take a vote on it if you like . . . [*Voices from the hall.*] . . . Only please bear in mind that there is no time to be lost and that our decisions can influence what is happening outside. On the contrary – [*A voice from the hall.*] . . . Yes? . . .

THE CHAIRMAN [*continuing*]: . . . Wait, Comrades, I know both Comrade Kreperát and Comrade Duba . . . among the various delegations, together with the Party Presidium. I think we must respect such proposals and take them into account. I only regret that you didn't make them a little earlier, because like this we are losing time. Now I would like to put it to the vote. Who votes for the proposal? Thank you. Who is against it? Comrades, anyone against? No? No one. Any abstentions? There don't seem to be any abstentions either. Oh, one abstention, please make a note of it in the minutes.

And now, Comrades, allow me to make a few organizational announcements.

1. Will Comrade Litera join the Electoral Commission immediately and take part in its work. And will the members of the Committee go to the organizational bureau, if they are not there already.

2. Comrades from West Bohemia have asked me to appeal to the leaders of the district delegations to go up to the balcony. The chief delegate wishes to consult them.

3. We have here a few items of news as broadcast by the radio. The legal Prague radio station has brought us some foreign news:

– Ceausescu:

The occupation of Czechoslovakia will have very serious consequences. The Romanian National Assembly has been in session since this morning to discuss the invasion.

48

- 14.15 hours:

  This is an item from the East Bohemian station: The head of the Administrative Department of the Ministry of the Interior, Lieutenant-Colonel Strnadel, condemns the actions of Colonel Šalgovič. The members of the Regional Administration of the Ministry also wish to dissociate themselves from Colonel Šalgovič, who has joined up with counter-revolutionary elements.

- 14.20 hours:

  Prague has again broadcast appeals for calm, asking the population not to allow itself to be provoked into conflict. There was also a special appeal not to take part in any demonstrations.

- 14.21 hours:

  An appeal from the former Central Committee and Central Control and Audit Commission was read, asking all members of the Central Committee and all candidates to attend the Congress.

- 14.22 hours:

  Yugoslavia – meetings are being held in factories, at which the workers are expressing full support for the legal Government and Party leadership in Czechoslovakia.

Comrades, please allow me to interrupt our proceedings in order to welcome most cordially in our midst members of our Czechoslovak socialist government. [*Tumultuous applause.*] We are now that much stronger, Comrades, we have with us some of the men who have for several months been at the helm of our State. It's good to be together like this. I should now like to ask Comrade Minister Machačová to speak to us.

MACHAČOVÁ: Dear Comrades, Delegates,

At its extraordinary session on 22 August 1968 the government of the Czechoslovak Socialist Republic asked me to convey to you its sincere greetings and to wish you every success in your deliberations. The government is convinced that your Congress will give unanimous expression to the will of the country's communists and that the resolutions it adopts will confirm the road taken by the Communist Party of Czechoslovakia and indeed the whole country since January. In spite of the exceptionally difficult circumstances caused by the unlawful occupation, and the internment of the Premier, Comrade Černík, the government is making every effort to fulfil its constitutional obligations towards the people.

At its extraordinary session yesterday the government decided that the Ministry of Foreign Affairs, through our ambassadors in Moscow, Warsaw, Budapest, Berlin and Sofia, should hand over a diplomatic note demanding the withdrawal of the troops of the five Warsaw Pact signatories from Czechoslovak territory.

The same demand was contained in a proclamation addressed to the governments of the Soviet Union, the German Democratic Republic, the Polish People's Republic, the Hungarian People's Republic and the Bulgarian People's Republic, together with an appeal for the cessation of armed acts resulting in bloodshed and the destruction of material values; and also for the immediate creation of normal conditions for the work of Czechoslovak constitutional and political organs whose interned members should be released, enabling those organs to resume work.

At the same time the government called on all our citizens to rally round the properly elected Czechoslovak government, to show their statesmanlike discretion once again and to help create the conditions necessary for normal life.

The government has also taken steps to ensure that the national economy functions as well as possible under the present circumstances. Yesterday members of the government visited the President, Comrade Ludvík Svoboda, and informed him about its work. The President expressed his agreement with what had been done and assured the government that it had his full support. The President promised to do everything he could to fulfil the government's demand that it should be enabled to function normally as soon as possible.

Dear Comrades, Delegates. Let me assure you on behalf of the government that it will do everything in its power to carry out, in these fateful moments, the task with which our nations have entrusted it, the task of building democratic socialism in our sovereign State, the Czechoslovak Socialist Republic. [*Prolonged and tumultuous applause.*]

THE CHAIRMAN: Comrades, permit me to thank Comrade Machačová-Dostálová most cordially for conveying to us the government's standpoint and its proclamation, and permit me also to take a vote on it. I should like all the delegates to vote on this

standpoint. Who votes in favour?.. Thank you?.. Who against?
.. No one. Any abstentions?... [*A voice from the hall.*] ...

THE CHAIRMAN: Excellent. Thank you for the suggestion. Comrades,
allow me on my own behalf to express my admiration to the comrades in our government, and in particular to Comrade Machačová-Dostálová, for everything they have done. They really deserve
our heartfelt thanks ... [*A voice from the hall.*] ... Yes, that also
helps. Comrades, we are near the main armoury and everything
can be heard there. We have been warned about this. That is why
we are now making less noise than we did earlier on. And we also
feel calmer now that you are in our midst ... [*A voice from the
hall.*] ... What was that?

Comrades, I think we should consider this proclamation to be
a completely independent one. That members of the Czechoslovak
socialist government are present at our Extraordinary Congress
and fully support its decisions ... [*Voices in the hall.*] ... Those
members of the government who are not interned – Yes? Please
try and help me by putting forward fewer proposals ... Yes, I'm
sure we shall do that ... [*Questions from the hall regarding the
whereabouts of the absent members of the government.*] ...

THE CHAIRMAN: Vice-premier Šik is in Yugoslavia, as most of you
know, Comrade Husák and Vice-premier Colotka are in Slovakia.
Comrade Valeš will give you a brief account.

VALEŠ: We're in contact with Comrades Hamouz and Štrougal.
They have approved what the government has done so far. For
various reasons which we accept they will of course not take part
in our sessions. We're keeping them informed, however, and are
in touch with them. That means they are not interned.

THE CHAIRMAN: Is that enough, Comrades?... Sorry ... [*Voices
from the hall.*] ... Yes, Comrades, your proposals are being
minuted and the appropriate committee will consider them in
keeping with the proposal I put forward that we should issue a
special proclamation or a special report on the Congress, telling
the public that members of the government are taking part in it.
I believe you are in agreement on this point. Yes?... Thank you.
And now, in consultation with the Working Presidium, I suggest
we take a short break .. But if you don't mind I'll first ask Comrade Machačová-Dostálová to be so kind as to introduce all
members of the government who have come to join us.

MACHAČOVÁ: The following members of the government have come to your Congress: Minister of the Interior Pavel, Minister of Education Kadlec, Minister of Foreign Trade Valeš, Minister of the Chemical Industry Rázl, Minister of Heavy Industry Krejčí, Minister of Health Vlček, Minister of Justice Kučera, Minister of Forestry and Waterways Hanuš, Minister of Transport Řehák – who is not present at the moment as he has been charged with a special task – Minister of Labour and Social Welfare Štancl, Minister of the Mining Industry Penc, Minister of Finance Sucharda, Minister Hůla, Chairman of the Prices Board, Minister of Culture Galuška, as well as Deputy Ministers Šmok, Comrade Dvořák for the Minister of Planning Vlasák, Comrade Toman for the Minister of Building – who happens to be abroad – and Deputy Minister Loukotka for the Ministry of Home Trade. Also the Minister of Agriculture Borůvka, and Comrades Řeháček for the Ministry of Power and Novák for the Ministry of Culture.

THE CHAIRMAN: According to my information, the Minister of National Defence is not a free agent . . . [*A voice from the hall.*] . . . Comrades, can I ask you to tell us why some of our government members are not here. Apart from those mentioned already?

VALEŠ: Comrade Černík – we all know he is interned. Comrades Štrougal and Hamouz have justifiable fears for their safety. Yesterday they were released by mistake, then shortly afterwards sought again. Their whereabouts are therefore being kept secret. With our knowledge. We have not managed to contact Comrades Husák and Colotka, most probably for the same reasons as those that prevented them from being present at the Congress. Comrades Šik and Vlasák are on holiday in Yugoslavia; Comrade Hájek is likewise in Yugoslavia; Minister Trokan is in America. Minister Korčák is in the Soviet Union. On official business. He left before . . . Comrade Pavlovský did not come to the first meeting of the government presided over by Comrade Černík shortly after the occupation started and he has not contacted us since, nor have we succeeded in getting him to take part in the work of the government . . . [*A voice in the hall.*] . . . Comrade Hruškovič, who is a member of the government, did not work in Prague, he was in Bratislava as the Industrial Secretary of the Central Committee of the Slovak Communist Party and, for the same reasons as Comrades Husák and Colotka, did not attend that first session conducted by Comrade Černík . . . We have no contact with Comrade Hofman, who was not a Minister but took part in the work of the government. We didn't try to establish contact with him as we knew he had been taken to the Soviet Embassy, and when he himself got in touch later we did not invite him to our government meetings.

THE CHAIRMAN: Thank you, Comrade Valeš . . There was one other comrade who wanted to ask something . . . [*Inaudible query.*] . . . Perhaps we should let Comrade Pavel say a few words about this. But please let's not prolong things any further by these questions. We really must get on. A great deal remains to be done. We can get our information by other means.

PAVEL: Yes, we did get such a report, and it was verified by the [parliamentary] Army and Security Services Committee in my presence. Comrade Šalgovič told us that he knew nothing about the arrest of Comrade Císař or about other similar cases, and that he would report to us in two hours' time. Two hours later he did report, saying that Comrade Císař had in fact been arrested, but that he, Šalgovič, had had nothing to do with it. I myself have no means of verifying this. You see, when I went to the Ministry the day before yesterday, it was already occupied. Since then I have been taking part in the work of the government and the Army and Security Services Committee of parliament.

THE CHAIRMAN: Thank you.

We have got through a large part of our agenda, Comrades, and now we'll take a short break. Only twenty or at most twenty-five minutes, if you please. Kindly remain in the hall.

[*Interval*]

THE CHAIRMAN: Let us continue. Comrade Hejzlar is down to speak.

HEJZLAR: I have only a brief note to the press, radio, and those who have already received copies of the draft proclamation. Once again, there seems to be a hidden hand working against us. There is a typing error on Page 2, where instead of saying that at twelve noon on Friday 23 August there is to be an hour's strike in protest, it says that there is to be a *general* strike in protest. Please put this right in your copies, and let those who work for the news

53

media bear this in mind. It's incredible, but it has happened. I am speaking especially to representatives of the press, radio and television, but we must all be quite clear about this error in the text.

THE CHAIRMAN: Comrades, this unfortunate mistake will be put right in future radio transmissions. It will be stated correctly that it is an hour's strike in protest. Kindly bear this in mind . . . [*Voices from the hall.*] . . . Will the leader of the East Bohemian delegation come forward, to the right of the rostrum. The leader of the delegation from East Bohemia. And now, Comrades, one more organizational matter. Those of you who are walking about in that corridor on the right-hand side, will you please resume your seats. Like this you are causing a distraction. It's in the interests of us all. Once again I ask you to go back to your places.

And now we have two important reports on the agenda. The first is by the Credentials Commission, and it will be presented by Comrade Kratochvíle. Will he kindly take the floor.

KRATOCHVÍLE: Comrades, Delegates. On behalf of the Credentials Commission I lay before the Fourteenth Extraordinary Congress of the Czechoslovak Communist Party the following report:

On the basis of credentials presented to us and verified by the district committees of the Party or personally by the heads of the regional delegations, a total of 1,112 properly elected delegates were present at the Congress at 14.55 hours. These include 1,044 men and 68 women. The number 1,112 represents 72·6 per cent of all properly elected delegates, this being more than a two-thirds majority, which means there is a quorum and the Congress is at this moment the sole and supreme body entitled under the Statutes to direct the activities of the Party. The Congress takes account of the fact that, owing to the occupation of the Republic by forces of the Warsaw Pact countries, the majority of the Slovak delegates have so far not been able to attend the Congress, and that Congress must therefore make sure the Communist Party of Slovakia is not put under any disadvantage by this fact. The Credentials Commission cannot at the present time provide any more information on the composition of the Extraordinary Congress, as it has no further detailed material to hand.

Thank you.

THE CHAIRMAN: Please stay here for the moment. Comrades, Delegates, have you any questions on the report of the Credentials Commission? . . . [*Voices from the hall.*] . . .

KRATOCHVÍLE: With your permission I'll repeat that sentence. It was not the way you understood it, Comrade. This is how it went: 'The Congress takes account of the fact that, owing to the occupation of the Republic by forces of the Warsaw Pact countries, the majority of the Slovak delegates have so far not been able to attend the Congress' . . .

THE CHAIRMAN: One of the members of the Working Presidium suggests that the Credentials Commission should give us another count of the Slovak delegates a little later. We're told that in the course of the past hour some more Slovak delegates have arrived. I would ask the comrades from Slovakia to help the Credentials Commission speed things up by putting down their names and whenever possible presenting themselves in person to the Commission so that they can be registered. Any more questions for the Credentials Commission? Yes? . . . [*Inaudible query.*] . . . Comrades, we have here a proposal that the report of the Credentials Commission should state how many members of the Central Committee, how many candidates and members of the various top Party organs are present at the Congress. Will you accept this proposal?

KRATOCHVÍLE: Yes, we'll do that as soon as we get more material. We haven't at our disposal all the documents from the occupied building of the Central Committee. That makes it very difficult for us to be accurate, but we did try in the extremely short time available. The Credentials Commission will continue to look into the number of delegates present and other details about the Congress and it will submit its report later.

THE CHAIRMAN: Thank you. Yes, Comrade? . . . [*A query from the hall.*] . . . Yes, we mean to talk about this very thing. Right, I would only like to repeat that proposal in more detail. The Credentials Commission is to ascertain the number of Central Committee members present at the Congress. Of course we can at the same time record how many members of the Central Committee were prevented from attending by intimidation, internment, arrest, and so on. Will the members of the Central Committee inform the Credentials Commission accordingly? . . . [*A query from the hall.*] . . . Yes? . . . That's right, Comrades, you have the proposal of the Credentials Commission. I'm sure there will be more comments from delegates – Sorry, I can't hear . . . It has been stated that a more detailed report will be made by the Credentials Commission later. That means everything that is usually contained in such a report. As far as we're concerned, the essential thing is the basic data – numbers of delegates, verified credentials, and so on. Everything else can be done later. The report has been presented by a member of the Credentials Commission, so that we should know for certain what we're doing and whether our resolutions have any validity. That is what counts at the moment. Nothing else is of any importance.

A DELEGATE: Forgive me for coming up here, Comrades, but I would like to draw attention to the fact that we really are attending an Extraordinary Congress, that we are practically working in conditions of illegality, so let's discard, at least temporarily, all the usual conference red tape, let's not meditate about the necessary, or as I see it unnecessary, numbers of delegates. In my view what *is* important is that we have a quorum, whether we are blonde or ginger is I think of little consequence just now. [*Applause.*]

THE CHAIRMAN: Thank you. We can end the discussion on this point, Comrades. I'll put it to the vote. Does the Congress approve the report of the Credentials Commission? Those in favour please raise their hands . . . Thank you. Anyone against? . . Any abstentions? . . I see that we are really unanimous. Thank you for your report, Comrade. And now I should like to ask the chief secretary of the district Party committee in Most, Comrade Mrázek, to present the draft election rules.

MRÁZEK: The Electoral Commission has asked me to report to you on the following:

1. Comrade Pacovský has been elected chairman of the Electoral Commission.

2. We have decided to submit the draft election rules in good time so that once we have compiled the list of candidates for the new Central Committee and Central Control and Audit Commission we can start the election right away and not be held up by points of procedure.

   Our Committee has agreed unanimously that we should put forward the proposal that has already been sent to you, with the exception of points 34 and 35, which state that the Electoral Commission should also concern itself with counting the votes in a particular way. Owing to the fact that the counting will have to be carried out manually, since the machines were originally ordered for 9 September and are not yet ready, we must now, and this will be our next proposal, elect the tellers.

There is another departure from normal Congress procedure, too. At a normal Congress we should first of all alter the Statutes. This would enable us to elect to the Central Committee comrades who have been in the Party for at least five years. This is not possible according to the present Statutes. We debated this for a bit and finally decided to change the Statutes in this one respect, otherwise we shan't alter them. That comrades who have been in the Party for at least five years can be elected to the Central Committee and the Central Control and Audit Commission. After that we can approve the election rules.

Perhaps I ought to sum it up, Comrades. First, a change in the Statutes on this one point; second, approval of the election rules as presented to you; third, our Commission suggests that you choose forty tellers, or in other words members of a committee of scrutineers, who will count the votes.

THE CHAIRMAN: Thank you.

A DELEGATE: I would like to ask something. Point 17 says: 'Before the vote is taken, each delegate will show his mandate to the Electoral Commission, which will mark it to show that he has taken part in the election.' How do you mean to do this when many of us have no written mandate and a number of the comrades who came in other ways than via the districts do not have the necessary documents? Can you answer that?

MRÁZEK: The Commission supposed that all the Congress delegates had their mandates issued by the district Party committees – as do those from our district. If that is not the case, I suggest that this be done now by the heads of the regional or district delegations, who have our complete confidence.

THE CHAIRMAN: Thank you. Comrades, will the Electoral Commission record all the proposals that are put forward – I cannot possibly keep track of them all – so that I can put them to the vote. All right? I want you to take down every proposal so that we can act on them later. Now are there any more? . . . [*A query from the hall.*] . . .

MRÁZEK: No, Comrades, I did not give these details. Even if it takes an hour or two, we'll try to provide a list of candidates as quickly as possible, certainly during this afternoon. This was the deadline, evidently. I'm sorry that I missed out these details.

THE CHAIRMAN: Any further questions? . . . [*Queries from the hall.*] . . . Perhaps we can sum up this proposal. I think we can ask the Electoral Commission to omit from the election rules all the clauses which presuppose a regular Congress and which cannot be met in our present conditions. I feel the Electoral Commission could draft the rules very quickly, so that we will have both proper election rules approved by the Congress and proceedings which will be in keeping with these rules. That is why I ask that all those clauses which cannot be complied with under these extraordinary circumstances should be left out, and it is for you, the delegates, to decide. I think the Party and its members will understand why we have had to do this.

Nevertheless, Comrades, in order that we can do our job properly, I recommend that we vote in favour of two things. First, that the present statutes should be changed in that either everybody is eligible for membership of the Central Committee* or only those who have been members of the Party for at least five years. At present we have two proposals before us. Kindly give your views on them. And secondly, we should elect a committee to count the votes. Everything else will be done in accordance with the recommendations of the Congress Working Presidium. Would you like to comment on these two proposals? . . . [*Queries and comments from the hall.*] . . . Thank you. This comrade would raise the minimum length of Party membership to ten years. Yes, Comrade Rázl.

RÁZL: If we do that we'll prevent the young people from being represented on the Central Committee . . . we should be guilty of keeping the young at arm's length ourselves . . .

THE CHAIRMAN: Thank you. Anyone else? Yes, Comrade . . .

A DELEGATE: I am for the five-year period. [*Cries of assent.*] I have seen at a number of Party meetings how necessary it is to give young people the opportunity of getting into the Central Committee. After all, they can become members of parliament at twenty-one. And many comrades, such as Indra, who have been in the Party for twenty years or more, are proof that length of Party

* *Editor's Note:* i.e. regardless of the length of time they had been in the Party.

membership is in itself no guarantee. We really must give the young the opportunity of becoming members of the supreme Party organ.

THE CHAIRMAN: Comrades, regarding the length of membership. I think we ought to keep the discussion brief. Yes?... [*A query from the hall.*] ... Yes, I agree we have to be consistent. Well then, we have here two proposals. One that we approve the five-year period of Party membership as a condition for election to the Central Committee, or even make that period longer; and secondly that we make it as short as possible or omit such a condition altogether – Yes – another comrade wishes to say something about this.

A WOMAN DELEGATE: ... If you please. Let's first of all discuss this properly, so that we really know what we're doing, but on the other hand let's not get bogged down in talk.

VOICES FROM THE HALL: ... on the one hand we support the idea of direct election and on the other we curtail it ...

THE CHAIRMAN: Please, Comrades, limit yourselves to proposals which have not been put forward already.

A DELEGATE: Why not make the following exception: the five-year period would not apply to Party members under twenty-three, for whom it would be impossible to have five years in the Party. This would enable young people to get elected to the higher central organs.

THE CHAIRMAN: As you can see, Comrades, a relatively simple question can easily lead to complicated discussions. Perhaps you would bear that in mind when you ask to speak. Yes?... [*A voice from the hall.*] ... Thank you. Has anyone anything to say that has not been said before?... [*A voice from the hall.*] ... [*Voices.*] ... Quiet, please. Comrades, can we have a little quiet. I'll consult the Working Presidium and then we'll decide what's to be done.

[*After the consultation.*]

Comrades, I suggest we end the discussion on this point, since it will not produce anything relevant beyond what has been said already. I'll therefore put it to the vote. The proposal is that the length of Party membership, any length, should not be made a condition for candidature to the Central Committee of our Party or to the Central Control and Audit Commission. Those in favour please raise their hands .. Thank you. Who is against?.. Quite a few, too. In that case we must count the votes. We'll have to take that vote again, I cannot possibly estimate the numbers from here. I am putting the proposal to the vote once more, Comrades. Before I do that, however, I'd like to ask the members of the Working Presidium to help in counting the votes. I repeat the proposal: election of members to the central Party organs with no condition as to length of Party membership. Who is in favour? . . Count, please . . Upstairs too. Now we can have a quick tally . . Is the count finished? . . It is? Thank you.

Who is against the proposal? Please raise your hands. And now the count . . Finished? Let us know the result as quickly as possible.

And now the last question. Who abstained? . . One, two, three . . four, five . . six . . on the balcony? . . Ten? That makes it sixteen altogether. Perhaps we can continue and not wait for the report. [*Addressing the chairman of the Commission.*]: Let's go on.

Comrades, I'd now like to return to the original proposal that the Electoral Commission change the election rules in such a way as to make them correspond to the circumstances in which our Extraordinary Congress is being held. The changes to be submitted to the Congress for approval. Who is in favour of this motion? The proposal is that the Electoral Commission will adapt the draft election rules in keeping with the extraordinary conditions of the Congress . . Thank you. Who is against? . . Who abstained? . . One. That means that this was, to all intents and purposes, carried unanimously. Comrades, you are to make what changes you consider to be clearly necessary in view of the extraordinary conditions of the Congress. And now, Comrades, we have to elect a committee responsible for counting the votes. It is to have forty members. Will the individual regional delegations put up candidates for this committee . . .

It is suggested that the leaders of the regional delegations should give the Working Presidium a written list of candidates, the Working Presidium should make a note of it, and the comrades whose names are put forward would then become the tellers who are to count the votes during the election. All right? . . That means that each regional delegation will put up four delegates. Right? Four each. If you would kindly agree on the names and pass them on to us at once.

A brief announcement, Comrades. Will Comrade Vyčítal from

Pardubice go to the right-hand corner by the Working Presidium table. And Comrade Pavlíček from Děčín, will he come forward and have his name registered.

One more important announcement – the committee which looks after the accommodation of the delegates asks that the leaders of the various district delegations come within the next hour to Room 8 on the ground floor. I repeat, will the leaders of the district delegations go to Room 8 on the ground floor within the hour and state their requirements as regards accommodation for their members. Otherwise they may find themselves without anywhere to sleep tonight. Let us hope this won't happen.

Comrades, I can't understand how this came about, there has been some mistake. The numbers I have been given on our vote just don't tally. They don't give even the approximate total of delegates at this Congress. In all probability there's nothing to be done but to take the vote again, in properly organized fashion. Will the tellers, when they have counted the votes, give their totals to the comrades at the Working Presidium table here on the right so that they can be added up and the result announced. I expect that with the numbers just being called out, some were not recorded, so it will be better to do it in writing on signed slips of paper.

A STEWARD: May I ask the delegates, on behalf of the stewards, to maintain discipline. Please take your places and follow the stewards' instructions. Thank you.

THE CHAIRMAN: Yes, thank you. Comrades stewards, we'll have to take the vote once more on the length of membership required as a condition for election to the Central Committee. Are you ready?.. Are you ready to count the votes?.. Hand in your slips of paper at the table here to the right so that they can be added up. Let's take that vote again. Who is in favour of Comrade Pavlíček's proposal that comrades be elected to the central Party organs regardless of the length of their membership in the Party? Who is in favour?.. Can the votes be counted? The Working Presidium? Finished? Thank you . . .

And now, who is against this proposal but wants the period limited to five years?.. How about the balcony, votes counted? Have the stewards finished? Thank you. Were there any abstentions?.. Oh, a very small number. Two, four, six.. how many on the balcony? None. That means six comrades. Please hand in your reports.

A delegation of the National Assembly, which has come to greet our Congress, asks to be allowed to speak. Will the head of the delegation take the floor.

HEAD OF PARLIAMENTARY DELEGATION: At today's meeting, which is being held in a building surrounded by the occupation forces, the National Assembly adopted the following message to the Fourteenth Congress:*

. . .

. . . We fully support the properly elected delegates of the Congress and wish them every success. Imbued by the ideal of socialist internationalism we appeal to the Central Committees of the Communist Party of the Soviet Union, the Workers' Party of Poland, the Hungarian Socialist Party, the German United Socialist Party, and the Bulgarian Communist Party to realize the gravity of the situation brought about by the occupation of our country. We ask them to acknowledge that only a Communist Party that enjoys the full trust of the Czechoslovak people and freedom to carry out its political work can resolve this very grave situation. We consider the fulfilment of these demands to be a basic condition if the Communist Party of Czechoslovakia is to enjoy the confidence of the people and play a leading role in the development of a socialist Czechoslovakia in the spirit of the post-January political course of our Party, as expressed in its Action Programme. This is of vital interest to the international workers' and communist movement and to all progressive forces the world over.

At the same time, Comrades, may I ask you to excuse those delegates who are attending the session of our parliament, as well as members of the Central Committee. I can give you their names . . . The National Assembly is in session . . . That is all I wanted to tell you. Thank you.

THE CHAIRMAN [*in Slovak*]: I would like to thank the deputy of the National Assembly for the greetings sent to us by its members. And now will the chairman of the Electoral Commission carry out the election of members of the Central Committee of the Party.

CHAIRMAN OF ELECTORAL COMMISSION: I'm afraid I must disappoint you, Comrades, but the Electoral Commission has not

* *Editor's Note:* The beginning of the message is almost inaudible on a new tape

finished its work yet. However, we have learned that you think we ought first of all to elect, by a show of hands, those eight members of the Central Committee who are interned. So, while the Electoral Commission continues its work, and it will try and be as quick as it can, I propose that the Congress agree to vote, by a show of hands, on the eight names of the interned members of the Central Committee as they are read out. Will the Chairman open a discussion on this point? Or, if there is no discussion, take a vote?

THE CHAIRMAN [*in Slovak*]: It has been decided.

CHAIRMAN OF ELECTORAL COMMISSION: I'll read all the eight names out to you, Comrades, and then repeat them one by one: Svoboda, Dubček, Černík, Smrkovský, Kriegel, Špaček, Císař, Šimon. And now I'll read them again, one by one, and the Chairman will ask you to vote on each individually. Ludvík Svoboda.

THE CHAIRMAN [*in Slovak*]: Comrades, will you please vote. Thank you. Has anyone abstained? . . Is anyone against? . . Comrade Ludvík Svoboda has been unanimously elected to the new Central Committee.

CHAIRMAN OF ELECTORAL COMMISSION: Alexander Dubček.

THE CHAIRMAN [*in Slovak*]: Thank you. Any abstentions? . . Who is against Comrade Dubček? . . The vote is on Comrade Dubček.

CHAIRMAN OF ELECTORAL COMMISSION: Perhaps it would be better, even though it is not customary, if I took the vote, so we don't have to repeat the names like this. We voted in favour of Comrade Dubček. I ask who is not in favour? . . Who abstained? . . No one.

Who is in favour of Comrade Černík? . . Thank you. Who is against Comrade Černík? . . Thank you. Any abstentions? . . No. Comrade Černík is elected unanimously.

Who is in favour of Comrade Smrkovský? . . Thank you. Who is against Comrade Smrkovský? . . One vote. Any abstentions? . . One. Comrade Smrkovský has been elected – Two abstentions? I am sorry, it seems there were two abstentions.

Comrade Kriegel. Who is in favour of Comrade Kriegel? . . Thank you. Who is against Comrade Kriegel? . . One vote. Any abstentions? . . Five. Comrade Kriegel has been elected.

Who is in favour of Comrade Špaček? . . . [*Voices from the hall.*] . . . Come, Comrades, do you think it is necessary to hold things up on that account? . . I always repeat the names. Comrade

63

Špaček. Who is in favour of Comrade Špaček?.. Thank you. Who is against Comrade Špaček? . . One vote. Any abstentions?.. Three.

Comrade Císař. Who is in favour of Comrade Císař?.. Thank you. Who is against Comrade Císař?.. Four against. Any abstentions?.. One, two, three, six – would you be so kind, Comrade, and help me count the votes. Anyone on the balcony?.. Four. Ten abstentions altogether.

Comrade Šimon. Who is in favour of Comrade Šimon?.. Thank you. Who is against?.. Anyone downstairs against?.. No. Any abstentions?.. Five have abstained.

These were the eight who are interned and who have now been elected to the new Central Committee of the Party. In the meantime the Electoral Commission has been busy and has drawn up a further proposal. As I did not take part in the last stages of its work, another member of the Commission will take over from me.

A WOMAN MEMBER OF THE ELECTORAL COMMISSION: Will the Working Presidium take charge of the election? We in the Electoral Commission have omitted the names of the comrades you have just elected. Of the other members of the existing Central Committee, we put forward Comrade Josef Černý. Who is in favour of Comrade Josef Černý?

A VOICE FROM THE HALL: But we didn't agree to vote like this!

MEMBER OF THE ELECTORAL COMMISSION: The Electoral Commission has been urged, by some of you and by others, to conclude its work. We called the heads of the regional delegations together and the regional delegations made their selection. The names I'm now reading out to you were put forward by the regional delegations at regional Party conferences. They were all members of the Central Committee. Apart from that, as you can see, I have material here from the individual regions, containing further proposals.

If, Comrades, you refuse to accept the work of the Electoral Commission then the situation is different and we'll resume our work. We were merely acting on the instructions we received from you, the Congress.

CHAIRMAN OF ELECTORAL COMMISSION: I suggest, Comrades, that you give us a little more time to prepare the proposal as a whole, which will then be read out to you so that you can get your bearings. Only when this has been done should the vote be taken. I am sorry that the list put forward by Prague has not been completed. If you give us another half-hour to put everything in order we'll come back then and put the complete proposal in front of you.

THE CHAIRMAN [*in Slovak*]: The Working Presidium recommends that the Electoral Commission be given more time to prepare the list of candidates for the new Central Committee. Who is in favour of this? Please raise your hands. Thank you. Any abstentions? . . Anyone against? . . One, two, three. The proposal has been carried by a majority. The Working Presidium recommends that we now take a fifteen-minute break.

[*Interval*]

CHAIRMAN OF CREDENTIALS COMMISSION: In accordance with the wishes of this Congress I state that there are present among the delegates twenty-nine members of the Central Committee and nine members of the Central Control and Audit Commission.

THE CHAIRMAN: The chairman of the Electoral Commission has still not arrived, so perhaps I can use this opportunity to deal with another matter. The news from Prague is that unfortunately an increasing number of incidents is taking place, involving our people, in particular the young, and units of the occupation armies. There is a danger of unnecessary loss of life. It has therefore been suggested that the Congress, even though it has done so already in its initial proclamation, should once more appeal to the public with the following short statement:

The Extraordinary Fourteenth Congress of the Czechoslovak Communist Party appeals to all citizens, and especially to the younger generation, not to take any action which may lead to clashes with troops of the armies of occupation and to the danger of unnecessary loss of life and sacrifice. We expect our people to show the same good sense and understanding of the situation that they have shown hitherto.

I recommend that we adopt this appeal, but perhaps the comrades can phrase it better than I have. I believe that our Congress carries great weight with the public and an appeal such as this could do much to calm things down, though unfortunately we cannot entertain any illusions that it will do so completely. I take it that none of you will be opposed to such an appeal. Are you in favour? . . Good. Will those in favour please raise their hands . . That's an absolute majority. Will comrades on the Press Commission draft the appeal on the lines I have indicated and use whatever means we still have to get it to the public.

Is the chairman of the Electoral Commission here now? Not yet. I'll therefore ask the secretary to find out whether the Electoral Commission can come and put its proposals to the Congress . . . It would be advisable to keep things as quiet as possible; it seems that the neighbourhood is being watched. Someone wants to say something over there . . .

[*A delegate asks whether Soviet tanks are encircling the building in which the Congress is being held.*]

THE CHAIRMAN: As far as I know the Working Presidium has not received any information of this kind. The chairman of the Electoral Commission has still not arrived, so Comrade Boček, the President of the Supreme Court, who is asking to speak, can perhaps tell us something of interest, since he was released yesterday after being interned, with the Premier, Comrade Černík. If there are no objections, then I'll ask him to speak.

BOČEK: I'll be very brief, Comrades. I must confess that I never thought I would have to make a speech like this at the Congress. Last night I was arrested in the building of the government Presidium, together with Comrade Černík.

The way in which the arrest was made was simply this: soldiers came in with machine-guns in their hands and took us prisoner. I don't know, but I have never in my life heard of a Prime Minister being arrested in this way, not to mention the Prime Minister of an allied State, and all the others. They took us and interned us for a time in the cellar, all the officials and the members of the Presidium. Even the gardener was there, who turned up in the pyjamas he was wearing when they dragged him out of bed, and with us also was Comrade Černík. After a short time I was taken away with Comrade Černík and both his deputies, Comrades Štrougal and Hamouz. They led us into the Premier's office, where everything was of course in the hands of soldiers.

At every step there were machine-guns at the ready, and broken telephones all over the place. Comrade Černík demanded to speak to Comrade Svoboda or Comrade Dubček. This was refused with the charming excuse that, as he could see for himself, the phones were out of order.

Then, when he asked to be put into any vehicle they liked, with any number of machine-guns guarding him, and taken to see Comrade Svoboda or Comrade Dubček, he was told this could not be done either. They had no orders to that effect.

Among those who were guarding us was a civilian, who it was said – mind you, I have not been able to check this at all – was a driver from the Soviet Embassy. He was a member of the NKVD and tried to make us believe that we were all counter-revolutionaries and that though he had nothing against Comrade Černík, he had been responsible for permitting this state of affairs in Czechoslovakia, and so on.

What is important for you, and this is the reason I have asked to speak – that is, if the chairman of the Electoral Commission has not yet arrived? He has? – In that case let me finish with the most important bit of information. I was with Comrade Černík till about seven o'clock in the evening. Until then I can vouch for it that he maintained a consistent standpoint, saying he would not in any way express approval of the occupation of Czechoslovakia, that he would not lend his name to any proclamation or statement and would not join any government or other organ that had not been formed in a constitutional manner. This he maintained staunchly, and although he was in great distress, understandably enough after what happened, I think it's important that you should know that he stuck to his guns.

One more thing, Comrades. Neither Comrade Štrougal nor Comrade Hamouz had until then – they remained there to wait for Černík – they too did not in any way agree with the occupation or with any change of attitude. Comrade Hamouz indeed flatly refused to discuss the matter. I only tell you this so that you should know how things stand. Of course I can only vouch for what happened while I was still there, that is until yesterday evening. Then Comrade Černík was driven away, and they told us that they had taken him to the Soviet Embassy. Whether there's any truth in that, I of course don't know. The members of the Presidium and I were released, whereas Comrades Štrougal and Hamouz stayed behind, saying they would wait for Comrade Černík to return from the Embassy. That's all I can tell you about it.

THE CHAIRMAN: Comrades, you know that the way the Premier and his deputies, as well as Comrade Boček, the President of the Supreme Court, were treated is tragic and shows such an incredible decline in conduct that it can scarcely be described.

The Electoral Commission is now present, Comrades. I believe that one of its members first wishes to say something about the election rules.

A MEMBER OF THE ELECTORAL COMMISSION: In accordance with your instructions we have adapted the election rules to the conditions under which we are working. Apart from approving a change in the Statutes in the sense that there is to be no condition as to length of membership governing candidature for the Central Committee or the Central Control and Audit Commission, I propose the following changes:

The abolition of Clauses 7–13 and 16–18 on holding a secret ballot. These are to be altered because of the extraordinary circumstances under which the election to the Central Committee and the Central Control and Audit Commission is taking place, and the vote will be taken by a show of hands. We leave Clauses 33, 34 and 35 to the tellers' committee. That is all as regards changes in the election rules.

THE CHAIRMAN: Comrades, you have heard a report on the necessary changes of the election rules and on supplements to the Statutes. Does anyone have anything to say on these two points? First let us take the question of electing the Central Committee by a show of hands. This proposal is supported by a number of regional delegations . . . Yes? . . . [*A voice from the hall.*] . . . We have here a proposal that we should have a secret ballot . . . [*Voices.*] . . . Just a moment, Comrades, I think it would save time if we took a vote on these two proposals. The election is meant to include members of the Central Control and Audit Commission, naturally.

Then there is a counter-proposal that the election rules should remain as they are, the election to be carried out by secret ballot.

Those in favour of this counter-proposal kindly raise their hands . . One, two, three. Three votes. That means the proposal is rejected.

Those in favour of a show of hands . . That is an absolute majority. Has anyone any comments on the other points of the report? If not, I'd like first of all – I don't know if the chairman of the Electoral Commission has done this – I'd like to make it clear that in this case the Central Committee we're about to elect will not be complete.

For one thing, there will be a provision for the representatives of the Slovak Communist Party to be elected to the Central Committee. Secondly, I am of the opinion that, as it has been suggested that the Congress should remain in existence, we ought to agree that more members from the Czech regions may also later be elected to the Central Committee. Because of the present circumstances it is of course quite possible that we shall discover that there are others who ought to be included on the Central Committee. But I expect I am anticipating what the chairman of the Electoral Commission wishes to tell us. Will he please take the floor.

CHAIRMAN OF ELECTORAL COMMISSION: Comrades, I'd now like to tell you what the Electoral Commission has been doing. I know we're in a hurry, but I ask your indulgence for two minutes by way of an introduction.

You instructed us to compile a list of candidates in the shortest time possible, and we have now done so. We were well aware of the need for a quick election of the Central Committee which could meet immediately and elect its Presidium, so that the public should be informed.

In this connection, Comrades, I ask for your utmost benevolence. In the very short time we had at our disposal – originally this was intended to take several days at the Congress – we could obviously not satisfy everybody. We recommend a large Central Committee with 150 members. This is because we were unable, when the delegations put forward their candidates, to adjust the numbers for the individual regions in any mathematical fashion. That would have led to absolute deadlock. We realize that this is a shortcoming. Another shortcoming, Comrades, is that we cannot give you a social breakdown. We naturally did our best to have all the main social strata represented. The regions bore this in mind and so did we in the Electoral Commission, but you must take my word for it we simply cannot say there are so many per cent of

69

those and so many of the others. And we are aware of yet another shortcoming, which lies in the fact that, based as it is on the proposals put forward by the regions and on the existing political practice, the list of candidates does not properly express the role played by women in this nation. We are aware of all these faults, and that is why I appeal to your magnanimity, so that we may prevent a long discussion which could easily follow among the regions and which might lead to our not electing the Central Committee at all.

We recommend the immediate election of the Central Committee, which is to start work at once, electing its First Secretary and Presidium. The Electoral Commission will then continue its session by drafting a list of candidates of the Central Committee and of the new Central Control and Audit Commission. We believe this to be practical in view of the possibility of outside intervention, in which case we should have at least got rid of the most important items on our agenda. So much then for my introduction, and now I'll slowly read out the names, telling you first of all which region has put up each candidate. Then there will be a discussion and we can take the vote.

THE CHAIRMAN: Do you agree with the procedure suggested by the Chairman of the Electoral Commission? . . . [*Voices expressing assent.*] . . . Any comments? . . . Yes? . . . [*A query.*] . . . Just a moment, I believe these proposals were debated in the regions. They were put forward by the heads of the regional delegations.

CHAIRMAN OF ELECTORAL COMMISSION: I can only add that this has not of course been done anonymously. We based our selection strictly on the nominations and short-listing done at regional conferences, and we naturally took into account the proposals voiced by the individual regions.

THE CHAIRMAN: May I interrupt just for a moment. I'd like to welcome Comrade Miková, Vice-chairman of the National Assembly, who has come from parliament. Also I'd like to inform those delegates who have not been able to secure accommodation for the night that they are to go to the Secretariat of the District Party Committee in Prague 9, which is only a short distance away in the Náměstí lidových milic, and they will be taken care of. The head of the delegation from the Nymburk district is to go to the accommodation committee, who need some additional information from him. That is all – will the chairman of the Electoral Commission please resume.

CHAIRMAN OF ELECTORAL COMMISSION [*reading out a list of candidates for the Central Committee and then continuing*]: . . . We propose that the Central Committee be elected as it stands, provided of course that the candidates receive the required number of votes, but that we delegates should agree among ourselves (unofficially, that is) that as soon as the Congress can start working under normal circumstances, as soon as the comrades from Slovakia are no longer prevented from coming here, we shall return to the question of their representation so as to comply fully with the requirement of equality for the Slovak communists.

A SLOVAK DELEGATE: May I recall what I said this morning and under what conditions we opened this Congress. I think we ought to return to it. I think that even though the Slovak delegation is not complete, the Congress ought to vote on the prepared list of candidates. But we made a condition, namely that the vote only becomes valid after the Slovak delegation approves our proposal by a two-thirds majority, or makes additional changes in the list. Do you understand me? Subject to this condition we agree that the Congress should vote on the Slovak delegates. Slovakia must have its political representation in that it will only become valid when two-thirds of the Slovak delegates have had the opportunity of either approving the vote or making alterations.

CHAIRMAN OF ELECTORAL COMMISSION: Agreed. I think that there is no fundamental disagreement between us. All I am concerned with is that when today we come to make the composition of the Central Committee public, we should not announce its provisional character. That, I fear, might detract from its authority. Otherwise I am in complete agreement with you that the Slovak comrades should reconsider it later.

In order to shorten the discussion, may I recommend the following, somewhat exceptional, measure: let us elect the Central Committee as proposed here, adding a rider that if a majority of Slovak delegates later decides on changes in the Slovak representation, the Congress will fully respect this.

Comrades, I have two more questions to discuss – [*A voice from the hall.*] Why, of course. The comrade says that this principle ought to apply to *all* the proposed members of the Central Com-

71

mittee and not only to the Slovak ones. I think that is a sensible suggestion. The Central Committee will thus be elected, but if the Slovak delegates so wish, there will be a new election and a vote will be taken again on those members to whom they may object.

THE CHAIRMAN: Forgive me for intervening, Comrades, but I have two important pieces of information for you. One about the South Moravian region, the other about Soviet armoured cars. As regards the first, the comrades suggest a change. In place of Antonín Morávek – would you cross him off your lists – put Karel Mrázek. The South Moravian region, Karel Mrázek instead of Antonín Morávek.

Secondly, and this is a verified report, there are Soviet armoured cars standing outside the factory gates. Perhaps we ought to speed things up a bit.

CHAIRMAN OF ELECTORAL COMMISSION: May I recommend that we take a vote on each name as it comes up. This is not to be the election proper, merely a vote on the inclusion of comrades on the list of candidates. It should go something like this: a name is suggested, there is a discussion, then the vote. But I do urge you to be as brief as you can.

THE CHAIRMAN: Can we decide whether to drop someone from the list or add someone else to it without a discussion? I have here a proposal that we include Comrade General Václav Prchlík. He is very well known to everybody. All those in favour of this proposal please raise their hands . . That, Comrades, is a minority, the proposal is rejected.

CHAIRMAN OF ELECTORAL COMMISSION: Comrades keep coming to me all the time with additional names. I can't work like this. I have read you the list of candidates, now please give us all your proposals in the normal way, that is, from the hall. I really cannot go on accepting any more.

THE CHAIRMAN: Comrades, would you agree that we call the names singly. It is impossible to put up ten names at a time, for we can't get anywhere like that. A comrade objected to the candidature of Comrade Kábele from the North Bohemian region, who played a part in an attempt to have her expelled from the Party in 1951. Has anyone anything to say on this – does anyone wish to voice an opinion? . . Yes . . . on this question, regarding Comrade Kábele . . . Please, comrades, we need absolute quiet . . . Otherwise I'll have to repeat things that are important . . . Quiet please. Make way for the comrade.

A WOMAN DELEGATE: Comrades, we are from the Děčín district, North Bohemian region. I'd like to ask how the candidates were selected, whether it was on the basis of the number of districts in a region or the number of communists. We have agreed on our candidate, Comrade Ťopek, and would very much like our region to have this one candidate extra. According to our reckoning, it seems to us that the North Bohemian region really has far fewer candidates than the others.

THE CHAIRMAN: Comrades, can we adopt a ruling that in its later stages the Congress, which as we have decided is to continue in existence, will deal with all additional proposals for candidates to the Central Committee. As the Central Committee is in this sense not meant to be complete, let us not for the time being discuss additions but only objections, if any, to those who are already on the list of candidates. Would you agree with this proposal, to leave the question of additional candidates and the rectification of any mistakes we might make, open? Those in favour please raise their hands . . Who is against this proposal? . . That's three . . six votes . . We are agreed then that the list of candidates is not to be supplemented, as this can be done at a later stage of the Congress. Let us therefore concentrate on the objections that are raised against the proposed candidates. We have, for instance, the case of Comrade Kábele. Yes, Comrade.

A DELEGATE: We have heard a serious charge against Comrade Kábele. In my view he must have the right to defend himself and give an explanation. Of course those of us who have worked with him for years know him as an extremely fine, honest and devoted worker, a Party member who in 1956 experienced a tragedy similar to that which the comrade from North Bohemia has told us about. And another in 1962. I therefore propose that we postpone a decision on this matter and take it off the agenda.

THE CHAIRMAN: Let us say that the story of this man shows how life taught him a lesson so that he learned to act in a way consistent with his Party membership.

A DELEGATE: I am Kábele from the North Bohemian region. I don't wish to hold things up with my personal affairs. But I think it would be impossible today to settle personal accounts between

73

myself, at the time a trade union official, and Comrade Chmelová, who was the managing-director of our works. May I just say this: if she claims that she was taken away handcuffed, in those days her husband, Chmel, was head of the police in Prague . . . [*Voices from the hall.*] . . .

CHAIRMAN OF ELECTORAL COMMISSION: There you are, I think the best solution is to vote. Now we know more about the case. The comrade has suggested that Comrade Kábele be struck off the list. He explained what happened. Let us therefore take a vote and get it over with . . . [*Voices from the hall.*] . . . I recommend that all supplementary proposals and comments, as we said at the outset, be laid before the Congress later on and that the Congress discuss them individually . . . [*Voices from the hall.*] . . . Well, I'm only trying to achieve some agreement on this point. Can we agree that all such additions are to be deferred, so that we don't hold up the election of the Central Committee? Those in favour please raise their hands – Yes, I do, I suggest we conclude the debate on this particular case.

A DELEGATE: May I second what was said by Comrade Belda. I have known Comrade Kábele since 1956, that's twelve years. He was the sole candidate and he was elected by all the organizations.

CHAIRMAN OF ELECTORAL COMMISSION: All right, Comrades, remember we recommended that he remain on the list of candidates. Let's stick to that, shall we . . . . Yes, Comrade Pokštefl . . .

POKŠTEFL: I think the Electoral Commission has left out two members of the Central Committee who are here with us, who have behaved most courageously over these past two days and who came over to us. I mean Comrade Vodsloň and Comrade Vaculík, and I move that they be included among the candidates.

THE CHAIRMAN: Yes, Comrade, what else?

A DELEGATE: I want you to consider the candidature of Comrade Mlynář, Secretary of the Central Committee, who was offered an important post and turned it down and who at the present time is not even acting as Secretary.

THE CHAIRMAN: Comrades, have you any comments on these three additional proposals? . . . [*Voices from the hall.*] . . . Comrade Miková has withdrawn as a candidate because she is Vice-chairman of the National Assembly. So we have additional proposals

for the candidature of Comrades Vodsloň, Vaculík and Mlynář . . .
Yes? . . .

I put it to the vote, who is in favour? . . Anyone against? . .
Thirteen . . .

Someone suggests we should vote for each of them separately. All right. Comrade Vodsloň. Who is in favour? . . Who
against? . . Twelve. Comrade Vodsloň is added to the list of
candidates.

Comrade Vaculík – Oh, are there any abstentions on Comrade
Vodsloň? Twenty-one . . . Yes, but I still think we should decide on
these three proposals. Who is in favour of Comrade Vaculík? In
favour . . Thank you. Anyone against? . . Forty-one . . . Yes,
Comrades, I admit I can't be completely accurate, it's getting very
difficult to see in this hall . . .

Comrades, may I repeat the condition under which I conducted
the business of this Congress earlier. Eleven hundred people are
present, and you can't hope to keep order from here under these
circumstances. So please be as disciplined as you can. Let us get
on – Oh, just a moment . . I have before me the proposals we were
discussing and I would like to finish them. The third concerns
Comrade Zdeněk Mlynář, a Secretary of the Central Committee.
Who is in favour of his being included on the list of candidates? . .
Thank you. Anyone against? . . Twenty. Any abstentions? . .
Forty-two abstained. That means that Comrade Mlynář is added
to the list of candidates.

And now, Comrades, let's take the list as it was originally laid
before you by the Electoral Commission. You comrades by the
rostrum, what is it you have to discuss?

A DELEGATE: I would like to say, on behalf of the delegation of the
Frýdek-Místek district, North Moravian region, that our district
conference stipulated in what order our members were to be put up
as candidates for the Central Committee, and we therefore suggest
that instead of Comrade Písek, Comrade Jarolím should be put on
the list. He was chosen as the first by the district conference. My
proposal has been discussed with Comrade Němcová, the head of
our regional delegation. Comrade Rudolf Jarolím instead of Comrade Písek.

THE CHAIRMAN: Just a moment. Are you agreed on this change, the
whole delegation?

ANOTHER DELEGATE: Yes, we are. This is the Frýdek-Místek delegation here on the balcony. All of us.

THE CHAIRMAN: You are all agreed? . . Right. Has any one of your members anything to say that might have a bearing on this? . . No. Thank you. We'll change the list of candidates accordingly.

Yes, Comrades? . . . [*A voice from the hall.*] . . . I understand perfectly what the comrade has in mind and I appreciate her integrity. We did make this mistake, I mean the way we took the vote. To a certain extent, though, the spontaneous agreement you have expressed with our proposals justifies our course of action. Comrades, I realize we have made certain mistakes, but I don't think we should now go over the same ground again . . . [*Delegates can be heard discussing among themselves.*] . . .

THE CHAIRMAN: We must orientate ourselves quickly, time is short. The views of the Děčín delegation were discussed with your regional and district delegations . . . all right, Comrades, I'll have a vote taken on this fourth proposal to add Comrade Topek to the list of candidates for the Central Committee. Who is in favour of this proposal by the comrades from Děčín? . . Thank you. Who is against? . . Sorry, but we'll have to count the votes in that case. Let me ask you again, Comrades. Who is in favour of this proposal by the comrades from Děčín? Raise your hands and we'll have the votes counted. Will the tellers please take a count . . . Comrades, quiet please, it isn't always the fault of the chair that we can't communicate properly . . .

Look, I have repeated that we are voting on the proposal by the comrades from Děčín to add Comrade Topek to the list of candidates; we have discussed this twice already. The comrades from Děčín quite justifiably object that three comrades have been added in contravention of the procedure we had previously agreed on, and so they again raise their own proposal, putting forward Comrade Topek as a candidate. Isn't that so? Yes, that's right.

Since this mistake has been made, going against the procedure we ourselves adopted, and because I don't want to go over the whole thing again from the start, I propose that we add Comrade František Topek to the list of candidates. Who is in favour of this proposal? . . Thank you. Who is against? . . Comrade, try and count – it's a minority. Visually it's quite clearly a minority . . . Any abstentions? . . Right, Comrade Topek is added to the list.

Comrades, forgive me for not counting the votes exactly, but the Working Presidium assures me that this is how the voting went ... Yes, Comrade, is it something to do with the list of candidates? ... Can't hear ... [*A voice from the hall.*] ...

CHAIRMAN OF ELECTORAL COMMISSION: I find that Comrade Borůvka has not been put up as a candidate. There was considerable discussion in the Electoral Commission on this point; some comrades spoke against him without stating their reasons. They did, of course, say that they were quoting what had been said at their district conferences and that for this reason Comrade Borůvka had not been chosen. We ought therefore to have a discussion here, but this time with concrete arguments. The only one that was raised before was that at one time Comrade Borůvka had publicly proclaimed views which made it look as if he were in favour of an Agrarian Party and so on.

THE CHAIRMAN: I would very strongly urge the chairman of the Electoral Commission to leave all further additional proposals to the end, as we have already decided to do, even if we have sinned against this procedure ourselves. Now can we turn to other motions. Yes. In accordance with our earlier resolution, I terminate the discussion and put the list of candidates to the vote. Please, Comrade, would you – [*A voice from the hall.*] ...

Comrades, I understand that, and I can see that the Electoral Commission has its reasons. Naturally in the case of every one of us who is put up as a candidate for the Central Committee reasons have been given to support the candidature on the basis of facts which you can read for yourselves and see that the nomination is in order. The Electoral Commission had these facts, these data, at its disposal. The Electoral Commission considered them and has now laid the list of candidates before us – Yes? ...

A DELEGATE: Comrades, about an hour ago I spoke on the phone to comrades whom we can implicitly trust. They confirmed the report that Comrades Kolder, Indra, Bil'ak, Rytíř and Pavlovský have expressed their willingness to accept functions in the Presidium of the Central Committee that is being formed at the behest of the Soviet authorities. Who else has accepted I don't know, but we know for sure that Comrades Šimon, Sádovský and Mlynář have not. That is a verified report we have received.

THE CHAIRMAN: Comrade Pelikán.

PELIKÁN: I would like to make the following appeal. We know some of the comrades proposed as candidates for the Central Committee and I think that many of us who do know them have certain reservations about them. But you must realize that this Congress is in an entirely new situation. We are concerned, as has been mentioned, to create a truly new, representative organ, to confirm the legality of this Central Committee. That is why I believe we ought to include even those members of the former Central Committee towards whom we may have certain reservations but who have taken a correct stand, that we ought to include them in the list of candidates because it is their present attitude that ought to be decisive. Also, this would help to maintain a certain continuity, so that the new Central Committee would truly represent a broad range of opinion within the Party.

THE CHAIRMAN: Thank you. Comrades, I think it is also necessary for us to achieve a certain unity, which we used to have on the Central Committee, as regards our views and attitudes to certain matters. This is of course not merely a question of tactics. We also wish to show our appreciation of the standpoint adopted by these comrades in the last few months. Among them are those we have named. I should moreover like to remind you that we have adopted a resolution according to which we shall not terminate our discussion on the composition of the Central Committee of the Party. For this reason petty arguments have no place here at this time . . . Now, would you – [*Hubbub in the hall.*] . . . I now hand over to the Chairman of the Electoral Commission.

CHAIRMAN OF ELECTORAL COMMISSION: Comrades, I have a choice of two different courses. Either to put the list of candidates to the vote as it stands, with the changes that have been made by the delegations and with those four additions, either by taking one name after the other, or *en bloc* . . . [*Voices of delegates raised in argument.*] . . . I think that in spite of the time factor, we ought to try and vote on each individual candidate, because to vote *en bloc* on the Central Committee is really unheard of. I think that if we hurry and with an optical count, it can't take more than half an hour, and I think we should devote that half-hour to it. That is just my recommendation, nothing more and nothing less . . .

[*His proposal is accepted, the Chairman of the Electoral Commission reads out the names of the candidates and a vote is taken on*

*each. The list of candidates thus elected to the Central Committee
appears below on p. 95.*]

. . .

THE CHAIRMAN: . . . Comrades, although it would be logical to
follow the election of members of the Central Committee by the
election of those who will sit on that Committee as candidates, it
would seem that it is more urgent to elect members of the Central
Control and Audit Commission, because that is yet another new
organ. If you agree, I think we should first of all read you the
names of the candidates.

Oswald Débrt, Leopold Hofman, František Hons, Václav
Hromádka, Bohuslava Křičková, Václav Pleskot, Jiří Rypel,
Ilona Pietropaulová, Karel Kaplan, Jiří Štika, Vladimír Bartoň,
Oldřich Kalda, Jaroslav Odstrčil, Milan Veit, Adolf Čechal,
Ladislav Jirků, Božena Šouláková, Zdeněk Braun, Miroslav
Šulda, Antonín Bízek, Vladimír Kolmistr, František Urban,
Václav Foltýn, Josefa Chmelová, Josef Krajča.

Slovak comrades: Július Pavlis, Martin Janečko, Vlasta
Baudišová, Vojtěch Hatala, František Myšeje, František Byzup,
Josef Raušman, Pavol Pavelka, Ján Jančík, František Bartík,
Ján Uher, Ondrej Michálik.

That's all. Comrades, we have here a proposal from the Congress
Working Presidium that after the usual discussion on the list of
candidates for the Central Control and Audit Commission we
vote on it *en bloc*. We cannot now waste a single minute . . . Yes?
. . . [*Voices from the hall.*] . . . The delegation from Litoměřice has
put forward Comrade Říčková [?Křičkovká – see p. 80] instead of
Comrade Barák . . . No, Comrade Barák instead of Comrade
Říčková, I beg your pardon . . . [*Prolonged interruptions from th
hall.*] . . .

. . .

Comrades, the Electoral Commission wants to propose that Comrade Stuchlík become a candidate of the Central Committee of the
Party, it's here ready. Is that right? Yes? Thank you.

Who else? . . . Thank you for the proposal. Have you made note
of it, Comrades? You haven't? Comrade Král. That's for which
organization? Karviná. Christian name, please . . . Vladimír Král.

Comrades, please bear the time factor in mind . . . Yes, Comrade? Comrades, give all names clearly and don't forget the Christian names. Comrade Jiří Loužil . . . Comrade Kalivoda . . . Look, Comrades, we can't possibly get anywhere like this. You have elected an authoritative Electoral Commission, we've elected it in the regular way, and this Commission has put its proposals before us. If you have no objections to these proposals, I suggest that we refrain from making any more or we'll never be finished . . . Comrade Kašpar from the Ministry of Transport is wanted in Election Room 8. From what I have said it follows that we ought to respect the changes made by the delegations themselves. Substitutions? Of course.

Would you repeat that, please. Comrade Barák – Christian name? Antonín Barák instead of Bohuslava Křičková. I take it that it is with the knowledge of the district delegation?

I have here another substitution. Jaroslav Horký instead of Hons, likewise with the consent of the district delegation. These aren't additional proposals, merely substitutions.

Well, Comrades, I have laid before you the draft of our list of candidates in which two changes have been made with the approval of the delegations concerned . . . [*A query from the hall.*] . . .

Comrade, we have already decided not to make any additional nominations and just to put it to the vote, naturally respecting the resolution we adopted earlier. Additions can be made later.

Now will the Comrade Chairman of – Comrades, the members of the Electoral Commission tell me that an army representative is there. Sorry, I don't know his name, I was just then . . . Štika, is it? . . The army is represented . . Yes?

A DELEGATE: Comrades, I have been a member of the Control Commission in the past and I am nominated for the new one as well. If we have acknowledged the part played by some members of the Central Committee, who showed themselves to be progressive, sticking their necks out for progressive ideas, I suggest that those comrades who did so should also be elected to the Central Control and Audit Commission. Two comrades are missing there: Jiří Loužil and Frýbert. They're not on the list and I recommend that they be added to it.

THE CHAIRMAN: But, Comrade, we have already made a ruling on this and we ought to abide by it. Comrade Chairman, will you please continue . . .

CHAIRMAN OF ELECTORAL COMMISSION: Well, Comrades, who is in favour?.. I think we should first of all take a vote on the proposal to vote *en bloc*. Please raise your hands if you are in favour. A clear majority...

Who is in favour that the proposal laid before you by the Electoral Commission, with those two changes, the two substitutions, Horký instead of Hons and Barák instead of Křičková, that this proposal be adopted as the Central Control and Audit Commission?.. Who is in favour?.. Thank you. Who is against?.. Can we have a count?.. Any abstentions?.. There were no votes against.. how many abstentions?.. downstairs six, yes, and upstairs.. none – six all told then.

The Central Control and Audit Commission has been elected. On behalf of the Electoral Commission I extend my congratulations and wish you a lot of courage.

Comrades, if you will allow me, and if the Chairman agrees, we have here a draft list of Central Committee candidates. We have already talked about this, and I think that it is a case in point that ought to be left to a later stage of the Congress. The most important organs have now been elected. I therefore propose that we postpone voting on the new Central Committee candidates. Who is in favour of this proposal?.. Who is against?.. Yes, also in the sense of the proposal made by Comrade Tabačka. Who is against this proposal?.. No one?.. One, two, three.. Any abstentions?.. Comrade Chairman, Comrades, my work is thus at an end. May I thank my colleagues on the Electoral Commission, thank you for the highly conscientious way in which you discharged your duties. As for all those who were elected today, we cannot wish them anything but a great deal of courage and integrity.

THE CHAIRMAN: I thank the Electoral Commission for its work. And now with your permission I'll ask Comrade Matějka to speak.

MATĚJKA: Comrades, forty-seven delegates to the Extraordinary Congress and the plenum of the regional committee of the Slovak Communist Party in Košice met today at a joint session, at which they unanimously passed the following resolution:

With sorrow and anger in our hearts we wish to express our resolute and unanimous protest at the way in which the Warsaw Pact forces have occupied a sovereign state. We categorically demand that Comrade Dubček and the Presidium of the Central Committee be enabled to carry out their normal tasks. In the interests of a renewal of civic rights and the normal activity of the legal Party organizations and organs we demand the immediate return to our political life of Comrades Svoboda, Dubček, Smrkovský. We reject and refuse to give our mandate to any group within the Central Committee, or any other group, which might try to replace the Party leadership or the government. We consider such actions to be blatant attempts to arrogate power and we reject them as being in contravention of the organizational principles of the Communist Party.

In conclusion we ask the majority of the Extraordinary Congress, now meeting in Prague, to consider this statement of ours to be a valid contribution to the proceedings of the Congress, which for the time being we cannot all attend because of the prevailing situation. We support the motion that the Extraordinary Fourteenth Congress be proclaimed a permanent one.

[*Applause.*]

THE CHAIRMAN: Thank you. And now, Comrades, a few more organizational matters. The newly-elected members of the Central Committee and the Central Control and Audit Commission will remain in their seats when today's session of the Congress ends. That is one announcement. And now permit me to read you a letter drafted by a group of our delegates and addressed to Comrade Dubček:

Dear Comrade Dubček,

The Fourteenth Party Congress, which met today, sends you warm comradely greetings. We wish to express our thanks for all the work you have done for the Party and the Republic. The chanted cries of 'Dubček, Dubček' from the lips of our young people as they carried a blood-stained Czechoslovak flag around Prague yesterday and sang the national anthem and the 'Internationale', bear witness that your name has become the symbol of our sovereignty. We protest against your illegal imprisonment, as well as against the imprisonment of the other comrades. The Congress has re-elected you to the new Central Committee, and we continue to see in you our chief representative. We firmly believe that the Czechs and Slovaks will again be masters in their own house and that you will return to our midst.

The Fourteenth Congress of the
Communist Party of Czechoslovakia

[*Tumultuous applause.*]

Comrades, we'll try to find ways and means of delivering this letter to Comrade Dubček. Are you in favour of sending it? Thank you for your agreement.

Comrades, our agenda for this part of the Congress is finished. We have successfully adopted the resolutions and carried out the elections which were the goal of today's session. The proceedings, today's proceedings, are almost over. We are bound by all the resolutions we passed here today, including the one that makes this a permanent Congress, which means that we consider today's session to be only the first stage of the Congress as such.

Much remains to be done. Allow me, before we wind up this session of the Congress, to call a Slovak comrade from Trenčín, who wishes to convey to us the greetings of Comrade Dubček's mother. If you please, Comrade.

A SLOVAK DELEGATE: Dear Comrade, Delegates, this morning, before I left Trenčín, Comrade Dubček's weeping mother implored me in great distress to greet you all and to appeal to you on her behalf to be as brave in the future as you have been till now. She is sitting in the Party Secretariat building and crying for her son.

THE CHAIRMAN: . . . Thank you, Comrade. And now, in conclusion allow me to give the floor to one of the oldest members of the Party, Comrade Vodsloň.

VODSLOŇ: Dear Comrades, this Extraordinary Congress which is now concluding, or rather interrupting, its work, has met under very dramatic circumstances, and so it would not be fitting to make any long speeches. I shall therefore, with your permission, confine myself to a few of the most important questions, which have to be stressed before we disperse to resume our work.

This Extraordinary Fourteenth Congress is an expression of the remarkable ability and preparedness of our Party. It gives expression to the will of the people, of both our nations, of all strata of our population. Our appreciation and gratitude belong to all the organizers and delegates, who displayed exceptional skill, discipline and understanding in the present situation. The impossible has become fact. There were many who doubted that it was really feasible to convene this Congress, whose successful work and resolutions will be of great, of exceptional, importance to our entire Party and to our socialist homeland, as well as internationally. It has met in dramatic times, seven and a half months after January,*

* *Translator's Note:* January 1968, the start of the Dubček era.

83

to which it has remained faithful. It expresses the will of our Party and our people in making its determined protest against the forcible occupation of our homeland by those whom we had trusted and believed in, confident that they would honour their obligations. That is why we demand an end to the occupation and express confidence in Comrade Dubček and his colleagues in the Presidium, who were treated in the same way as Comrade Černík, about whose experiences you have heard. The party needs the trust of our people, which we shall continue to win by means of our active and disciplined work and exemplary behaviour.

Everything else is insignificant in comparison with the lofty and noble aims of our Party, and in comparison with the obstacles it has to surmount at the present time. For this reason, Comrades, I would like to appeal to you to discard all pettiness in our work. The unity, sovereignty and victory of our just cause must lead to more and more perfect freedom and socialism in our country. We appeal to all our members to be brave and calm, to uphold their communist and national pride and our correct and heartfelt attitude to internationalism.

We shall remain faithful in our work to the legacy of January and to the resolution, the last resolution passed by the Presidium of our Party.* We shall consistently implement the resolutions adopted by our Congress not to slacken our activity until such time as our people are once more able to go about their business in peace, freedom, and sovereignty. [*Applause.*]

THE CHAIRMAN: Thank you. Comrades, I'd now like to ask a representative of the Proposals Commission to read us a resolution they have drafted. If you please, Comrade.

CHAIRMAN OF PROPOSALS COMMISSION: Final resolution of the Extraordinary Fourteenth Congress of the KSČ:

The Extraordinary Fourteenth Congress of the KSČ met at its first session in Prague on 22 August 1968. Despite the difficult conditions, 1,182 properly elected delegates took part, out of a total number of 1,540. Despite great efforts some of the Slovak delegates were unable to attend, being prevented from doing so by the occupation forces. The Congress agenda consisted of the following points:

* *Editor's Note:* This is a reference to the resolution of 21 August 1968, condemning the invasion of Czechoslovakia by the armies of occupation as quoted on pp. 15–16.

1. The opening political proclamation.
2. An appeal to the communist and workers' parties of the whole world.
3. Annulment of the mandate of the Central Committee of the Party.
4. Election of a new Central Committee.
5. Owing to the prevailing conditions, the Congress was unable to deal with the whole prepared agenda. It therefore proclaimed itself to be in permanent session, leaving the Party Statutes, questions of the future character of our State, and other important problems, to its next meeting.

In all its work and in its resolutions the Congress adhered to the post-January Party line, reiterating the importance of the Action Programme, which the Party wishes consistently to implement. The Congress confirmed the Party's determination further to develop democratic and humane socialism. In its relations with the international workers' movement, the Party will work towards its unity. Inspired by the will of the entire nation, the Party will implement its policy with the nation's immediate participation and support. The Congress again solemnly declares that it rejects the violation of the sovereignty of the Czechoslovak Socialist Republic and demands the immediate withdrawal of the occupation armies. Having the vital interests of our people at heart, the Party will endeavour to normalize the economic and political life of the country.

A necessary condition for this is the resumption of the work of our lawfully appointed State and political organs led by their elected representatives, President of the Republic Ludvík Svoboda, First Secretary of the KSČ Alexander Dubček, Premier Oldřich Černík, Chairman of the National Assembly Josef Smrkovský, and Comrade Kriegel. The newly elected Central Committee will continue to strengthen the unity of the Party and the whole nation.

The Congress appeals to all citizens to devote their energies to strengthening the Czechoslovak Socialist Republic, and to ensuring that its economy is kept running, all this in a dignified and calm fashion to show their determination to manage their own State and national affairs.

The Congress concludes its first session convinced that the whole nation will understand the gravity of the situation, will support it in its work, and will implement its resolutions.

The first session of the
Fourteenth Congress of the K S Č,
Prague, 22 August 1968

THE CHAIRMAN: Thank you. I shall now ask you for your comments on this resolution, Comrades. Perhaps you will permit me to give you mine first of all. Where the election of the Central Committee is mentioned we should add: 'and the Central Control and Audit Commission as the highest elected organs'. Also it is necessary to add to the points of our agenda the words, 'The Congress also adopted a proclamation to the Slovak people as one of the Congress documents'. And also a letter to Dubček, a personal letter to Dubček. That is all as far as I'm concerned. Any other comments? . . . [*Voices from the hall.*] . . . Yes, I think I agree. Anyone else? . . . [*Voices from the hall.*] . . . Comrades, leave the actual drafting of the letter to the newly elected Central Committee of the Party. Are there no other important points you wish to raise? Yes? . . . Please remember, Comrades, that there are now 1,290 delegates present. This number will probably increase still further . . . May I remind you that minutes are precious now. Yes? . . .

[*So ends the penultimate tape. The recording omits further discussion of the resolution and its unanimous approval by the Congress. The last tape then continues*]:

. . .

THE CHAIRMAN: . . . A few more organizational items before we conclude our session.

. . . The military commandant of Prague and the Central Bohemian region, Lieutenant-General Velichko, has ordered a curfew between the hours of 10 p.m. and 5 a.m. It is therefore necessary to decide on our organized departure from the Congress. There are two possibilities. We have buses waiting outside in the factory yard which can take you to Slovakia, South Moravia, North Moravia, East Bohemia, South Bohemia, North Bohemia, and Central Bohemia. This is for delegates who have not got their own means of transport – they can ask the drivers to take them to their region or district, or even their home town. There are two buses for each region, the first carrying an inscription in each case. That is one possibility. The curfew is due to start officially at 10 p.m. A lot of ground can be covered in an hour.

The other possibility is for you to spend the night at the accommodation we have found for you. If you decide to leave for home we must give the necessary instructions, for we cannot call the stewards together. The stewards would then have to arrange for the buses to leave by various gates, not only by gate Number Two, at intervals, so that it should look as if the afternoon shift was going home.

That's one thing. I repeat, Comrades, that we do have accommodation for you. Or rather, those of you who have not yet done anything about their accommodation, please go to the District Committee of the Party here in Prague 9. It's only a little distance away, in the Náměstí lidových milic.

Another item of information – Quiet, please! – Will the members of the Central Committee and the Central Control and Audit Commission gather here to the right of the Presidium and then hold their first meeting in other parts of the building, now, tonight.

And a final announcement. A number of delegations have come to me with the request that we convey their thanks to the workers and communists of the Vysočany works which played host to this Congress. I am sure we'll gladly convey this message to all the organizers, workers and communists of the Vysočany organization.

Now perhaps you will permit what is really a final word. Comrades, our first session is over. I think we can say it was a successful session. There is no better organized force in our country than this very Congress. It has shown its strength, expressed its standpoint, influenced political developments in this country. I believe that with these documents which it has adopted it has fulfilled its great role at this grave hour.

Comrades, I beg you to heed all the organizational instructions you have received. Do not give the slightest cause for conflict.

Will the Slovak delegates also remain behind in this building when we disperse, and will they wait outside the library on the ground floor.

. . . And now, Comrades, at the end of our session let us sing the 'Internationale'.

[*The delegates rise and sing the 'Internationale'.*]

Thank you, Comrades. Long live the Communist Party of Czechoslovakia! [*Tumultuous applause.*]

IV

Conference Documents

1. Proclamation Adopted at the Opening of the Congress

Comrades, citizens of Czechoslovakia,

Today, on 22 August 1968, began the Extraordinary Congress of the Communist Party of Czechoslovakia, attended by its properly elected delegates. The Congress adopted the following proclamation:

Czechoslovakia is a free and sovereign socialist State, founded on the will and support of its people. However, its sovereignty was infringed on 21 August 1968, when it was occupied by the armed forces of the Soviet Union, Poland, the German Democratic Republic, Bulgaria and Hungary.

This act is explained away by assertions that socialism was in danger and that certain leading Czechoslovak representatives had asked for the intervention. As was made clear in yesterday's statement by the Central Committee of the KSČ, the second broadcast made by the President of the Republic, the proclamation issued by the National Assembly and the government of the Republic, as well as the statement put out by the Presidium of the Central Committee of the National Front, no responsible Party or constitutional body had asked for troops to be sent.

There was no counter-revolution in Czechoslovakia, nor was her socialist development threatened in any way. The people and the Party were perfectly capable of resolving the problems that had arisen by themselves, as was borne out by the tremendous trust enjoyed by the new Party leadership headed by Comrade Dubček. On the contrary, Czechoslovakia was about to put into practice Marx's and Lenin's fundamental concepts of socialist democracy. Czechoslovakia did not violate her obligations towards her allies, nor has she the slightest interest in hostility towards the socialist States and their people in the future. However, these obligations have been violated by the armed forces of the occupying powers.

They have trampled on Czechoslovakia's sovereignty and on their own obligations as allies, as well as on the Warsaw Pact and the agreements signed at Čierná and Bratislava. Several leading Czecho-slovak representatives have been wrongfully arrested, isolated from the people and prevented from carrying out their duties. A number of government and Party offices have been occupied. All this amounts to a grave injustice.

The Congress categorically demands that normal conditions be created immediately for the work of Czechoslovak constitutional and political organs and that the arrested representatives be released without delay, so that they may return to their duties.

At this time of crisis, the unity of all our people, the unity of our two nations and the unity of both with our Party has become the most urgent problem of the day. Not even armed intervention has prevented the Czechoslovak people from remaining the one and only rightful and sovereign ruler of its own country. The defence of free-dom in our socialist homeland is not the concern of the communists alone, but of all the Czechs and Slovaks and the other nationalities, of all workers, farmers, members of the intelligentsia, and of the young, of all who have the dignified and free life of our socialist country at heart. The communists can play their leading part by becoming the most active and self-sacrificing organizers of the cam-paign for the withdrawal of foreign troops. They can achieve this aim in the closest unity with all patriots and with all the active demo-cratic forces in our society.

The situation that arose in our country on 21 August cannot last. Socialist Czechoslovakia will never resign itself to being administered by the military occupation authorities, nor will it accept any col-laborationist regime dependent on the armed might of the occupants.

The Extraordinary Fourteenth Congress declares that it recog-nizes only the lawfully elected constitutional representatives of this country, the President of the Republic Ludvík Svoboda, the Chair-man of the National Assembly Josef Smrkovský, the Premier Oldřich Černík, and others, just as it only recognizes Alexander Dubček as leader of the Party. It refuses to recognize, even as Party members, those members of the former Central Committee who fail in this difficult test.

Our basic demand must of course be the withdrawal of foreign troops. Should the above demands not be complied with; if, in par-ticular, negotiations for the departure of foreign troops are not started within twenty-four hours with our constitutional and Party representatives, these being again free men; and if Comrade Dubček does not within that time-limit announce this to the nation; then the Congress asks all workers, led by members of the Communist Party, to carry out a one-hour protest strike at twelve noon on Friday 23 August. At the same time the Congress has resolved that if these demands are not met it will continue to take all necessary measures, and once the new Central Committee has been elected will entrust the carrying out of such measures to the Central Committee as the only lawful representative of the Party.

The Congress appeals to all communists and all Czechoslovak citizens to maintain law and order, to keep calm and behave in a disciplined fashion, thus ensuring that we on our side do not provoke incidents that could result in serious loss of life and damage to property.

The Congress entrusts all Party organizations and organs with the full implementation of this resolution.

[The text of the proclamation is reprinted from the magazine *Politika*, No 1, published in Prague on 24 August 1968.]

2. Appeal Addressed by the Congress to the Communist Parties of the World

In the afternoon the Extraordinary Fourteenth Congress adopted its second resolution, addressed to all the communist and workers' parties of the world:

We appeal to all the communist and workers' parties of the world, and in particular to the Party and people of the Soviet Union, the Polish People's Republic, the Bulgarian People's Republic, the German Democratic Republic and the Hungarian People's Republic, whose armed forces have occupied our homeland.

In January our Party set out on the road to a renascence of socialism, laying greater emphasis on its democratic and humanist principles in keeping with the conditions of our society at its present stage of development. It believed that its allies would respect the principles of sovereignty and non-intervention and that all outstanding problems would be resolved by negotiation. This was the starting point adopted by our Party leadership in all its post-January bilateral and multilateral negotiations. This policy, as contained in the Action Programme of the Central Committee of the KSČ, and its gradual implementation, gave our Party unprecedented authority and earned it the support of the nation. The safeguarding and accelerating of this course was to be discussed at the Extraordinary Fourteenth Congress, preparations for which were in their final stages. On the eve of that Congress, the armies of the Soviet Union, the Polish People's Republic, the Bulgarian People's Republic, the German Democratic Republic and the Hungarian People's Republic, without any justification for such action and without the consent of our lawful government and Party representatives, against the will of our people forcibly occupied our territory, brought chaos to the country, and made it impossible and are continuing to make it impossible for us to proceed on the road upon which we have set out. We are faced with the bitter truth that the armed forces of countries we have come to regard as friends are behaving like an occupying power. The constitutional representatives of our State and the representatives of our Party cannot continue to carry out their duties. They are unable to use the normal constitutional channels to discuss the present situation. They have no contact with the news media. Our leading representatives have been interned. There can be no doubt that this action is bound to have disastrous effects on the entire international and communist movement. We declare that our people and our Communist Party will never acquiesce in it, that they reject it and will do everything in their power to renew normal conditions in our country.

That is why the required quorum of delegates to the Extraordinary Fourteenth Congress, elected at district and regional conferences, have met in compliance with the wishes of the Czechoslovak communists and of the nation as a whole and now turn to you with this urgent appeal and request for help.

If we are freely to continue on our socialist road, the following demands must immediately be met:

1. All the interned representatives of the Party, government, National Assembly, Czech National Council and National Front must be released at once. They, as well as the President of the Republic, must be enabled to carry out their duties without hindrance.
2. All civic rights and liberties must immediately be restored.
3. The armies of occupation must commence their withdrawal without delay.

The Extraordinary Fourteenth Congress declares that it does not recognize any representatives of the Party and government but those who were elected by normal, democratic means.

Having regard to the tragic consequences of the occupation of our country for the cause of socialism the world over, we ask you, Comrades:

Give political support to our just cause and make your views known to the representatives of the parties responsible for the action that has been taken against our country. Consider whether it would be advisable to call a conference of communist and workers' parties, which would be attended by our delegation. Deal only with those representatives of our Party who are elected at our Congress.

Let us defend the human face of socialism! It is our international duty to do so.

The delegates of the Extraordinary
Fourteenth Congress of the KSČ.

[*Rudé právo*, 23 August 1968 – special Congress number. Reprinted from the book *Seven Days in Prague, 21–27 August, 1968, documents and study material*, published by the Historical Institute of the Czechoslovak Academy of Sciences, Prague, September 1968, pp. 97–9.]

3. *Message to the Slovak Communists and People**

The Extraordinary Fourteenth Congress of the KSČ has met under very difficult conditions and we very much regret that, through no fault of their own, not all the properly elected delegates from Slovakia have as yet arrived to take part in it. The delegates of the Extraordinary Congress have met for a conference demanded by various Party organizations under the stress of the exceptional situation caused by the presence of the occupation forces as well as by the incorrect behaviour of certain members of the former Central Committee of the Party, and since 1,170† properly elected delegates with the right to vote were present, it was decided to commence the Extraordinary

---

* In Slovak.

† The number of delegates arriving at the Congress grew hourly. Finally, 1,290 of the 1,543 delegates elected at the regional conferences attended.

Fourteenth Congress of the KSČ. The Congress confirms and wishes to assure the people of Slovakia and Slovak communists that it unequivocally insists on the implementation of the Action Programme of the Party; the basic questions of equality of rights as between our two nations will thus be settled by means of a socialist federation, though this has not as yet been discussed at the Congress.

We ask you fully to support the resolutions and the results of the Congress, and in their spirit to activate the work of all Slovak Communists, National Committees, and the entire Slovak people.

Only if all of us living in this country remain firmly united can we hope to make good the consequences of the tragedy that has befallen our two nations.

We assure you that all the decisions taken at the Extraordinary Congress will subsequently be discussed with the absent Congress delegates from Slovakia.

Those Slovak delegates who *are* present at the Extraordinary Congress of the KSČ consider the acceptance by Slovak communists and the Slovak nation of the resolutions adopted by the Congress to be a basic condition of further action by the whole Party. These resolutions, and the other documents of the Extraordinary Congress of the KSČ, must become the strongest link between Slovak and Czech communists in the present political situation and in its solution. Follow the instructions of the newly elected Central Committee! We appeal to the Slovak members of the Committee to organize active political life in Slovakia and the activity of the Slovak Communist Party in the spirit of these resolutions.

You must realize, Comrades, that some of the members of the former Central Committee, now abolished by the Congress, are also meeting in Prague. By continuing to meet they are infringing the unity of the Party and of our nations. The standpoints adopted by certain members of the former Central Committee serve only to sow confusion in the ranks of the Communist Party, and in particular of Slovak communists. These comrades have refused invitations to the Extraordinary Congress and persist in holding their own conference.

We hope you will appreciate the gravity of this situation and organize Slovak communists for the implementation of the tasks adopted by the Congress. The Slovak delegates present at the Congress will do everything in their power to influence it in the right direction.

Slovak communists, Slovaks, members of national minorities!

The Czech and Slovak communists taking part in the Extraordinary Fourteenth Congress of the KSČ are thinking of you and are convinced that they are acting in accordance with their communist convictions and their communist honour, being guided by a single aim – to give support to Comrades Dubček, Svoboda, Černík and Smrkovský and to insist on the restoration of normal conditions for the work of the Party and State organs of which these comrades are the leading representatives.

Have faith in us and do all you can to ensure responsible and, in particular, active support on the part of Slovak communists.

The Extraordinary Fourteenth Congress of the KSČ

[The text of this proclamation has been taken from *Rudé právo*, Saturday 24 August 1968, p. 1.]

4. *Appeal by the Congress to the Whole Public and to the Young* ·

We appeal to you, as the constitutional organs of our Republic have done already, once again to show common sense, calm and national pride. All these you will not manifest by public demonstrations or by ill-considered meetings and protest marches. Do not help the foreign troops; take no notice of them, ignore them.

Do nothing that could lead to unnecessary conflicts and loss of life, to injury and to damage of national property.

Young friends! Provocation is not our weapon. That is the weapon of those who would like to give a legal semblance to the occupation of our country and thus provide the pretext for brutal intervention. You know already that the unanimous opinion of the delegates of this Congress is identical with yours – we demand the withdrawal of the occupation forces from our country and the liberation of all our representatives, the restoration of our Republic's sovereignty.

We urgently need your help. That is why we are making this appeal to you, so as to bring this struggle to its victorious conclusion.

The Fourteenth Congress of the KSČ

[The text of this appeal is taken from a leaflet printed by the Central Committee of the KSČ. It is the final version of the appeal whose first draft is given on p. 65 as recorded during the Congress debate.]

5. Report on the Congress and Inaugural Session of the New Central Committee

'We reject the occupation; we insist on the withdrawal
of the foreign troops; our weapon is a general strike.'

Yesterday, on 22 August 1968, at 21.15, the Fourteenth Congress of the KSČ ended the first part of its session. It elected a new Central Committee of 144 members, as well as 37 members of the Central Control and Audit Commission. It pledged its full support to the Party's Action Programme and our post-January course. It adopted a resolution on the situation in the country, which is printed elsewhere, and an appeal to all communist parties, asking them to assist in bringing about an end to the occupation of Czechoslovakia. The Congress was attended by 1,219 out of the 1,543 properly elected delegates – many were unable to be present because they were detained by the occupying powers; by the end of the day's session some fifty Slovak delegates were present, their arrival having been hampered by various obstacles. The Congress decided to make its session a permanent one and to continue discussing further important problems as soon as conditions allow. Shortly before dawn on 23 August, the new Central Committee concluded its first meeting, having re-elected as its First Secretary Alexander Dubček, who is still interned, and having decided to entrust the direction of the Party Presidium temporarily to the newly elected Secretary Věnek Šilhan, a leading economist.

Communists, citizens! From now on obey only the instructions issued by this new Central Committee, which is the sole Party representative, enjoying the confidence of our entire people. Do not lose sight of the fact that the occupants will try to find traitors among former Party officials.

6. The New Central Committee: List of Members

The delegates of the Fourteenth Congress of the KSČ elected the following comrades to the new Central Committee:

1. Dubček, Alexander
2. Černík, Oldřich
3. Svoboda, Ludvík
4. Špaček, Josef
5. Císař, Čestmír
6. Smrkovský, Josef
7. Šimon, Bohumil
8. Kriegel, František
9. Černý, Josef
10. Hájek, Jiří
11. Hrdinová, Libuše
12. Kadlec, Vladimír
13. Krejčí, Josef
14. Slavík, Václav
15. Starý, Oldřich
16. Šik, Ota
17. Kabrna, Vladimír
18. Šabata, Jaroslav
19. Ondráček, Karel
20. Přibyl, Josef
21. Vojáček, Bohumil
22. Zuda, Josef
23. Pavlištík, Karel
24. Vojáček, Bořivoj
25. Petránek, František
26. Salák, Libor
27. Klága, Petr
28. Doležal, Zdeněk
29. Soukalová, Olga
30. Mrázek, Karel
31. Šmidke, Vlado
32. Ploss, Jiří
33. Mára, Josef
34. Rybář, Jaroslav
35. Polívka, Miloš
36. Bejček, Karel
37. Hlaváček, Mojmír
38. Králík, Bedřich
39. Hašek, Josef
40. Zelenková, Jiřina
41. Svoboda, Jaroslav
42. Částečka, Jan
43. Smolík, Zdeněk
44. Matějíček, Vojtěch
45. Dejl, Ladislav
46. Kábele, Antonín
47. Faloušek, Rudolf
48. Káninský, Josef
49. Černý, Rudolf
50. Klinger, Miloslav
51. Jindřich, Václav
52. Sýkora, Jaroslav
53. Loskot, Josef
54. Paulus, Zdeněk
55. Svoboda, Josef
56. Trojánek, Vojtěch
57. Šauer, Břetislav
58. Šimeček, Václav
59. Stoklasa, Jiří
60. Klánský, Jan
61. Koubek, Josef
62. Kratochvíl, Zdeněk
63. Tousa, Václav
64. Jeřábek, Jan
65. Němcová, Jarmila
66. Jarolím, Rudolf
67. Šimek, Miroslav
68. Kargel, Vladimír
69. Frank, Jaromír
70. Oldina, Josef
71. Popluda, Jaromír
72. Falc, Jaroslav
73. Plšer, Josef
74. Hejzlar, Zdeněk
75. Hrobek, Antonín
76. Jelínek, Jan
77. Haur, Josef
78. Burián, Václav

79. Šmidka, Josef
80. Galuška, Miroslav
81. Goldstücker, Eduard
82. Hanzelka, Jiří
83. Pavel, Josef
84. Erban, Evžen
85. Pelikán, Jiří
86. Hübl, Milan
87. Litera, Jaromír
88. Pavlíček, František
89. Šilhan, Věnek
90. Brož, Bohumil
91. Judl, Jiří
92. Kosík, Karel
93. Kratěna, Josef
94. Moc, Zdeněk
95. Němčanský, Miloš
96. Sochor, Lubomír
97. Vorel, Karel
98. Záruba, Antonín
99. Vodsloň, František
100. Vaculík, Martin
101. Mlynář, Zdeněk
102. Ťopek, František
103. Šišovský, Jozef
104. Husák, Gustáv
105. Hladký, Milan
106. Colotka, Peter
107. Pavlenda, Viktor
108. Zrak, Jozef
109. Kočtúch, Hvezdoň
110. Novomeský, Ladislav
111. Števček, Pavol

112. Sádovský, Štefan
113. Sedláková, Mária
114. Klokoč, Ondrej
115. Turček, Július
116. Való, Ján
117. Neoveský, Kliment
118. Malý, Jozef
119. Opavský, Jozef
120. Har, Jozef
121. Jankech, Anton
122. Ťažký, Anton
123. Pepich, Egyd
124. Repáš, Milan
125. Dzúr, Martin
126. Skalka, Jozef
127. Belaj, Jaroslav
128. Koscelanský, Ján
129. Batta, Alojz
130. Beder, Jozef
131. Pirč, Ján
132. Faraga, Michajl
133. Sabolčík, Juraj
134. Varga, Pavol
135. Pezler, Otto
136. Puzlová, Pavlína
137. Marko, Ján
138. Petruňa, Fedor
139. Tröml, Augustin
140. Procházka, Jan
141. Graca, Bohuslav
142. Zamek, Andrej
143. Machačová, Božena
144. Borůvka, Josef

7. *The New, Properly Elected Central Committee of the KSČ and the New Central Control and Audit Commission: Report on Inaugural Session*

Less than half an hour after the end of the first day's session of the Extraordinary Fourteenth Congress, Comrade Vodsloň opened the meeting of the newly elected Central Committee and the Central Control and Audit Commission. At its first session the Central Committee elected a new Presidium and discussed the tasks for the coming hours and days. The meeting of the Central Committee of the KSČ ended in the early hours of Friday, so that we shall be publishing further Congress material and a list of the members of the new Presidium in our next issue, if we succeed in producing one.

[Taken from the magazine *Politika*, No 1, 24 August 1968, p. 1.]

Our weakness lies in an incorrect view of the relationship between the Party member and the expert, between the administrator and the scholar or publicist . . .

V. I. Lenin, *Collected Works*, vol. 32, p. 144

We must learn to respect scholarship, to reject the 'communist' arrogance of the dilettante and the bureaucrat . . .

V. I. Lenin, *Collected Works*, vol. 32, p. 143

Ignorance is a demon, and I fear that it will yet cause many a tragedy; the great Greek poets were right to depict it as a tragic Fate in their terrible dramas of Mycenean and Theban royalty . . .

Karl Marx

V

Memoranda Compiled for the Fourteenth Congress

Preparation and Outline of a Long-term Programme:
[A draft for the Fourteenth Congress]

A. THE NEED FOR A PARTY PROGRAMME

The time has come when it is absolutely necessary to draft the Party's programme on the basis of Marxist theory, the contemporary development of science, and the experience gained by the socialist movement.

The reasons that have led us to this decision are the following:

Every section of the international workers' movement which has embraced Marxism has in so doing undertaken to guide and gauge its daily progress by the yardstick of a socialist and communist programme and by a never-ending process of scientific perception. Since the time of the *Communist Manifesto* the truly revolutionary character of any movement has been tested by asking whether it makes a correct assessment of the trends and possibilities of social development in any given epoch and country, and whether it critically links its present activity to its long-term aims.

In spite of the fact that a programmed activity forms one of the basic pillars of the communist movement we have to admit that our Party has in the past not managed to work out a programme for itself that respects the special conditions of this country and the traditions of our nations. This *programmatic weakness* has historical roots. There were three important periods in the history of our movement during which attempts were made to bring our programme in line with its goals: first the efforts made by Šmeral and the Marxist Association in the early twenties, when the Czechoslovak Communist Party came into being – efforts discontinued after the general adoption of the programme of the Communist International in 1928 which had summarized, but also simplified and schematized, the revolutionary experience of Soviet Russia; then there were the attempts by Czech and Slovak Marxist thinkers of the thirties, sparked

100

off by the crisis brought about by sectarian tendencies at the time of the struggle against Fascism, these attempts giving the Party its great authority in the resistance movement and the national and democratic revolution; and finally the endeavours which gave birth to the blueprint for Czechoslovakia's road to socialism in the years 1945–8 and which paved the way for the success of February,* but were then abandoned at the height of the 'personality cult'.

So far none of these attempts has led to a clarification in depth of the Party's aims, nor to the adoption of an integrated programme. On the contrary, the lack of such a programme proved progressively more acute until, in the last two decades, it *became* a programme in itself. This, unfortunately, happened at a time when the Party was faced with the very task of elaborating the true aims of socialism.

It is only very recently, in connection with the renascence of socialism in our country, that the conviction has gained ground in the Party that its entire activity must be based on firm programmatic foundations. The Action Programme, unanimously approved in April 1968 by the Central Committee of our Party, was the first step in this direction, however limited in scope. Now it is necessary to take the Action Programme as a starting point, to make use of the ideas and experience gained in the course of its preparation and to start work on a new, long-term Party programme.

A/b

The fact that the Party has hitherto not had a programme must be considered *abnormal* for several reasons.

Firstly, a Party which accepts responsibility for the leadership of our two nations without presenting them with a programme starts off by introducing into our national life the principle of arbitrariness. If the Party means to continue seeking the people's confidence, if it wishes to gain its permanent support, it must lay before it a consistent, feasible, scientifically based programme which will show it to be the force capable of uniting, in this country and at this particular point in history, the various social groups in our society, the force capable of giving meaning to the life of the workers, capable of solving the problems with which men are beset, capable of bringing to a successful conclusion the brave socialist experiment for which we have

* *Translator's Note:* The communist takeover of power in Czechoslovakia in February 1948.

accepted responsibility before the whole workers' movement and indeed the world.

Secondly, a Party which makes membership dependent on agreement with its programme, when in point of fact it has no such programme, builds its internal life on the principle of arbitrariness. If our movement is to undergo a genuine renascence and to remain a living, indomitable body inspired by revolutionary ideals and standing in the eyes of all its members for a true treasure-house of ideas and feelings, then the Party must build its internal life on the principles of a programme capable of uniting communists and giving real meaning to comradely relations between people.

It is obvious that the non-existence of a programme had gone hand-in-hand with the bureaucratization of the Party and with the crisis that had for years plagued the life of this country; and this weakness contributed to the disparity between socialist and communist ideals and actual everyday practice, preventing the application of science to the direction of social processes.

The statement by A. Novotný that the programme of the Communist Party of the Soviet Union was also our own programme merely served to conceal the absence of our own socialist and communist orientation. The time has come when the Party has to overcome the lack of its own creative application of Marxism, when it can no longer be content to copy foreign models, when it must stand firmly on its own feet as far as its programme is concerned.

A/c

The widespread concepts of socialism and communism which are still used as a programme arose in conditions of acute class conflict in the period of the dictatorship of the proletariat, the period of industrialization, when the revolution gave the class enemy a taste of his own medicine. In this way certain temporary, emergency measures and institutions which in many instances are not at all socialist in character have survived and are being placed in opposition to the humanitarian aims of the movement. The clarification of its programme, the revival and further development of the basic ideas of Marx, Lenin and the other socialist and communist thinkers, of Marxism as a whole, in a way that would be in keeping with the present state of society, is one of the fundamental conditions that must be fulfilled if the movement is to achieve a rebirth.

The extent of the disorientation which afflicted the Party in recent years and the magnitude of the social crisis brought about by the negation of socialist democracy made it imperative for the Party to devise a programme. The problem took two forms:

- first, the need to formulate *the humanist mission* of the communist movement;
- second, the task of conceiving *a new model of socialism*, corresponding to Czechoslovak conditions, and a concept of the Party appropriate to such a model.

A/d

The drafting of a Party programme under our present conditions requires:

- an analysis of the conflicts and future prospects of the contemporary world; an analysis of the whole range of questions connected with the development of the socialist countries, the advanced capitalist countries and the 'third world'; an explanation of the dynamics of the forces operating in the conflicts between the world's different systems and inside those systems; a survey of the dangers resulting from the existence of imperialism under these conditions. At the same time it is necessary to take cognizance of the changed situation of mankind, conditioned by the growth of modern civilization and culture as well as by the profound social changes that have taken place in this century;
- a confrontation of socialist and communist ideas with the experience of the revolution, its triumphs and its defeats, this being an essential component of the Party's programme, which can no longer confine itself to a critique of capitalism but must also continually analyse and critically assess its own theoretical premises and practical achievements; the Party's programme must unceasingly examine its own concepts, comparing them with other currents of contemporary humanism and with the results of scientific analysis;
- the maintaining of harmony between the aims and the means used to achieve them, between the transformation of objective conditions and the betterment of the individual; for experience teaches us that false means give birth to social forces hostile to socialist aims; the programme is not supposed to prescribe how

people should live but rather to clarify the conditions under which socialist interests are formed and reconciled, conditions under which the free activity of men may gradually acquire communist features;

– the drafting of a programme for the various stages and methods of realization of socialist changes in such a way as to utilize all the possibilities of rapid expansion in our country and to prevent subjectivism and the omission of individual stages;

– at the same time it is necessary to bear in mind both the true interests and aspirations of world socialism and the interests and aspirations of our own workers, our own nations; the decisive factor is the welfare of the international communist movement as a whole, but that movement can only be strong – especially under present conditions – if every single member is strong too. That is why we link the principle of international solidarity, of closest solidarity and closest collaboration between socialist countries, between communist, workers' and other progressive forces in the world, with the other principle of independent action by each Communist Party, the principle of respect for the individuality and the traditions of each nation and the sovereignty of each socialist country.

Only if these conditions are met can we hope to find a socialist solution to the present crisis, to offer our people a humanist alternative to modern society, to discover practicable applications of socialism in the solution of the basic social and human problems of our time.

B. ON THE AIMS OF THE PARTY (MAIN POINTS)

A Marxist party, in formulating its long-term programme at a time when it is trying to liberate itself from the Stalinist, bureaucratic deformation of Marxism and socialism, must above all make it quite clear how Marxism sees the problems of the liberation of man in a socialist and communist society; it must develop the basic values of Marxism and of the revolutionary movement which contain the ideas and emotions forming the basis of its practical activity.

Marxism does not see socialism and communism as the final goal of history, but rather as a means of humanization, i.e. of the maximum satisfaction and development of the needs of highly civilized and cultivated human beings. Socialism represents a society created by the outstripping, in every respect, of advanced capitalism – the most advanced system of exploitation of man by man – and providing the fundamental social conditions for man's liberation. Communism gives people the opportunity to implement freedom in the widest sense.

The liberation of man is thus the basic aim of socialism and communism.

Human liberty cannot be understood merely as 'perceived necessity'. It consists in the free choice of activity, naturally influenced by the existing level of development of the general conditions of human life, which to a lesser or greater extent facilitate or debar free human activity.

The founders of Marxism based their teaching on the knowledge that the conditions for achieving a higher stage of human freedom and removing social inequality included not only the abolition of the actual forms of the capitalist order, but also the overcoming of the alienating power of objects over people and of the role played by the division of labour in creating class distinctions. This is almost diametrically opposed to those concepts of socialism which, now as in the past, aim at putting everyone on the same social level and ignore the need for material and cultural advancement in socialist or communist society as a fundamental condition of human freedom. Such concepts are far below the standards of Marxist thought.

It was Marxism that discovered the fundamental motive forces in the emancipation of man.

It discerned, first and foremost, that the social force whose historical activity is capable of creating the necessary conditions for the universal realization of human liberty is that class of society which, though it carries on its shoulders the main brunt of the material production of goods necessary for human life, is yet denied, more than any other, free human activity in those conditions. The proletariat has been shown to be that class. The proletariat does not of course strive for socialism in order to establish a permanent dictatorship of a new class over the other social groups, as used to be the case earlier, but rather so that it may abolish itself, transform itself, together with the other social groups, into a sovereign producer in a socialist society, which will develop in such a way as gradually to create conditions for a human freedom that is no longer conditioned or limited either by class or social distinctions.

Marxism has likewise shown that correct perception, illuminating the road to the emancipation of the working class, and thus also the emancipation of man in general, is a basic condition for the achievement of these aims. Socialism grows out of the association of science with the revolutionary movement, with which it stands or falls. And communism can only be achieved on the basis of activity that makes this association possible.

In the Marxist concept of socialism and communism, the collective is not one-sidedly elevated above the individual. On the contrary, Marxism has from the very beginning opposed the abstract elevation of society over real people and their mutual relations. This remains true even if in the process of liberating the individual the interests of individuals and groups have to be balanced and the interests of joint revolutionary action taken into consideration. Marxism is the programme of a truly individual freedom of man, which cannot of course come into its own until man's personality is given the opportunity to create and absorb the values of a society organized on socialist lines. This is what makes the socialist and communist programme so fundamentally different from the bourgeois, liberal idea of individual freedom, which permits an individual to be free at the expense of others.

The Marxist concept of freedom is based on the total liberation of every member of society; it cannot therefore lead to the 'socialization of misery', but on the contrary to socialized prosperity. The prosperity of such a society is not an end in itself, it merely forms an essential foundation on which the full liberation of each single man can be achieved, and with it also relations resulting in the mutual enrichment and development of man by man.

C. TOWARDS THE CREATION OF A PARTY PROGRAMME (THE MODEL OF SOCIALIST DEVELOPMENT)

C/a. The paths of revolution

The creation of conditions for free human activity, which the founders of Marxism called a communist revolution, includes the overthrow and transformation of the entire way of life of bourgeois industrial civilization, passing through several stages that transform politics, economics, the production forces and culture.

By gaining political power and socializing the means of production, the working class ushered in a socialist revolution, making it possible to start the process of the gradual liberation of man's life. However, socialism as a socialist way of life was understood in the model that was used in this country to be a mere discarding, a pure negation, of the social reforms achieved under capitalism. It was thus reduced to nothing more than the nationalization of capitalist property, the bureaucratic management of the economy from the centre, and a monopolistic power-political system. Yet this is not enough. Within these confines neither the working class, nor the peasants, nor yet the working intelligentsia can develop as the creators of new human relationships. Socialist relationships are formed only on the basis of a constructive replacement of the political and economic foundations of the old society, which leads in the course of socialist development to a gradual constructive replacement of the living conditions of bourgeois civilization and culture in general.

The distorted model of socialism was applied in this country in the past to all intents and purposes as a slavish imitation of the prevailing Stalinist concept which had trimmed socialism back to its primitive assumptions. It deformed and generalized aspects which may perhaps have suited the conditions and needs of countries on the threshold of industrialization but which did not suit the real aims of socialism, and that model was bound to come into conflict with our more advanced way of life. In contrast with this concept of socialism, in which the idea of the liberation of man has lost all contact with reality, a contemporary concept must demand a positive liberation of man to take place gradually in every sphere. Such a process includes the overthrow of bourgeois political power and private ownership by capitalists, as well as the tyranny of things over people in the traditional industrial civilization. In every case new conditions and greater scope are being created for man's free activity: the development of democracy and extension of freedom for all, the building of a more effective system of socialist enterprise, and the improvement of man's culture and living style.

Socialism arises as a society freed from class antagonisms and the exploitation of man by man; it is based on the linking of work and enterprise, a society having at its disposal the economic system of a planned exploitation of the market, a society that is just both in a social and in a national sense, a society that is free and organized on

107

democratic lines, an industrially advanced society intensively developing its production forces, a society with a civilized way of life and managed by competent people, a society whose material wealth makes possible dignified human existence and comradely relations of mutual co-operation among people, a society gradually providing increased scope for the development of the human personality.

This humanist model of socialism, in keeping with Marxist ideas, can of course work only as a whole; if any of its major components are missing, the entire socialist project loses its meaning.

On the contrary, a full implementation of this model is both a condition and the goal of truly communist relations between people, which will of course become decisive only when the structure and dynamics of production forces change completely, when they fully cross the frontiers of industrial civilization, and when man's universal progress becomes the real be-all and end-all of everyday life.

C/b. Changes in the social structure

The very first step in the socialization of the means of production, *viz.* their nationalization, led to the end of class antagonism. The class struggle has ceased to be a fundamental aspect of the social processes within the country. The position and role of the classes and groups in our society have changed and are continuing to change.

It will depend to a decisive degree on the working class whether we shall succeed in putting into practice the new model of socialism, whether we shall find the means to bring about further revolutionary development. The socialist working class, which still has to bear the heavy burden of division of labour inherited from the past, has a deeply based objective interest (irrespective of how far any particular individual is aware of it) in changing these conditions of life and thus bringing to completion its own elimination as a class. Herein lies concealed a profound source of the historic revolutionary role of the working class, which it can of course fulfil only in co-operation with science and its exponents among the progressive intelligentsia, and with the increasing integration of the other social groups in the formation of a socialist society.

The socialist co-operative farmers, who have in the past been forced in many respects into an unequal position in comparison with other sections of the population, have benefited from the development of their economic and social relations and from the mechanization of production, and are rapidly approaching the conditions enjoyed by other workers, thus gaining new scope for their socialist activity.

The progressive role in society of the intelligentsia grows in step with the development of socialism as it strengthens its ties with the workers and widens the range of its own participation – especially as science is becoming the decisive production force, thus giving greater importance to pre-production stages and welfare considerations.

These far-reaching changes have given rise to the class unity of socialist society, but they do not of course remove all social differentiation between individuals and groups and their various interests. The structure of socialist society is, on the contrary, based on a network of different social roles linked with a qualitatively transformed division of labour and distribution of social activities in general.

Socialist society is characterized by the general applicability of the principles of performance and equal opportunity of self-fulfilment. This does not in any way impede the growing differentiation of needs, interests, and aspirations of individuals and social groups; on the contrary, it is one of the most important aspects of the dynamic character of socialist society.

The manner in which these individual, group, and national interests are reconciled makes it possible for people to become more deeply involved with the socialist society, with its major governing principles and values.

Provided a socialist society does not become enmeshed in bureaucracy, and provided the old class-conflicts stemming from property relations are not superseded by new ones emanating from power relations, there will be a gradual increase in social differentiation based on the different work people do and the different reward they receive for that work. A socialist society must reckon with the factual inequality between those on the one hand whose jobs give them only a very limited opportunity for free self-fulfilment as human beings, whose working hours and wages make it almost impossible for them to achieve this outside their work, and who are therefore forced to depend on the mass-consumption system, and those on the other hand who do work that possesses, in however limited a fashion, features of genuine human self-fulfilment but who can as a result easily become complacent in this respect. This kind of social differentiation no longer has a class character; it is common to all the social groups. It makes it possible to reconcile the interests of all the social groups, provided the necessary conditions are created for this. On the one hand, a socialist society must in every possible way mobilize the interests of the people in the first group, *viz.* those who are seeking escape from the limitations imposed by their work and their consumption, and can find it only in a revolutionary transformation of society and of the foundations on which human civilization is based. On the other, socialist society must provide scope for the interests of the second group, those who are able to utilize their energies and talents in highly skilled work that helps to transform the social and cultural conditions of human existence. The Marxist blueprint for the liberation of man from social and objective conditions that stand in the way of his self-fulfilment represents the common denominator of these social interests, mutually linking the two motive forces behind the socialist development of society.

It is to be expected that in the long term an increasing proportion of society will be motivated by free creative activity and will, in one way or another, be able to participate in it. At a certain level of development this will lead to the merging together of the social groups, which will overcome the differences that used to exist between them; and this in turn will lead to the creation of a truly classless communist society, i.e. to a solution of the conflict between social equality and human freedom on the basis of the general development of man.

C/c. The solution of the problem of nationalities

One very important aspect is the position of nations and nationalities, who must find in socialism their opportunity to enjoy full equality and unhindered political, legal, economic and cultural development, all this to be achieved on the basis of a profound understanding between nations and mutual international assistance.

The Marxist concept does not exclude any form of mutual relations, provided it is based on equality and prevents the overruling of a smaller nation by a larger one, provided it gives them the opportunity for maximum development within a framework of harmonious universal growth, and provided it corresponds to the wishes of the nations concerned. In this sense a republic set up on the principle of federation, union or confederation – depending on conditions – or any other form of self-determination of nations including secession, is fully in keeping with socialism.

At the present time – in view of the history of the relations between the Czechs and the Slovaks – the main task appears to be the working out of a federal system which could become the basis for an exemplary socialist solution to the problem of nationalities in our country.

Such a solution is all the more important since the future poses for our country the problem of such an improvement of fraternal socialist relations between various nations and nationalities as would pave the way for ever higher forms of international co-operation across national and State frontiers.

C/d. Socialist democracy

The very content and meaning of our revolution presupposes a profound transformation of the socio-political system and all its institutions. Such a transformation can of course only take place to the extent that a new social structure is created, a socialist economy is functioning, and the advancement of society alters the material conditions of human existence.

What is needed above all is a new model of democratic socialism to replace the bureaucratic system. Having outgrown the class struggle, a socialist society must gradually begin to curtail and liquidate the executive and repressive functions of its organs, to de-monopolize politics and to extend civic liberties and the free self-determination of the individual as much as that of nations.

Democracy is a basic and indispensable aspect of socialist development. The actual socio-political system of socialism grows out of a temporary dictatorship of the proletariat, by means of the replacement of traditional class democracy, the generalization of democratic principles, and the elaboration of a new content and new forms of democratic decision-making. Socialism requires more, not less, freedom than any previous type of society: freedom of the press and of expression, of assembly, movement, travel and so forth; it requires more, not fewer, human rights: the right to own a home, the right to work, to self-fulfilment, education and opportunity to develop one's talents, to social welfare, private property, democratic representation, the protection of one's interests and participation in decision-making – and all this for all members of society.

The whole purpose of socialism as a socio-political system is to

111

mediate and guarantee these rights and freedoms, which in their totality form the actual content of a workers' State; this requires that use be made of representative democracy (in particular of parliament) and that direct and indirect democracy be linked, with a view to strengthening self-administration in every sphere of social life, in places of work as well as in areas of residence, where it can help to overcome the shortcomings of representative democracy, where the conditions have been created for the free self-determination of man and the widening of his real participation in decision-making.

According to the level of development of the social structure and the extent of creation by socialist society of its own economic forms, there will be scope for greater democracy in political decision-making on the basis of confrontation between ideas and between people, of opposition and mutual control through political parties and national organizations which can independently propose and represent various methods of achieving modern humanist socialism, and through the National Front, which provides a common platform with socialist foundations for working people.

Socialist society now at last offers an opportunity to make use of the scope for strengthening democracy inherent in the otherwise equivocal development of the media of information and mass communication; to increase the number of people who decide, the number of matters submitted for decision, the number of alternative solutions offered, as well as to make the selection of competent decision-makers more impartial and to bring science into the whole business of decision-making.

All these roads to socialist democracy are both a preparation and a framework for the gradual long-term phasing out of the State's repressive power, which will then spread to other spheres of life. This will make it possible to leave discussions to organs of self-administration, thus excluding political interference, or to the people themselves. All in all, this development towards communism is intended gradually to replace the system of governing people by a system of managing affairs.

C/e. The economic system of socialism

The transfer of the means of production into the hands of the State has abolished capitalist exploitation but has not replaced it by constructive forms of socialist economy. Under the present system the

State has administered the economy in the name of society as if it were one huge industrial enterprise. Economic forms, considered to be 'alien' to a socialist society, have given way to State instructions which virtually prescribed, down to the last detail, what is to be done by the individual workers.

In an industrially advanced country, however, such a system of centrally direct administration of the national economy was bound to prove cumbersome and highly inefficient. Instead of being an organ of the workers, the State became their sole employer; the national economy was turned into a machine that went on running for its own sake; and the entire administration became hopelessly bureaucratized. While abolishing incentives typical of capitalism, the system did not succeed in replacing them with sufficiently efficacious incentives of a new, socialist kind. Thus the producers continued to a certain extent to be deprived of the ownership of the means of production.

The socialist programme, however, stipulates not merely formal but genuine 'socialization', i.e. the creation of an economy that would make it possible for all the workers really to be in charge of the process of reproduction and of creating wealth rather than serving it.

This can be achieved only through economic means that are in keeping with the given standard of industry and which, on this level, make it possible to give the workers an interest in socialist enterprise. Such a solution needs to be based on the planned exploitation of a market economy.

A doctrinaire, rigid application of State ownership cannot provide an answer; it must therefore make way for the concept of structured social ownership depending on the standard of workers' skill and the size and nature of the enterprise. According to how social production forces are formed in each particular case, and according to the degree to which they are in practice truly social, the socialist society makes use of a broad range of forms of ownership, from large State enterprises through national and co-operative ones, down to small private undertakings, thus mobilizing all the resources and all the initiative of the workers.

Independent socialist enterprises are set up as the basic elements of a socialist economy and as the agents of a market economy; they are independent of the State, entering into economic associations of their own choosing, exposed to the pressures of the market and of economic competition.

These economic conditions – influenced by the central authorities in a planned manner if necessary – can link maximum output with a maximum of consideration for the needs both of the individual and of society as a whole. If a socialist enterprise is to hold its own under such conditions, it must be capable of harnessing all the skill of its workers, it must choose the most capable executives with the most up-to-date ideas, and it must succeed in combining expert management with democratic self-administration.

A great deal of help can be afforded by variously constituted organs of self-administration, the workers' councils – provided they combine the immediate interests of the workers with the wider interests of the enterprise and of society as a whole and furnish a firm and dynamic basis for expert, technically and organizationally skilled management. Subsequent changes in the technical equipment, structure of work, and level of qualification may in future make these organs of self-administration, as the basic devices for worker participation in economic management, part of a higher order of economic administration on a national scale.

The State does not enter the process in order to supplant the other factors of economic movement, but to create – in accordance with an overall plan and on the basis of economic rules and instruments – conditions under which the interests of the workers become concomitant with the interests of the whole of society; to direct them in the most progressive economic directions and towards the easiest means of exploiting national resources; finally, to influence the creation of social wealth wherever market criteria prove insufficient or where it is necessary to decide in favour of social or human values, as in questions affecting the environment, culture, etc.

This indirect planned management is influenced and raised to a higher, more dynamic level than the traditional directive approach by the fact that it does not presuppose a passive role for the workers but, on the contrary, plans the development of an active role for labour at all stages, giving the workers the opportunity to act independently and, by their initiative, to add new dimensions to economic life.

Socialism will not reach the point of standing on its own feet until it produces an economic system all its own, which will generalize socialist enterprise and open up the sphere of human interests to new impulses of civilization and culture.

This approach puts the replacement, in a communist society, of old economic forms such as the market, value ratios, etc., in an entirely new light. As opposed to the traditional view, which simply foresaw their abolition, modern organizational techniques would now seem to make it possible – at a certain level of development – for these forms to be systematically utilized and to become the means for a consistent shaping of processes aimed at achieving a planned objective.

C/f. Social justice

Socialism abolishes ancient class privileges, demands that everyone should work for his living and provides equal opportunity for self-fulfilment. These principles constitute a higher form of social justice, which does not aggravate social disparities more than the present limitations necessitate, which at the same time respects the diverse needs, interests and aspirations of people and does not stifle their initiative, skill and ability in levelling tendencies, sacrificing the newly acquired freedom to achieve a mere formal equality.

Socialism has proclaimed the universal right to work as one of its most outstanding benefits. If, however, it is to keep this promise, it cannot interpret it one-sidedly as a guaranteed right to a certain kind of activity – for instance the particular work a man has been doing hitherto – without regard to its economic effectiveness and social importance (which would tend to undermine all economic and social advancement) but, instead, as an assurance that everyone will be given the opportunity to work, as a guarantee of social utility in rapidly changing conditions, and as an entitlement to be transferred to other work and to acquire new or superior qualifications.

Socialism has proclaimed the principle of performance, the right to a reward consonant with work done. If it is to fulfil its mission, it must consistently demand that rewards are everywhere paid according to results; and it must also find a new, broader approach that includes not only reward for the individual, but also for the economically verified result of the work of the whole collective.

Socialism has proclaimed the universal right to human dignity. If it does not wish to break its own resolutions, it must also secure truly dignified living conditions for all those who for reasons of age

115

or health cannot work, and who need social and human assistance.

This social welfare already contains the germs of a future, higher, form of social justice, transcending the bounds of civic justice and the principle of work. However, these aspects will fully come into their own only when they are backed by a wealth of resources making it possible for man himself, his requirements and abilities, to become the actual criterion by which human activity as well as the distribution of wealth are governed.

C/g. Basic amenities in modern life

Socialism cannot exist in any genuine form unless it is based on a civilization which, by the nature and extent of the human endeavour it demands and by the standard of the material and spiritual resources it affords, is in keeping with the requirements of socialist life; and which generates universal interests in society that of their own accord, without outside pressure and as a result of free human activity, influence daily life in a socialist direction.

An advanced industrial system is thus an indispensable basis for socialist life. In its historical beginnings the socialist movement lacked such a basis – it had to create one. These specific historical circumstances once placed industrialization on the agenda of socialism. Yet industrialization, consisting in the main of the extensive growth of industrial production forces – machines and manpower – does not belong to the historic tasks of socialism. It is, rather, a necessary condition for the birth of socialism, and represents in fact a stage in civilization which is actually in contradiction to socialist development. As long as society boosts production at the cost of limiting the growth of consumption for the majority, as long as it multiplies its production forces by increasing unskilled industrial work, as long as it introduces scientific management by depriving the majority of any share in that management, as long as it creates an artificial environment and civilization at the cost of devastating the nation's living conditions and relegating culture to the fringes of life, as long, that is, as general expansion is forcibly achieved by hampering the advancement of the majority of the workers, there can be little hope of making human relationships truly socialist, even though exploitation has been done away with.

Socialist life can develop fully only if society has attained such a structure of production forces that the further improvement of amenities can be achieved not by extensive growth – which puts the main emphasis on industrialization of wider areas – but by intensive growth in which the chief concern is the utilization and improvement of existing industrial potential, the development of services, of pre-production techniques and of social welfare.

Experience shows that in our country the tasks of extensive industrialization have now been fulfilled, its possibilities exhausted. To adhere to this traditional orientation leads only to technical obsolescence, to a catastrophic condition in the service industries, to a waste of human endeavour; it is responsible for our not making sufficiently good use of science and of intellectual resources in general which, under modern conditions and in particular in our society, could well become a decisive source of national wealth. The model of socialist development that would correspond to our specific conditions is thus in every way dependent on gradual changes in the structure and dynamics of the production forces; it would make use of the immense resources of contemporary science as the most incisive production force of all, facilitating, step by step, better living conditions for all workers, which would alter man's whole position in the world of production forces. What this means is that we should seek our own approach to the scientific-technical revolution which is beginning to make itself felt below the surface of the contemporary world.

It is obvious that a democratic, humane socialism cannot simply be grafted on to traditional industrialization; such a democracy would be incapable of affecting the lack of freedom that most people encounter in their daily work – unskilled, monotonous, purely productive activity; as for humanity, it would not abolish the deprivation felt by many workers within the limits of their consumption and in their hours after work, but would instead only enhance their equality of deprivation.

No permanent socialist development is possible unless the limitations created by traditional industrial labour are removed. In the short term this will mean a consistent humanization of existing labour processes on the basis of rational organization, increasing the workers' share in management, improving the culture of work and the working environment, linking work with education, and so on. In the long term, however, the only solution is the gradual abolition of all unnecessary and ineffective, obsolete, unqualified labour by making use of the achievements of modern science and technology,

117

gradually transferring human labour to the pre-production stages, and finally giving man every opportunity for creative self-fulfilment as a result of a radical change in the technology of production and a drastic reduction of working hours.

Socialist development is equally impossible if man remains enslaved by the daily worry of earning a living. In the short term, then, we must achieve a growth of consumption in keeping with modern civilization which would fully satisfy the existing requirements of human life. In the long term, however, the only solution lies in creating such prosperity and such unlimited productivity as will make possible the continuing creation of new, higher requirements and the cultivation of human interests.

The new society thus has to work towards a state of affairs where it can overstep the boundaries of industrialization; it must gradually discover ways and means of achieving a higher structure of the productive forces of human life and of achieving the scientific-technical revolution. This in turn requires the increasing participation of science as a production force at the very root of industry and the growing automation of production processes so that man can be liberated more and more from the immediate production process. It must provide basic amenities for human life, with whose help fundamental changes in human activity, consumption, living environment and life in general can be brought about, raising every member of society above the poverty line, liberating him from the burden represented by the division of labour and basing human relationships on mutual development so that life can be devoted to the free cultivation of man's talents and abilities.

Whereas at the outset of the socialist revolution the liberation of all was a pre-condition for the liberation of the individual, the free development of the individual will gradually become a pre-condition for the free development of all.

C/h. Cultivation of human resources

Cultural development, seen in its broadest sense as the cultivation of the living environment as well as of man himself, is an indivisible, vital part of the revolutionary process. Culture has its source in man's creative work and the utilization of the results of that work, whether in the material or the spiritual sphere.

In previous societies – and equally so in the new society as long as it is marked by extensive industrialization, the directive system of management and bureaucratic power – culture has been regarded as a special sphere, sharply divided from the rest of life, which was governed by the cult of utility. Culture was thought to be more or less unimportant for human progress. This prepared the ground in daily life for a contemptuous attitude towards created values, for an unfeeling approach to a balanced life-environment, for a disregard of Nature, for lack of concern regarding human labour and man's daily worries. Culture itself, viewed as the private affair of a narrow section of society, was left to its own devices at the fringes of life, being subjugated to the whims of the powers-that-be. This led to a loss of social importance on the part of the arts, which had no connection with the business of daily living. Such a connection can be established only by the cultivation of human resources. This is of vital importance to socialism, especially in our country, in which the relatively high potential of science and erudition has for years not been practically utilized for the benefit of society and its development.

If we wish to orient socialism towards the modern trends of civilization, towards the scientific-technical revolution, we must rely on people with outstanding intellectual abilities, highly developed senses and emotions, dynamic will-power and sensitivity to the human aspect of things. We must open the door to everyone capable of creating such wealth and passing it on to others.

Socialism must be based on a free, autonomous and completely unhindered development of science and scientific research. There is no conflict between the revolutionary workers' movement and science: the greater and freer the scope of scientific research, the more relevant it is to the workers' interests. Only a society in which scientific knowledge is used at every level that influences further development can be a truly socialist society.

Socialism must, furthermore, be based on a free and autonomous flowering of the arts, safeguarded by the autonomy of culture, the absolute freedom of artistic creation and a universal right of access to the cultural heritage. Only a society which knows how to appreciate the role played by art, which is capable of protecting it against bureaucratic interference and commercial debasement, can be a truly socialist society.

Socialism must also necessarily rely on an educational system which can make the best use of all the talents of every member of society and which is at their disposal throughout their life. This can put a socialist country well ahead as regards the quality of its education.

And finally, communism will open the door for culture to influence the entire life-environment, at work as well as at home, in leisure as well as transport, in social life as well as in the field of human relationships, thinking and behaviour. It is to be expected that the cultivation of human resources will prove to be a decisive factor in social development, that it will become the life-giving force of our Party.

Herein lie all the great and fundamental elements on which socialism and communism can rely in the world of today.

C/i. The international standing of our revolution*
C/k. The tradition of our nations

A feeling for the history and culture of our nations forms an important part of the programme by which Czechoslovak communists have been expressing their views on the specific road of the Czechoslovak people to socialism and communism.

In our struggle for a just, free and sovereign society, based on the maximum freedom of every individual, we consider as our predecessors and the pioneers of our own endeavours all those personalities and social movements in the history of our nations who worked towards the same goals.

The ideals of humanism, social justice and civic national freedom have always provided strong incentives for revolutionary and reformist endeavours in Czech and Slovak history. That is why the communists of today are fully justified in accepting the Hussite legacy and the humanitarian ideals of the Czech and Slovak Reformation; why they respect the defenders of Bohemian sovereignty in 1618 and sympathize with the peasant revolts that took place in the age of feudal oppression; why they draw inspiration from the brave stand for freedom in 1848 and 1849; why they appreciate the democratic and progressive movements of the late nineteenth century as well as the statesmanlike wisdom of the great figures of the Czechoslovak Republic and of our entire history. They are the natural heirs of the finest traditions of the workers' movement from its very beginnings in Social Democratic and anarchist form; they admire the intrepid struggle of those who took part in the resistance movement in the

* *Editor's Note:* C/i exists only as a heading; C/j not at all.

two world wars, of the fighters in the Slovak National Rising and on the Prague barricades; they continue the work of the Czech and Slovak *avant-garde* Left between the wars and of the generations of workers, revolutionaries and communists who founded the Party, guided it through a period of class struggle and won our people over for the building of socialism.

Our nations, living as they do at the crossroads of various historical currents, have a turbulent history behind them. Our culture, our social feeling and upbringing are imbued with that tradition, which represents an important factor making for consolidation and survival in Central Europe.

Our people has passed through a period when it was threatened with complete annihilation; it learned to be grateful for the help provided by the Soviet people and for the international unity of socialist forces, considering these ties, based on sovereignty and fraternal co-operation, to be a permanent condition of national life.

Czechoslovakia set out on the road of socialist development as an industrially advanced country with a large and highly skilled working class, an exceptional standard of education, a mature progressive culture, deeply rooted traditions of democracy, a living awareness of all the former struggles for freedom, national independence and national sovereignty that had formed part of her history for many centuries. All this gives us today an exceptionally good opportunity to foster in this country a humane, democratic socialism which will bring worthy fulfilment to the legacy of our past history.

C/1. The mission of the Party

The Marxist-Leninist Party, which is capable of creating and developing a new society on a scientific basis and rallying the majority of the workers for the fulfilment of this task, has its inalienable place in the realization of democratic socialism and of the humane aims of communism. In order to do this the Party must of course bring about its own profound renascence; its external action and inner life must be cleansed of the bureaucratic silt that has smothered them. It must renew itself as a movement serving the whole of society and visibly striving for the general acceptance and realization of the aims it has adopted; it must cease to be a power institution which decides every single action of every member of society.

The original concept of the Party as a vanguard of the working class fighting for the implementation of the communist programme based on science was reduced, in the Stalinist version, to 'the instrument of the dictatorship of the proletariat', an organ of industrialization. As it acquired power, it increasingly lost its character as a movement. In its inner life the Party created a hierarchy; it did not implement the principle of democratic centralism in order to give greater scope for initiative to individual communists, but rather to tie their hands with directives; all this gave rise to a closed system, both internally and externally.

In our own age, with its changing economic and social structure, communists must gain a fresh understanding of their tasks and their methods of work. The Party undoubtedly remains the defender of the vital interests of the workers, but it can no longer act as the representative of one single social class. It has a more far-reaching mission as the vanguard of contemporary progress, linking the creative forces and endeavours of the workers as they attempt to build a classless society, a movement which tries to solve the fundamental human problems of present-day civilization.

This presupposes a fundamental change in the inner composition of the Party as well as in its standing in society.

It will be necessary to create a Party in which new and truly democratic methods of decision-making are applied, making use of all available information both in the Party and in society as a whole. It will be a Party made up of members whose own activity implements its programme, members who have a genuine right to form their own opinion and to associate with other members in order to defend that opinion, and a minority will have the opportunity to try, with the whole Party looking on, to become a majority. The law of diversity and re-creation of unity must therefore apply. It will be a Party in which the choice between alternatives and the establishing of a political line will be the result of initiative from both the top and the bottom, a Party with a mind open to science and possessing an organization that allows scientific knowledge to infuse its whole activity. It will be a Party in which the role of the professional apparatus in drafting and implementing policy will be limited to technical and organizational work and where elected workers are not permanent professional office-holders but the temporary representatives of the movement, democratically elected from among people of good character and natural authority who are respected by the public at large.

As a pioneer of democratic socialism our Party will unceasingly strive to hold such a position in the political system as will make the control of power possible on the basis of partnership and opposition, on the basis of a contest between ideas and between people, at the same time providing a guarantee that there can be no reactionary backsliding. In addition to its traditional political operations, the Party should be a pioneer in the sphere of self-governing bodies, whose internal work must no longer be dictated by Party directives.

At its very first Congress our Party resolved not to be merely a political party in the accepted meaning of the term, but rather to become 'the *avant-garde* of a new life', a movement that realizes that all its changing forms are pre-conditioned by circumstances and that its very existence as a party is justified solely by its aims and within the limits of the struggle to realize those aims.

D. HOW TO DRAFT THE PROGRAMME

The drafting of the Party's programme must be regarded as a long-term and exceptionally important task for the Party. The resolution of the Fourteenth Congress merely provides an introduction to this programme, work on which will take many years. The Congress therefore sets up a Party Programme Committee (alternatively: charges the Central Committee to set up such a committee) and formulates the basic concepts.

Work on the Party programme represents an integral part of the rebirth of socialism and of the Party, a pre-condition for overcoming the movement's ideological and moral crisis.

The draft programme is of course not intended to, and indeed cannot, impose any final set of ideas upon our nations; it merely provides an impulse for the public formulation of such ideas on the basis of Party proposals and of the clash of opinions. Once the programme has been drafted with the aid of many experts and cultural workers, the Party will organize a long-term discussion both within the Party and outside it, giving the nation an opportunity to express its views on it. The Party Press, and in particular the periodicals dealing with political theory, will play a permanent part in this work. The participation of the news media in general is recommended.

Provided the main problems are solved and unity is achieved, the Fifteenth Party Congress will be able to approve the programme; but again not without proper debate, which must form a regular part of the preparation of every Party Congress. Then the Congress can go on to supervise the implementation of the programme and amend it as necessary, in accordance with the experience gained in its operation and as a result of a new scientific knowledge.

The programme was drafted by a committee composed of the following members:
R. Richta, B. Levčík, D. Bárta, E. Bartoš, V. Blažek, J. Bodnár, J. Cvekl, I. Dubská, J. Hanzelka, J. Hermach, J. Hronovský, F. Hronský, Z. Javůrek, M. Kaláb, R. Kalivoda, O. Klein, J. Hopčok, J. Kosta, M. Král, E. Löbl, K. Lukeš, K. Minárik, E. Novák, O. Pavlík, D. Pokorný, S. Provazník, M. Průcha, R. Selucký, J. Sláma, J. Strinka, Z. Strimiska, J. Šindelář, M. Švermová, I. Vojtěch, J. Zumr.

No discipline obliges the members of the Party blindly to sign all draft resolutions presented by the Central Committee. Never have there existed anywhere rules that would cause Party organizations to relinquish the right to their own judgement and become mere signatories *of Central Committee resolutions.*

V. I. Lenin, *Collected Works*, vol. 10, p. 500

At the same time it is essential that all *members of the organization should* independently *and* separately *express their opinions on disputed questions of interest to the whole organization when electing their representatives. Democratically organized parties and associations simply cannot do without this canvassing of the opinions of all their members without exception – certainly not in serious cases and in particular when involved in a political action in which the* masses *act independently* . . .

Why do we insist that all *Party members be asked for their opinion, i.e. a so-called 'referendum'? Just because the voluntary participation of every single worker is indispensable to the success of mass campaigns.*

V. I. Lenin, *Collected Works*, vol. 11, p. 432

Every political problem cannot be solved by asking all members of the Party; such a course would be a never-ending, exhausting, fruitless ballot. But the most important problems, and especially those that are directly linked with action by the masses *themselves, must be solved, in the name of democracy, not just by sending representatives but by consulting every member of the Party.*

V. I. Lenin, *Collected Works*, vol. 11, p. 433

Communist arrogance means that a man who is a member of the Communist Party and has not yet been expelled after a screening thinks that everything can be solved by communist dictatorship.

V. I. Lenin, *Collected Works*, vol. 33, p. 69

The principle of democratic centralism and autonomy of local institutions means the freedom *to* criticize, *always and everywhere, as long as this does not impair the unity of a* particular campaign, *and the inadmissibility of* any *criticism which undermines or makes difficult the* unity *of a campaign on which the Party has agreed.*

V. I. Lenin, *Collected Works*, vol. 10, p. 440

It is high time to discard the traditions of sectarian secrecy and – in a party based on the masses – *to raise a resolute slogan:* more light, *let the Party know* everything, *let it have at its disposal* all, absolutely all *the material for the assessment of disagreements, lapses into revisionism, breaches of discipline, etc. Let us have more faith in the independent thinking of the mass of Party workers.*

V. I. Lenin, *Collected Works*, vol. 7, p. 112

The political struggle cannot be conducted unless the Party as a whole expresses its views on all political problems and gives impetus to the individual phases of the struggle.

V. I. Lenin, *Collected Works*, vol. 4, p. 221

VI

Draft Party Statutes:
Preliminary and Final Versions

Introductory Note

The preliminary and final versions of the new draft Party Statutes prepared for the consideration of the Fourteenth Congress are presented side by side on the following pages. Since it was the final version which alone appeared in print (as a special supplement to *Rudé právo* on 10 August 1968) and was publicly discussed before the Congress, this is printed in full on the right-hand side; on the left is a skeleton version of the preliminary draft, as it had emerged from a working party of experts on 4 July, with corresponding paragraphs printed as close to one another as variations in length and order allow. (Where paragraphs or sections of paragraphs in the preliminary version were adopted with no change this is indicated by the letters [NC], while the numerals in brackets on the left-hand pages give the cross-references to the corresponding paragraphs in the final version.)

The chairman of the Commission for the Preparation of Statutes, who was chiefly responsible for the differences between the two versions, was none other than Alois Indra – a man who subsequently emerged as a leading apologist for the Soviet invasion and who had, indeed, been earmarked as the potential Premier of a collaborationist government. It is thus unsurprising that the changes are almost without exception in the direction of tighter discipline and more conservative language. It is only the later version, for example, that speaks of the Party's need to wage a 'consistent struggle against all forms of bourgeois ideology' and a 'war on nationalism' in its opening section. Both versions specify – in contrast to the existing Statutes – the rights of minorities within the Party, though overruled, to ask for their views to be reconsidered in the light of possible fresh facts; but the minority's right to have its opinions *published* in the Party press is only specified in the earlier draft (para. 5), like the member's right to 'associate temporarily' with like-minded comrades

128

(para. 21 (f)). The later version adds a requirement of five years' Party membership for aspirants to Central Committee membership (para. 39 (c)) – a provision which, as we have seen, attracted some discussion at the Fourteenth Congress itself where there was an urge to introduce fresh blood. It is symptomatic that the competence of Party organs in cultural policy, abandoned in the July draft, is reintroduced in the August one (para. 41 (a)).

Both versions, it will be noticed, assume (para. 37 preliminary version, para. 38 final version) that a new *Czech* party organization is to be set up as a counterpart to the Slovak Communist Party which had long enjoyed a dubious status under the umbrella of the effective Czechoslovak Communist Party. Despite the introduction of a thoroughly federal Constitution in other respects at the beginning of 1969, however, symmetry in the *Party* arrangements was never achieved – presumably because of Russian fears that a purely Czech Communist Party would be too 'progressive'.

Needless to say, neither the earlier and more liberal draft of the new Statutes, nor even Indra's more cautious one, were ever adopted. The Fourteenth Congress had no time to consider them and the previous Party regulations, as revised under Novotný in 1962, remain in force.

Draft Statutes of the Czechoslovak Communist Party
[Preliminary Version]

Compiled on the basis of comments from members of the Commission of the Czechoslovak Communist Party Central Committee for the Drafting of New Statutes, as well as by other members, and by some branches and organs of the Party.

The following Party members took part in the compilation:
Dr Miroslav Havlíček, Vladimír Bernard, Dr Jindřich Fibich, Stanislav Jägermann, Dr Karel Hanka, Dr Vladimír Kneř, Vladimír Kůš, Miroslav Láb, Eng. Josef Podroužek, Ilja Sychra, Dr Milada Srovnalová, Dr Marie Tichá, Martin Vaculík, Jaroslav Zíma.

Prague, 4 July 1968

*

The Czechoslovak Communist Party is a voluntary association of the most enlightened members of the working class, farmers and intelligentsia, joined together to implement the programmatic aims of socialism and communism.

The party interprets the humanist and deeply democratic principles of socialist society as meaning the satisfaction of man's material, cultural and ethical needs and the creation of conditions for the expansion of the human personality in all directions.

Draft Statutes of the Czechoslovak Communist Party
[Final Version]

The Presidium of the Central Committee of the Party submits for internal debate these draft Statutes of the Czechoslovak Communist Party. The draft was prepared by a working group under the leadership of Comrade Dr M. Havlíček, Deputy Head of the Department of Political Theory and Activity at the Klement Gottwald Military and Political Academy.

It was considered at two successive meetings of the Commission for the Preparation of Statutes set up by the plenum of the Central Committee. A working variant was discussed by the Central Committee's Presidium and by the Political Commission for the Preparation of the Extraordinary Fourteenth Congress of the Party.

Following these discussions the working group submitted an amended draft for final assessment by the Presidium, which after very detailed discussion unanimously approved the text now submitted for internal Party debate.

Individual familiarity with the text is an essential prerequisite for useful discussion of it at members' meetings in August, which will express their views on the draft. Primary Party organizations will hand in specific proposals and comments to the Central Committee through their district committee in writing.

In view of the shortage of time and our anxiety to process all comments we ask primary organizations to ensure that observations or proposals relating to particular articles or paragraphs are written on separate sheets marked with the number of the relevant article.

Primary organizations of railway workers will pass their comments to the Central Committee through the Party committees of the political branch of the Czechoslovak State Railways. Primary organizations in the army will observe a corresponding procedure subject to instructions from the army's main political administration.

Primary organizations will submit their statements of views, proposals and comments to district committees at the latest by 25 August 1968.

*

The Czechoslovak Communist Party is a voluntary association of progressive and politically active members of all social groups, joined together to implement in their country the programmatic aims of socialism and communism and thereby to create conditions for the complete liberation of man.

The party interprets the humanist and democratic principles of socialist society as meaning the satisfaction of men's material, cultural and ethical needs and the expansion of the scope for fulfilment of the human personality in all directions.

The basis of the Czechoslovak Communist Party's activity is the true understanding of social development through the teaching of Marxism-Leninism. The Party strives to see Marxism-Leninism creatively extended and to see scientific Marxist theory linked to practice, and in this way it creates conditions for people's enlightened social activity.

The Communist Party follows on in the national, democratic and revolutionary traditions of our people. In building a socialist society and in striving for the further progressive development of the country, it starts from the specific living conditions of our two nations. The Party is an inseparable component of the international communist and revolutionary movement, acknowledges the legacy of the Great October Socialist Revolution and exploits the useful experiences of the communist and workers' parties. It actively promotes and defends the principles of proletarian internationalism and socialist patriotism, contributes to the consolidation of the fraternal relations and co-operation of our people with the nations of the Soviet Union and the other socialist States, and with the working people of all countries, and supports the revolutionary socialist and national liberation movements.

The Communist Party arose as the organization of the revolutionary struggle of the working class, which can only achieve full and final liberation if it frees all who are exploited and oppressed. During the class struggles with capitalism, during the fight against Fascism and for national liberation, and in the course of the socialist revolution, the Communist Party became the organization of all working people.

In a period when socialist changes have already been achieved the Party strives, in reliance on the progressive sections of the working class, farmers and intelligentsia, toward the growth of productive forces with the help of the scientific and technological revolution, and toward the growth of socialist relations in society by the extension of socialist democracy.

The Party helps to create a system of political relations within society, in which every citizen in the Republic can have a share of decision-making and authority.

The Czechoslovak Communist Party bases its activity on the scientific theory and method of Marxism-Leninism. The Party strives to see Marxism-Leninism creatively applied and developed in the light of the latest findings of the social sciences and linked to social practice. In view of the objective existence of class antagonism between the forces of socialism and capitalism in the world, the Party wages a consistent struggle against all forms of bourgeois ideology.

The Czechoslovak Communist Party follows on in the national, democratic and revolutionary traditions of our people and in the progressive traditions of the revolutionary working-class movement. It is the Party which successfully led the working people to overthrow the exploiting classes and to construct a socialist society. The Party is a consistent guardian of the basic values of socialism. It posits its efforts for the further progress of socialist society upon the actual living conditions of our two nations and the national minorities, and it fosters their sense of belonging to a socialist fatherland. The Party is an inseparable component of the international communist and revolutionary movement. It creatively applies in the actual circumstances of our own country the experience of the various communist and workers' parties, and especially of the Communist Party of the Soviet Union. It consolidates the fraternal relations and co-operation of the Czechoslovak people with the Soviet people, with the nations of the socialist States and with the workers of all countries, according to the principles of proletarian internationalism and socialist patriotism. It supports the socialist, communist, national liberation and peace movements in their struggle against imperialism.

The Communist Party aims to give expression in a socialist society to the long-term progressive interests of all classes and groups in society. The Party believes that under conditions of socialism, and in the course of the scientific and technological revolution, the working class is the main social force whose historic mission and special interest is to set up a communist society. After the disappearance of class antagonisms, however, this class changes its nature, and so do the applications of its social role. In this historic function the working class is irreplaceable.

The Communist Party bases its activity on the support of progressive forces in all social groups and amongst the young.

As the leading and unifying force in our system of political and social relations, the Party elaborates its programme and its concept of the growth of socialist society on the basis of scientific analysis, and organizes the workers with a view to implementing them.

It supports the democratic principles inspiring the work of the repre-

The Party regards the National Front as the natural foundation for its co-operation with the integrated social organizations of the working people, and with the other political parties, on the basis of equal rights and responsibility in fulfilling the agreed socialist programme. The Czechoslovak Communist Party strives to achieve the leading political role in the National Front by dint of its unceasing renewal of the workers' confidence, its initiatives in the field of political ideas, and its efforts to create conditions for the fulfilment of the progressive interests of all classes and groups in society.

The Party consistently supports the democratic functioning of socialist State authority, the independence of representative and State organs, and their responsibility to the whole people. As a politically unifying factor in society it strives for the full equality of the Czech and Slovak nations and respects the rights of all the minority nationalities in the federal arrangement of the Czechoslovak Socialist Republic.

It is the Party's ambition to become a true *avant-garde* in the struggle of our nations for the renewal of socialism, human rights and freedoms and the humanist ideals of communism in our land.

The Party maintains and strengthens its role as leader and revolutionary transformer by the continual conquest of its own deficiencies, by the repeated rebirth and further growth of its own organism, in harmony with the known laws of social evolution and by the united exercise of its revolutionary will and its ideological, political and organizational energies.

sentative bodies and their responsibility to the whole public and strives to ensure that they truly represent the people, defend its socialist achievements and strictly comply with socialist legality.

It regards the National Front as the foundation for its co-operation with the social organizations of the working people, and with the other political parties, on the basis of their common share in, and responsibility for, the fulfilment of the agreed socialist programme. The Czechoslovak Communist Party continually renews its leading political role in the National Front by dint of its unceasing initiatives in the field of political ideas, and its activity in the field of political organization. It is mindful that it derives its strength from close contact with the people, with their life and with their needs. In all its work, therefore, it seeks their confidence and voluntary backing, and submits to their control.

At the present time the Party's efforts are aimed at promoting the growth of socialism as a form of society without class contrasts, and based on the unity and variety of social interests; a society free and democratically organized; a society profoundly international and committed to social justice, rewarding its citizens according to their qualifications and the results of their labour: a society industrially advanced, possessing a flexible economic system and expanding its productive forces by intensive means; a society able through the wealth of its resources to offer a worthy level of cultural life, to promote comradely and co-operative relations between people and progressively to enlarge the scope for the flowering of the human personality. The Party's ultimate aim is to build a classless communist society, and it takes care accordingly to ensure the continuous growth and consolidation of socialist production relations. It strives for the extension of socialist democracy and for the realization of the programme of communist humanism.

The Czechoslovak Communist Party is a deeply populist one; as the heir to progressive revolutionary and national traditions it works for a better future for the Czechs and the Slovaks. As a unifying factor in society it fights for the progress and full equality of the Czech and Slovak nations and of all the minority nationalities in our Czechoslovak socialist society. At the same time it wages a war on nationalism and, on the foundations of socialist internationalism, deepens the brotherly ties between the workers of all our nations and nationalities.

It is the Party's ambition to maintain its role as an *avant-garde* in our nation's joint fight for socialism, democracy, human rights, freedom and the humane ideals of communism in our country. It sees its chief missions in serving the people and serving progress.

I. BASIC PRINCIPLES OF THE PARTY'S INTERNAL LIFE AND ACTIVITY

(1) The Czechoslovak Communist Party conducts its activity on the basis of democratic centralism, which represents a complete system of basic principles for recognizing, forming and directing all relationships within the Party, at all levels. The consistent application of democratic socialism makes systematic progress possible in the growth and activity of the Party, so encouraging the democratization of the whole of socialist society.

The essential principles of democratic centralism are these:

(a) the whole system of Party organizations and of elected organs of leadership and control is created from below, starting with the individual members and unit branches and involving their widest possible participation, either direct or – through their elected delegates and organs – indirect. The most important channel of influence by the members on the Party's internal activity and on its policy toward society is the equality of rights and duties among members and the democratic system of exchange of views, elections of officials, and selection, evaluation and control of those appointed to further the Party's policy in the machinery of State or in society;

(b) to ensure the Party's unity in thought and deed, its members and their unit branches or 'primary organizations' link together in an integrated structure of temporary or permanent organs and organizations, transferring the necessary portion of their autonomous rights and competence to higher elected organs who then decide joint procedure in wider and more general matters, and co-ordinate the work of the associated branch members;

(c) the supreme Party organs are under obligation to take as their starting point society's need for progress, and all programmatic documents, instructions and resolutions must together form an objective analysis of the situation and must exploit to the greatest degree possible the methods and findings of science and the experience of Party members. The programmatic documents, resolutions and instructions issued by the higher Party organs are under Party discipline binding upon lower organs and organizations and upon all Party members. [1]

(2) The unity, efficiency and *avant-garde* role of the Party in society require an appropriately flexible, uniform and efficient expansion of the basic content of the Party's activity, together with the exercise of its external function (requiring a uniform and disciplined procedure) and its internal function (requiring the greatest possible growth of inner-Party democracy).

(3) In order to ensure unity, democratic initiative and the implementation of Party policy, the Party employs the following basic approaches and working methods:

136

Draft Statutes: Final Version

I. BASIC PRINCIPLES OF THE PARTY'S INTERNAL LIFE AND ACTIVITY

(*1*) The Czechoslovak Communist Party conducts its activity on the basis of democratic centralism.

Democratic centralism implies:

– the democratic creation of the Party's programme and political line as the outcome of creative Marxist-Leninist activity informed by the most modern scientific findings; confrontation of different views and consideration of ideas from both communist and non-communist sources;

– participation of the members at large, and of the subordinate links in the Party's structure, in the formation and implementation of Party policy and in continuously checking its correctness in the light of practice;

– equal opportunity for all members to express their views on Party policy, to make proposals and to criticize any member, branch or organ of the Party;

– creation of the whole system of leading bodies and control organs within the Party by the democratic method of election, evaluation and control of officials from below;

– the regular rendering by Party organs of accounts and reports on their activity to the branches which elected them and by this means to all Party members. Subordinate Party units and their organs inform higher organs of their activity and their fulfilment of Party resolutions. Programmatic documents and resolutions adopted by higher organs are binding upon lower units and their organs and upon all members of the Party.

(*2*) Decisions are taken in Party branches and organs by a simple majority of the votes of those present, after collective discussion. Annual members' meetings, plenary sessions of organs, conferences and congresses are qualified to pass resolutions if over one half of the members or duly elected delegates are present.

The method of voting in Party organs is laid down in the rules of procedure.

Before making substantive decisions, the Central Committee of the Czechoslovak Communist Party (or the central committees of the national-territorial organizations) will organize a discussion or referendum within the Party. Party members will be informed of its results.

(*3*) In the spirit of democratic centralism a minority submits to the majority and carries out its decisions. A minority has the right:

– to formulate its viewpoints and ask for them to be entered on the record;

– to persist in its opinion and on the basis of new evidence and de-

(a) confrontation and unification of individual and group interests with those of society in general;

(b) a Marxist approach to problems affecting the Party and broad social processes;

(c) confrontation of views and exercise of the right of every member to put forward a question for inner-Party debate;

(d) free exchange of practical and scientific information between members, branches and organs, and between the Party and the general public;

(e) collective assessment and settlement of the main political and doctrinal problems arising from alternative suggestions and viewpoints and pointing toward optimal uniform solutions (if a fifth or more of members present so request, each issue must be voted upon separately);

(f) formulation of resolutions and instructions with binding force for the further public and internal activity of the Party;

(g) elaboration and controlled implementation of important Party resolutions;

(h) the election and subsequent control of responsible leading organs and officials, and the allocation of authority and responsibility within the Party;

(i) internal Party inquiries, referenda and discussions prior to important decisions. The Party membership at large has then to be informed of the outcome by the organ in question.

(4) Voluntary and enlightened Party discipline is indissolubly connected with independent thinking and objective advocacy. It implies freedom of discussion and criticism within the Party and demands above all:

(a) consistent fulfilment of the programme and political line in the formation of which Party members have taken part;

(b) constant confrontation of Party resolutions with the whole Party's practice and experience;

(c) the opportunity openly to criticize any Party member, or organ, and to submit viewpoints on Party policy to Party organs. [4]

(5) All decisions of Party organs are taken after democratic, collective discussion and approval by the majority of those present. In the implementation of a resolution the minority is obliged to carry out the decision of the majority.

Party organs may reject minority viewpoints but must respect minority rights. It is only permissible to use argument as a means of influencing adherents to minority views, provided these are not in fundamental conflict with the Party's programme or Statutes. Even after the majority has made its decision the minority is entitled to persist in its view, to continue defending it and measuring it against actual practice, and to ask for it to be termination of the effect of the original resolution to ask for its viewpoints to be reconsidered by the appropriate Party branch or organ.

It is only permissible to use argument as a means of influencing adherents to minority views, provided they are not in fundamental conflict with the Party's programme or Statutes.

It is not permissible to invite support for minority views outside the terms of the Statutes, nor to form groups of Party members with their own rules of discipline as Party fractions.

(4) Voluntary and enlightened discipline is a prerequisite for the effectiveness of the Party as a whole and of its individual branches and organs. It arises from a deep grasp of Marxism-Leninism, of the aims and needs of the Party and of the devotion of communists to the cause of socialism.

(5) Party branches and organs conduct their activity in accordance with the programme, Statutes and resolutions of higher organs which are binding upon them. It is the duty of the higher organs to create conditions which will give the lower organs scope for their initiative and independence. In the settlement of political and organizational questions within their own sphere of activity all branches and organs make their decisions independently. In cases of conflicting opinion they are entitled to appeal to a higher organ, a Control and Audit Commission, a conference or congress.

reconsidered by the appropriate Party organ. A minority has the right to ask for its view to be published alongside the majority decision.

This right to criticize, take initiatives and compare opposing views is limited by the principles and declared aims of the Party's programme and Statutes. It is not permissible for adherents of an active minority policy to organize themselves outside the provisions of the Statutes; the formation of organizations or organs subject to their own separate discipline is in particular forbidden. [3]

(6) Party members, their designated representatives, branches and elected organs may, before important questions are due to be discussed, in Party branches or organs, enter into direct contact and temporarily associate together for the purpose (according to their division of functions) of mutual consultation, or information, or for *ad hoc* joint campaigns, and then submit their viewpoints to the appropriate organs. Members, branches or organs in question must apprise the appropriate higher organs of any such intention to co-operate. [6]

(7) A prerequisite for unity of outlook amongst all Party members and branches in their participation in forming policy is an efficient and relatively independent information system, based on scientific principles and on generalizations drawn from working people's experience. Democratic centralism enables this system to permeate the Party from top to bottom in all directions, making collective awareness and decision-making as democratic and efficient as possible.

Among the most important elements in the Party's information-gathering and distributing system are these:

(a) continuous training of all Party members in ideas and theory on the basis of the most modern Marxist-Leninist findings and of the social sciences;

(b) acquainting the whole Party, and the public, with various alternatives and viewpoints of a programmatic or conceptual sort;

(c) systematic analysis of the political situation and of the consequences of Party decision-making at all levels;

(d) exchange of internal Party information in all directions, upwards and downwards and between bodies at the same level;

(e) systematic publication of news about Party activities through the communication media;

(f) a well set up and democratically operating system of information centres, libraries and archives available to all Party members. [11]

(8) As a complex social organism the Party consists of equal members, enjoying rights and fulfilling duties. As a result of different degrees of knowledge, ideological maturity and opportunity for political action, and as a result of the division of labour and different positions in the Party's

(*6*) Party members, branches and organs concerned with a given field of socio-political activity may with the permission of higher Party organs hold joint consultations to co-ordinate their work, or to draw up statements of view or alternative proposals for the consideration of Party branches or organs.

(*7*) Party members combine to form primary organizations (branches) in their place of work or residence. These primary organizations in localities, workshops and enterprises are standardized as local, city, factory or enterprise branches. Branches with a territorial membership normally rank above all other branches operating in the territory in question.

A chairman (president) is elected to lead every organ at all levels.

A Party Congress acts in the name of the Party as a whole, as does the Central Committee in the intervals between Congresses or, in particular cases, delegations or organs authorized by the Central Committee. The other organs and branches act in their own name.

(*8*) All Party organs are elected by secret ballot. Those communists are selected for office who, because of their political, professional and moral qualities and their experience in Party or public service, enjoy prestige and the workers' confidence. To ensure compliance with these principles the Central Committee of the Czechoslovak Communist Party will approve a uniform code of electoral procedure.

structure, the following basic elements come naturally into being within the Party:

(a) a voluntary spearhead or *aktif* of members and officials, anxious to increase their competence and their share in the development, direction and control of Party policy and representing an inexhaustible reserve of potential cadres; [9]

(b) the elected organs of Party leadership, equipped with due authority and responsibility for moulding and implementing the political line and doctrinal orientation of the Party, and so organized and articulated amongst themselves as to lead to a democratic division of labour and mutual control;

(c) executive members of a paid *apparat*, entrusted with a sharply defined area of service and assistance to the elected organs and their members, to the voluntary *aktif* and to the Party organization.

Members of the Party form unit branches or 'primary organizations' according either to their place of work or their place of residence, and can decide voluntarily in which of them to be organized. Branches in cities, enterprises and factories constitute municipal, enterprise or factory organizations, which link up in turn to form district and national-territorial organizations. Branches with a territorial membership normally rank above all other Party organizations operating in parts of the same area. [7]

(9) In addition to the general meetings of the primary organizations, which represent the most authoritative organs of direct decision-making by all fully-enrolled members, a crucial role is played by the democratically elected leading organs.

A chairman is elected to each such organ at all levels, as representing the Party's voluntary *aktif*.

By means of its elected delegates a primary organization transfers the necessary portion of its overall powers to conferences and Congresses. A further portion is transferred to the elected committees. The narrow elected bodies – committees, presidia and secretariats – are subordinate and responsible to the organs and to the electors or organizations who gave them their powers.

(10) All Party organizations and organs are autonomous within their own political and organizational area. They make political and organizational decisions of local or sectoral significance by dint of their contact with the working people and general conclusions drawn from their experience.

They are guided in their activity by the Party Statutes, programme and resolutions of higher organs. Resolutions of higher Party organs should be of such a nature as not to constrain the initiative and independence of lower organs and organizations.

Resolutions of higher organs are binding on lower ones. In cases of con-

(9) Branches and organs at all levels rely on the voluntary *aktif* of members and officials, and create *ad hoc* democratic forms by which members can take part in running their own affairs. For this purpose they can set up temporary or permanent commissions or working groups from rank-and-file members or members of branch organs, as well as other experienced officials and specialists capable of displaying initiative.

Such commissions and working groups submit the results of their activity and their proposals for action to the branch or organ which set them up, and these will then discuss them in their presence.

flicting opinion lower organizations and organs are entitled to appeal against resolutions to a higher organ, to the appropriate Control and Audit Commission, to a conference or to Congress. [5]

(11) Elected organs at all levels co-operate constantly with the broad voluntary *aktif* of communists. For the purpose of examining basic conceptual issues of Party policy, and for elaborating specific political plans, permanent or temporary working commissions or initiative commissions are set up, together with groups composed of members of such commissions, experienced *aktif* members, and interested experts. Elected organs may transfer part of their powers to such commissions. They must accord every respect to their standpoints or alternative proposals.

As a co-responsible element and organ of direct participation by the voluntary Party *aktif* in the development and direction of the Party policy, a commission must not in any circumstances be subordinated to the Party *apparat*. [9]

(12) The elected organs form their own ancillary *apparat*. A Party *apparat* is subordinate to its own elected organ and has no right to intervene directly in the affairs of lower Party organizations, nor in the activity of communists in State, economic or social organizations. It plays an active role in helping to implement the resolutions and instructions of elected organs. Persons appointed to a Party *apparat* will be experienced members with suitable political and specialist qualifications. Their work is evaluated according to objective criteria of performance and effectiveness in public political activity. [10]

(13) The successful fulfilment and progressive extension of the Party's basic practical tasks and functions depends on correct cadre policy. The Party's cadre policy aims above all at finding communists of good character, politically and professionally mature, with initiative and talent, for carrying out various Party and public functions and playing an active role in the Party's policy. At the same time it strives to create fair conditions so that every Party member's ability and energy may be utilized to the utmost.

The Party tries to see that the quality and performance of cadres, subjected to public control and criticism, are the main criteria for promotion both inside and outside the Party. It adheres to the principles of natural, open and well-informed choice, frequent changes of personnel and appointment to posts on the basis of secret election. The Party seeks, supports and recommends suitable delegates and applicants for posts in the Party and in public political life.

Cadre policy and the solution of personnel issues is chiefly the business of the primary organizations and elected organs, without whose comments and consent their members cannot be proposed for any office. Under no circumstances can cadre decisions be made by a Party *apparat*. [12]

(*10*) For the fulfilment of their political and organizational tasks, Party organs can set up their own *apparat* which is subordinate to them and whose activity they supervise. An *apparat* cannot assume the prerogative of a Party branch or organ or of communists working in State, economic or social organizations or institutions. It takes an active part in the drafting and implementation of resolutions. Persons appointed to a Party *apparat* will be experienced Party members with good political and specialist qualifications.

(*11*) A prerequisite for unity of outlook and internal Party democracy is a system of information-gathering and distribution which embraces

- a synthesis of scientific findings with generalizations based on the experiences of Party members and workers in general;
- the exchange of internal Party information in both directions, upwards and downwards;
- availability of information and documents of Party branches and organs to their members;
- exchange of opinions and information between the Party and the general public through the communication media; and
- systematic use of expert assessments and scientific research in the work of decision-making and propaganda.

An important part in the system of gathering and distributing information is played by the Party press. Every Party paper is managed by the organ which issues it.

(*12*) The following principles are observed in personnel ('cadre') policy:

(*a*) Personnel questions are decided exclusively by Party branches and elected organs.

(*b*) Party branches and organs strive to extend the skills and activity of every Party member.

(*c*) Selection of cadres takes place in the presence of the Party membership at large.

(*d*) When cadre appointments are under discussion there will normally be two or more alternative proposals to choose from.

(*e*) In seeking and recommending candidates or applicants for Party, public or economic posts, only considerations of quality will carry weight.

(*f*) Branches and organs are responsible for enabling officials to carry out the functions assigned to them and for regularly assessing their work.

(14) All the Party's leading organs are elected in a consistently democratic manner, from below upwards, by secret ballot. Communists are only chosen for office because of their political, professional and moral qualities, their experience in the Party or public service, and the personal authority and confidence they enjoy among the workers. Proposals for membership of any committee are selected well in advance, with the broad participation of Party members, branches and organs. Names of candidates are first submitted for preliminary comment to primary organizations and their members by internal Party channels and also, where possible, through the Party press. The Party's membership at large should be aware of the attitudes of proposed candidates toward current Party questions. To ensure compliance with these principles the Congress of the Czechoslovak Communist Party is approving a uniform code of electoral procedure. [8]

(15) In order to prevent excessive concentration of power in single hands, to avoid stagnation and to assure the flow of fresh blood into the Party organs, the following principles will be applied in the selection of candidates and election of officials:

(a) NC

(b) NC

(c) Except in the primary organizations, an official cannot be elected to the same organ more than three times in succession in the case of two-year electoral periods, or more than twice in the case of four-year periods. [13]

(16) The Party's control system is an inseparable part of its fact-finding and decision-making activity. It furnishes democratic control over the formation, implementation and subsequent checking of the Party line and resolutions of Party organs and organizations. It watches over and evaluates the fulfilment of duties by members and organs, and the creation of conditions enabling them to enjoy their rights to the full. In this way it assists the integration of Party members, branches and organs and the consolidation of discipline and of a sense of responsibility toward the whole Party.

The control system comprises

(a) the members, organizations and organs of the Party themselves, in their mutual relations and *vis-à-vis* communists in the State and economic administration and in the social organizations;

(b) communists in the public, State, economic and social organs, organizations and institutions *vis-à-vis* Party organs and organizations; and

(c) the Control and Audit Commissions as relatively independent organs elected by the Congress and conferences of the Party, to which alone they are responsible for the exercise of their functions.

The position of the Communist Party in society demands a high level of

(13) In order to prevent excessive concentration of power in single hands, to avoid stagnation and to assure the flow of fresh blood into the Party organs, the following principles will be applied in the selection of candidates and election of officials:

  (*a*) Leading Party, State and public functions should not be combined when to do so would confer a position of privilege on the person involved and make it harder to control his activity effectively.

  (*b*) Measures should therefore be taken to ensure that a single person does not concentrate in his own person a number of prominent Party posts.

  (*c*) Except in the primary organizations, an official cannot be elected to the same organ more than three times in succession in the cases of two-year electoral periods, or more than twice in the case of four-year periods, though in exceptional cases these terms may be extended by one period of office in each case. Any such exceptions must be approved by a two-thirds vote of delegates at a conference or Congress.

(14) It is the task of the Party's control system to confirm whether a Party's work accords with its programmatic aims, whether its policies respond to the needs of a socialist society, how far its Statutes are complied with and what styles of Party work are being adopted in the branches and their organs.

Control is effected in these ways:

– through self-control exercised by members, branches and organs at all levels, primarily through the encouragement of criticism and self-criticism;

– by the independent system of Control and Audit Commissions; and

– through public control exercised by society.

self-control from the Party at all levels of its structure, and of submission to control by the public, whose confidence the Party unceasingly solicits.[*14*]

II. MEMBERSHIP IN THE PARTY

(17) Any citizen of the Czechoslovak Socialist Republic may become a member of the Party if he is in agreement with its programme and Statutes, anxious through political commitment and public work to take part in the collective creation of a socialist society, and prepared to undertake active work in a Party branch and pay his dues.   [*15*]

(18) NC   [*16*]

(19) Party members are united by the ideas of Marxism-Leninism, their common tasks and aims, mutual comradely assistance, trust and criticism as a higher stage in human relations.

Each member is an active and decisive factor in the Party organism. By his political and professional qualities, his character and moral traits, he wins personal authority and helps to enhance that of the whole Party.

He is organized in one of the primary branches in his place of work or place of residence and under the leadership of that branch or of some higher organ to which he may belong he performs his active political work.   [*17*]

(20) The following principles are observed in the acceptance of new members:

sixteen*

(a) Any citizen over the age of eighteen* years of age who wishes to apply for Party membership submits an entry form to the appropriate primary organization together with letters of recommendation from two Party members and a *curriculum vitae*.   [*18a*]

(b) Each application is discussed and decided upon individually by public vote at a general meeting of the primary organization. Membership is granted to applicants who receive the supporting votes of a majority of those present.   [*18b*]

(c) NC   [*18c*]

(d) Every new member will be issued with a membership book by the district committee, who will then maintain his records.   [*18d*]

(e) Upon termination of membership the membership book is returned to the member's primary organization.   [*21*]

(f) A member must report the loss of his membership book to the committee of his primary organization.   [*18d*]

* Alternatives in the draft.

II. MEMBERSHIP IN THE PARTY

(*15*) Any citizen of the Czechoslovak Socialist Republic over eighteen years of age may become a member of the Party if he is in agreement with its programme and Statutes, willing to commit himself in political and public activity and to play his part in the growth of a socialist society, and prepared to undertake active work in a Party branch and pay his dues.

(*16*) A citizen enters the Party voluntarily and can leave it of his own free will.

(*17*) Party members are united by the ideas of Marxism-Leninism, by the struggle for common ends, by comradely co-operation, enlightened discipline, mutual trust and criticism.

The members of the Party are the active and paramount factors in its organism. Each member is organized in one of the primary branches and it is under the guidance of that branch, or of some higher organ to which he may also belong, that he performs his political activity. A communist in regular employment is in principle organized in the branch of his worksite; this branch may consent to his becoming a member of the branch at his place of residence or, with the agreement of the district committee, some other branch.

(*18*) The following principles are observed in the acceptance of new members:

(*a*) An applicant for membership submits an entry form to the appropriate primary organization together with a *curriculum vitae* and letters of reference from two members who are personally acquainted with the applicant and have been in the Party for more than three years.

(*b*) Each application is discussed and decided on individually by public vote at a general meeting of the primary organization. Membership is granted to applicants who receive the supporting votes of more than half the members present.

(*c*) Acceptance of foreign members and the procedure for recognizing membership in other communist and workers' parties is governed by a directive of the Central Committee of the Czechoslovak Communist Party.

(*d*) Every new member will be issued with a membership book by the district committee, which will then maintain his records. Loss of a membership book will be reported by the member to the committee of his primary organization.

(*19*) All Party members are equal, regardless of sex, race, nationality, class origin, education, office or social status. Membership of the Party is in-

(21) All Party members are equal, regardless of sex, race, nationality, class origin, education or social status. The Party expects of its members independent creative thought and active participation in politics and the running of the Party. Membership confers no privileges or advantages. Enlightened Party discipline applies equally to all communists, regardless of their past deserts or offices held.

A Party member is entitled

(a) NC   [*19a*]

(b) NC   [*19b*]

(c) to be kept informed about all important questions affecting the Party's policy and about the activity of Party organs and their members; to demand any information or documents concerning the activity of branches or organs to which he belongs or under whose guidance he works;   [*19c*]

(d) NC   [*19d*]

(e) while respecting and carrying out the will of the majority to retain his own opinion, compare it with the facts and re-submit it to the appropriate organs;   [*19e*]

(f) to associate temporarily with other members for the discussion or recommendation of proposals for solving questions of Party policy, or for the drafting of viewpoints, comparisons of opinion or alternative proposals for the solution of problems, and to submit these to the appropriate organs;   [*19e*]

(g) to submit questions, comments and proposals to Party organs at all levels, including the Czechoslovak Communist Party Congress. [*19f*]

A Party member is obliged

(a) NC   [*19a*]

(b) to comply with the Party's Statutes;   [*19b*]

(c) NC   [*19c*]

(d) NC   [*19d*]

(e) NC   [*19e*]

(f) NC   [*19f*]

(g) to pay the prescribed membership dues;   [*19g*]

(h) NC   [*19h*] compatible with any kind of racial, social or national discrimination, or with the dissemination of such views and doctrines.

Membership confers no privileges or advantages. Enlightened Party discipline applies equally to all communists, regardless of their past deserts or offices held.

A Party member is entitled

(*a*) to take part in the formulation and implementation of the Party's programme, Statutes, political line and tactics;

(*b*) to elect and be elected to Party organs, and to resign from them;

(*c*) to be kept informed about all important questions affecting the Party's policy, and about the activity of Party organs and their members; to demand any information or documents concerning the activity of branches or organs to which he belongs;

(*d*) to give open and critical expression at Party meetings or in the Party press to his opinions on the activity of the Party and of its organs and members, regardless of any office they may hold;

(*e*) while respecting and carrying out the will of the majority, to persist in his own opinion and on the basis of new evidence and determination of the effect of the original resolution to ask for his viewpoints to be reconsidered by the appropriate Party branch or organ;

(*f*) to submit questions, comments and proposals to Party organs at all levels, including the Czechoslovak Communist Party Congress;

(*g*) to take part in meetings of Party branches and organs where his work is being evaluated and decisions made that affect him personally; to be aware of opinions and comments passed on his activity and behaviour, and to put his own arguments in reply; and to appeal on Party matters to Party organs up to and including the Czechoslovak Communist Party Congress.

A Party member is obliged

(*a*) to play an active political part in Party branches and other organizations, to promote acceptance of the Party's policy and win public support for it;

(*b*) to comply with the Party's Statutes, carry out its resolutions and attend members' meetings;

(*c*) to strive for the growth of critical comradely relations in the Party as in society, and to defend the democratic rights and freedoms of all working people;

(*d*) to act truthfully and honourably in Party and civic life;

(*e*) to extend his knowledge of Marxism-Leninism and use it to assist the progressive development of socialist society;

(*f*) to reinforce the authority and effectiveness of the Party by enhancing his specialized knowledge and qualifications and by fulfilling his

III. ORGANIZATION AND STRUCTURE OF THE PARTY

Primary organizations (*branches*)

(22) NC [22]
(23) NC

Basic organizations are active in all spheres of public life and to a great extent decide the success or failure of the Party's policy ... NC

NC

They stimulate Party members in National Committees and in social, political and interest-group organizations to play an active part, so that they can effectively contribute to the fulfilment of the tasks and missions of these very organs and organizations.

NC
NC

They render account of their activity to higher Party organs and expect them to fulfil this duty themselves.

[NC] They administer their own finances and property.

[*add.*] Primary organizations may temporarily associate with other primary organizations, or with higher organs, for the joint discussion of common problems and drafting of proposals for their solutions, and for the adoption of viewpoints and the submission of suggestions to higher Party organs. They will inform the appropriate higher Party organ of any such intention. [23]

Party, civic and working duties in an exemplary manner;

(*g*) to pay his stipulated membership dues; and

(*h*) to report changes in his place of work or residence to his primary organization.

(*20*) If a Party member fails despite repeated warnings from his committee and personal discussion of the case to fulfil the basic duties of membership, but has committed no other offence, a general meeting of branch members is empowered to cancel his membership.

(*21*) Membership lapses upon resignation, cancellation, expulsion or death. After termination of membership, a membership book is returned to the primary organization.

III. ORGANIZATION AND STRUCTURE OF THE PARTY

Primary organizations (*branches*)

(*22*) Communists are associated together in primary organizations which constitute the unit link in the Party's structure and the foundation of its activity. Five or more Party members can establish a primary organization after obtaining the consent of a district committee.

(*23*) Primary organizations deal openly with the public, consult them, respect and utilize their opinions and suggestions and sound them to determine the effectiveness of their own work.

Primary organizations are active in all spheres of public life. By stimulating ideas and making proposals they play a role in the formation of the Party's general line, whose implementation they ensure within their own field of action. On the basis of their knowledge of local conditions they form and implement their own independent policy in harmony with the Party's general line.

They expound the Party's political aims and intentions and by the attractive effect of their ideological and organizational work in their local environment they win over members of the public to help solve specific problems in their own area of activity and to take part in the growth of socialist society. They seek to recruit the most active members of the public, particularly amongst the young, as new members of the Party. They lead Party members in the National Committees and in the social, self-managing and interest-group organizations to play an active role in fulfilling the tasks and the special functions of these various bodies, and provide them with the information they need.

They organize training in Marxism-Leninism for both members and non-members of the Party, inform them objectively and obtain for them information on important social problems and current events.

They provide Party members with the conditions they require to meet

(24) The supreme element in the primary organization is its general members' meeting, which is summoned by its committee as often as needed to ensure the uninterrupted political activity of the organization.

The committee is also under obligation to convene a general meeting whenever so requested by

   (a) NC   [*24* – at end]

   (b) one-fifth of branch members, or whenever so required

   (c) NC

General meetings of members

   (a) evaluate the degree of fulfilment of previous resolutions, assign tasks to all members of the primary organization and check their fulfilment;

   (b) assess the work of their own committee, of their individual Party groups and of all their officials and members, and change the composition of their committee;

   (c) NC

   (d) NC

   (e) NC

   (f) approve Party members as candidates for National Committee membership, assign tasks to communists working in social organizations and their organs, and discuss their proposals and comments;

   (g) NC

. . . NC [but last part placed earlier in paragraph]   [*24*]

(25) Meetings of primary organizations are normally public. The committee invites either interested non-Party circles, or the general public in the locality or work-site in question, to take part.

At these meetings it is the duty of communists to create an atmosphere such that members of the public can put forward their own viewpoints and ideas and address themselves critically to the work of the primary organization and to the policy of the whole Party.   [*25*] obligations ensuing from resolutions of higher organs and to fulfil tasks assumed by their own branch. They support the principle of personal and social accountability of Party members.

They keep higher Party organs informed of their own activities.

They administer their own finances and property.

(24) The supreme executive organ of every primary organization is its general meeting of members.

General meetings of members

(a) assess the branch's political activity, pass resolutions on the basis of their analysis of the situation, assign tasks to all members and check their fulfilment;

(b) evaluate the work of their own committee, of their individual Party groups and of all their officials and members, and change the composition of their committee;

(c) adopt standpoints towards the work of high Party organs, particularly their district committee, and towards the whole Party's policy;

(d) induct new members;

(e) elect their chairman, committee members and Control and Audit Commission or Economic Auditors for a two-year term of office, and also delegates to conferences;

(f) approve Party members as candidates for National Committee membership, assess their work and that of Party members in social organizations, and discuss their proposals and comments;

(g) make decisions on the institution of disciplinary proceedings, set up groups to carry out Party inquiries in connection with complaints or offences of Party members, and impose Party penalties.

A members' meeting can approve certain exemptions from the fulfilment of Party obligations for sick and aged members, or in other deserving cases.

A members' meeting is summoned by the branch committee as often as necessary to ensure the uninterrupted progress of the branch's political work, but at least once in every two months.

The committee is also obliged to summon a members' meeting whenever so requested by

(a) any Party group, or

(b) one-third of branch members, or whenever so required

(c) by a resolution of a higher Party organ.

(25) Whenever serious problems affecting the majority of working people are to be discussed, the committee will in addition to convening a members' meeting invite interested groups of non-communists to attend, or else summon a public Party meeting.

At such meetings it is the duty of communists to create an atmosphere

(26) The committee of a primary organization inspires the political activity of the branch members. It attends to the fulfilment of resolutions passed by branch meetings and directs the work of Party groups between general meetings.   [*26*]

(27) NC   [*27*]

(28) NC

[*add.*] Party organizations in cities and localities set up municipal or local Party committees.

NC

NC

While preserving the greatest possible independence of the primary organizations, the municipal, local, enterprise and factory committees integrate the efforts of communists and their primary organizations in any given work-site or locality and organize and carry out mass political and ideological work in co-operation with them.

They propose Party members as candidates for membership of municipal and local National Committees, or of trade union, enterprise or self-management organs; co-operate with them during the pre-electoral periods and evaluate their work. They assign tasks to communists in the social organizations and their organs, and discuss their ideas and comments.

[rest NC]   [*28*] such that members of the public are able to put forward their own views, proposals or critical comments.

(*26*) The committee of a primary organization stimulates the political activity of the branch members. It attends to the fulfilment of resolutions passed by branch meetings, directs the work of Party groups and works individually with Party members between meetings. It provides members' meetings with regular reports on its activities.

(*27*) In accordance with the particular conditions of the area or work-site in question, primary organizations set up Party groups which elect their own leaders. It is through the agency of these groups that the branch committee attends to the fulfilment of Party tasks between general meetings, recruits Party members for active work and makes use of their proposals and comments.

Party groups operate in close contact with all working people and consult them over the best approach to problems in their area or work-site.

(*28*) All factory and local branches within the area of a town or village operate as a single entity, constituting one local or city branch.

In large factories, work-sites or other installations where there are a number of primary organizations, a factory committee or enterprise committee is formed.

Municipal, local, factory and enterprise committees, as well as Control and Audit Commissions, are elected at conferences or plenary anniversary members' meetings for a term of two years.

While encouraging the independence of primary organizations, the municipal, local, enterprise and factory committees will establish a uniform procedure for dealing with political, economic, ideological and cultural problems within their field of activity, and co-ordinate the efforts of Party members and their primary organizations in the place of work or residence in question. They will co-operate with them in organizing mass political and ideological activity.

They propose Party members as candidates for membership of municipal and local National Committees, or of trade union, enterprise or self-management organs, and co-operate with them systematically during the pre-electoral periods.

They lead Party members in the National Committees and in the social, self-management and interest-group organizations to play an active role in fulfilling the tasks and the special functions of these various bodies. They provide them with the information they need, evaluate their work and discuss their proposals and comments.

National-territorial Central Committees may accord some, or all, of the rights of a district committee to specified municipal, enterprise or factory committees.

District Organizations of the Party

(29) NC   [*29*]

(30) NC [throughout; but continue with]   [*30*]

An Extraordinary conference is called by the district committee

(a) NC

(b) at the request of one-third of the members or of the primary organizations;

(c) by unanimous decision of the District Control and Audit Commission, or

(d) NC

Extraordinary conferences are held within not more than one month of the time when conditions make it possible to hold one.   [*31*]

District Organizations of the Party

(29) Party organizations within the borders of a district constitute a district party organization.

(30) The supreme organ of the district organization is the district conference. This consists of delegates with full voting rights, elected by their primary organizations, and delegates with advisory voting rights, namely current members and alternate members of the district committee and members of the district Control and Audit Commission unless these were elected as full delegates.

A district conference

(*a*) assesses the political work of the district organization over the preceding period and defines its future tasks;

(*b*) discusses reports on the activity of the district committee and district Control and Audit Commission;

(*c*) elects a district committee and district Control and Audit Commission;

(*d*) elects delegates to congresses of the national-territorial organizations and to the Congress of the Czechoslovak Communist Party;

(*e*) makes decisions on requests, complaints and appeals from Party members;

(*f*) discusses and formulates the district-organization viewpoint on the work of higher Party organs and on Party policy; and

(*g*) discusses and makes district-organization proposals for membership of Central Committees.

A district conference will be convened by the district committee once in every two years. Its date and agenda will be announced by the district committee at least two months beforehand.

(31) An extraordinary conference is called by the district committee

(*a*) in pursuance of a two-thirds majority decision by a plenary session of the district committee, or

(*b*) at the request of one-third of all members of the district organization, or

(*c*) at the request of the district Control and Audit Commission with the support of a four-fifths majority of its members, or

(*d*) by the decision of a higher Party organ.

Requests for the convocation of an Extraordinary district conference are submitted by Party members of primary organizations to the district committee and to the district Control and Audit Commission. These organs are obliged to inform Party members at large of the number of such requests submitted.

Extraordinary conferences are held within not more than one month after the announcement of their convocation.

(31) The supreme organ of a district organization. . . NC   [*32*]
   [the following passage corresponds to *last* part of *32* in final draft]
   A meeting of the district committee can be summoned by its presidium
   (a) by its own decision; [NC]
   (b) NC
   (c) at the request of one-fifth of the members of the plenum;
   (d) NC
   (e) at the recommendation of a higher Party organ.
   A Party district committee [now return to beginning of *32*]
   (a) NC
   (b) NC
   (c) while respecting their autonomy directs the work of lower Party
       organs and organizations, and assists them in their activity;
   (d) NC
   (e) elects its presidium, chairman, leading secretary and secretaries;
   (f) NC
   (g) elects a council of elders;
   (h) NC [as *32g*]
   (i) sets up and directs the press organs of the district committee and
       elects their editors;
   (j) approves its own budget and ensures compliance with it.
[*add.*] A district committee may temporarily associate with other district
or higher organs for consultation on common problems and agreement on
how to solve them, or for drafting comparisons of views, proposals and
ideas for higher Party organs. They will inform a higher Party organ of any
such intention.   [*32*]

(*32*) The supreme organ of a district organization in the period between conferences is the Party district committee.

A Party district committee

(*a*) establishes, on the basis of systematic information-gathering and in harmony with the Party programme and with resolutions of higher organs, an independent procedure for dealing with political, economic and social problems within the district;

(*b*) takes part in the creation of political decisions by higher Party organs and by the whole Party, and ensures their implementation within the district;

(*c*) directs the work of subordinate Party branches and organs while respecting their independence in dealing with local questions, and assists them in their activity; dissolves primary organizations when the number of their members falls below the stipulated figure;

(*d*) directs ideological work throughout the district organization, sets up Party schools and institutes for training Party officials;

(*e*) elects the presidium, chairman and secretaries of the district committee;

(*f*) elects the commissions of the district committee, and their chairmen;

(*g*) renders account of its activities to the district conference and Party organizations, and keeps all higher organs informed;

(*h*) approves Party members as candidates for membership of the district National Committee, approves its representatives for service on district organs of the National Front, co-operates systematically with Party members serving on National Committees, National Front organs and in the social and interest-group organizations, establishes conditions for their successful activity and makes use of their experience and proposals and discusses its decisions with them beforehand;

(*i*) approves its own budget and ensures compliance with it; administers its own funds and the property entrusted to it by the Party;

(*j*) supervises and evaluates the work of the district committee's *apparat*.

A district committee meets at intervals of not longer than three months, depending on the political situation and on the tasks assigned to the district organization.

A district committee meeting can be summoned by the presidium

(*a*) by its own decision;

(*b*) by decision of the committee plenum, or in accordance with its working plan;

(*c*) at the request of one-third of the committee's members;

(*d*) at the suggestion of the district control and audit commission;

(*e*) at the request of one-third of the basic organizations; or

(*f*) by decision of a higher Party organ.

(32) NC [*33*]

(33) NC [*34*]

[*add.*] Such a fraction

(a) discusses and lays down the line to be taken by communist Deputies in local politics;

(b) helps to draft decisions of the district committee concerning communal affairs;

(c) submits proposals to the Party's district committee;

(d) adopts viewpoints toward Party policy and its implementation in the representative organs.

The members of the fraction elect their own chairman and secretary.

(34) The council of elders is an advisory organ of the district committee. It consists of Party members with good records and long experience of Party and public life.

Either on its own initiative or at the request of the district committee or its presidium, the council of elders may express its opinion on particular issues concerning the political and organizational life of the district organization. [no equivalent]

(35) NC [*35*]

(36) The municipal organizations in Prague, Bratislava and other charter cities enjoy a special status. They comprise ward and other organizations with the status of district organizations.* [*36*]

The National-Territorial Organizations of the Czechoslovak Communist Party in the Czech Lands and in Slovakia

(37) NC

[*add.*] They comprise the Party organizations in the areas in question.[*38*]

(38) NC [1st para of *39*]

[next para brought forward from end of *39*]

A Congress of each national-territorial organization is convoked by its ~~every two years†~~

Central Committee ~~every four years.†~~ The date and agenda are announced by the Central Committee.

The Congress of each national-territorial organization

(a) assesses the political work of the national-territorial organization over the past period and lays down guidance for its further activity;

(b) NC

* *Editor's Note:* This preliminary draft assumes that regional committees will have lapsed, whereas Indra's later version, in its Article *37*, assumes their continued existence.

† Alternatives in the draft.

162

(*33*) The presidium of a district committee is its executive organ and, in the periods between its sessions, ensures the fulfilment of tasks ensuing from resolutions of the district conference or district committee. It directs and supervises the work of the *apparat* and carries out activities assigned to it by the district committee. The presidium is accountable to the district committee and submits to it regular reports on its own work.

(*34*) Communist members of the district National Committee constitute a Communist Deputies' fraction, and this fraction works under the guidance of the district committee plenum and in accordance with its resolutions.

(*35*) In those municipal organizations which have been accorded the status of district organizations by the Central Committee of their national-territorial organization, ward committees may be formed, operating with the status of local Party committees.

The Central Committees of the national-territorial organizations may in case of need set up other organizations, according them some of the rights of district committees or giving them equal status with district organizations.

(*36*) The municipal organizations in Prague, Bratislava and other large charter cities enjoy a special status. They set up municipal committees which direct the work of ward and other organizations with the status of district organizations, and co-ordinate the efforts of Party members in creating and carrying out policy throughout the city.

(*37*) Regional committees in general conduct their activities in accordance with resolutions applicable to district organizations, extended to their own area of activity, and with resolutions of the Central Committees of the national-territorial organizations. These Central Committees may, in agreement with the Central Committee of the Czechoslovak Communist Party, set up special bodies to assist district organizations.

The National-Territorial Organizations of the Czechoslovak Communist Party in the Czech Lands and in Slovakia

(*38*) The Communist Party of the Czech Lands and the Communist Party of Slovakia are national-territorial organizations of the bi-national Czechoslovak Communist Party. They accept its programme and its Statutes, and their members carry uniform membership books.

(*39*) The supreme organs of the national-territorial organizations are the Congress of the Communist Party of the Czech Lands and the Congress of the Slovak Communist Party respectively. A Congress consists of delegates with full voting rights, elected by district conferences, and delegates with advisory voting rights, namely current members and alternate members of the Central Committees of the Communist Party of the Czech Lands and

(c) elects a Central Committee and a Control and Audit Commission;
[No minimum length of membership was stipulated in this draft
for membership of these bodies.]

(d) NC

(e) NC

[*add.*]   [*39*]

(f) discusses and recommends proposals of the national-territorial
organization for membership of the Central Committee of the
Czechoslovak Communist Party and the Central Control and Audit
Commission.

[the rest corresponds to para *40*]

An Extraordinary Congress is convoked by the Central Committee of
the national-territorial organization

(a) by decision of a two-thirds majority of members at a plenary session
of the Central Committee;

(b) at the request of one-third of members of the organization, or of
primary organizations, district committees or district conferences;

(c) NC

(d) NC

NC

An Extraordinary Congress is held within not more than one month of
the fulfilment of conditions for holding it.   [*40*]

(39) The supreme organ of each national-territorial organization in the
period between Congresses is its Central Committee. This meets at times
depending on the political situation and on the tasks lying before the
national-territorial organization. A plenary session of the Central Committee is summoned by its Presidium [following section from penultimate
part of *41*]

(a) by decision of the Presidium itself;

(b) by decision of the Central Committee plenum or in compliance with
its working plan;

(c) at the request of one-fifth of the members of the plenum;

(d) at the request of the Control and Audit Commission of the national-
territorial organization; or

(e) at the invitation of the Central Committee of the Czechoslovak Communist Party.

The Central Committee of each national-territorial organization [pick
up from 4th line of *41*]

(a) NC [but no reference to 'cultural problems' in this draft]

(b) NC

(c) while respecting their autonomy, directs the work of lower Party
organs and organizations and assists them in their activity;

Slovak Communist Party respectively, and members of the Control and Audit Commission, unless these were elected as full delegates.

The Congress of each national-territorial organization

(a) assesses the political, economic, ideological, cultural and social problems of its organization and the manner in which they have been met during the preceding period, and lays down guidance for activity in the next period;

(b) discusses the report on the activity of the Central Committee and Control and Audit Commission of the national-territorial organization;

(c) elects a Central Committee and a Control and Audit Commission (only persons who have been Party members for at least five years may be elected to either body);

(d) makes decisions on requests, complaints or appeals from Party members and organizations;

(e) discusses and formulates the viewpoints of the national-territorial organization on the work of the Central Committee of the Czechoslovak Communist Party and on Party policy.

A Congress of each national-territorial organization is convoked by its Central Committee within four years at the latest. The date and agenda are announced by the Central Committee.

(*40*) An Extraordinary Congress is convoked by the Central Committee of a national-territorial organization

(a) by decision of a two-thirds majority of the Central Committee members;

(b) at the request of one-third of its members;

(c) at the request, supported by a four-fifths majority, of the Control and Audit Commission;

(d) by decision of the Central Committee of the Czechoslovak Communist Party.

Requests for the convocation of an Extraordinary Congress are submitted by members, primary organizations, district committees or district conferences to the Central Committee and the Control and Audit Commission of the national-territorial organization. These organs are obliged to inform the membership at large of the number of requests received.

An Extraordinary Congress is held within not more than three months from the announcement of its convocation.

(*41*) The supreme organ of each national-territorial organization in the period between Congresses is its Central Committee.

The Central Committee of each national-territorial organization

(a) strives independently to solve the political, ideological, cultural, economic and social problems of its own national territory on the

(d) elects its Presidium, Secretariat, Chairman, Leading Secretary and Secretaries;
(e) NC
(f) elects a Council of Elders of the national-territorial organization;
(g) NC [*41f*]
(h) NC [*41g*]
(i) sets up and directs the press publications of the national-territorial organization and elects their editors-in-chief;
(j) approves its own budget and that of its institutes and ensures compliance with them.

NC ['Each Central Committee . . . political situation.' Rest brought forward.] [*41*] basis of systematic fact-finding and in harmony with the programme of the Czechoslovak Communist Party;

(b) takes part in the designing of political decisions by the Central Committee of the Czechoslovak Communist Party, and ensures their adequate interpretation and implementation within its own area of activity;

(c) directs the work of subordinate Party organizations and organs, while respecting their independence in dealing with questions within their own area of activity, and assists them in their work;

(d) elects its Presidium, Secretariat and Secretaries;

(e) elects Commissions and their chairmen;

(f) renders accounts of its activities to its Congress and to lower Party organizations and organs and keeps the Central Committee of the Czechoslovak Communist Party informed;

(g) approves Party members as candidates for membership of the Czech National Council and Slovak National Council, approves its representatives for service in the national governments and organs of the National Front, co-operates systematically with communist Deputies in the National Councils and with communist officials in the national government, in organs of the National Front and in the social and interest-group organizations, establishes conditions for their successful activity, makes use of their experience and proposals and discusses its decisions with them beforehand;

(h) sets up and directs the press publications of the national-territorial organization and approves their editors-in-chief;

(i) establishes Party enterprises and institutes and approves their directors;

(j) approves its own budget and that of its institutes and ensures compliance with them while administering its funds and the property entrusted to it by the Party.

Each Central Committee meets at intervals of not more than three months, depending on the political situation. A plenary session of either Central Committee can be convened by the Committee's Presidium

(a) in compliance with the Committee's working plan;

(b) by decision of its own plenary session, or of its Presidium;

(c) at the request of one-third of the members of the Committee;

(d) at the request of the national-territorial Control and Audit Commission;

(e) at the request of one-third of the district committees; or

(f) when asked to do so by the Central Committee of the Czechoslovak Communist Party.

The Central Committees of the national-territorial organizations may

167

(40) NC   [*42*]

(41) The Secretariat attends to the practical aspects of the fulfilment of tasks ensuing from resolutions of the Central Committee or its Presidium, organizes and directs day-to-day activities and executes other tasks assigned to it by the Central Committee.

NC   [*43*]

(42) NC [but *add.*]

The fraction

(a) discusses and lays down the line to be taken by communist deputies in the national-territorial legislatures;

(b) helps to draft decisions of the Central Committee of the national-territorial organization affecting the area in question;

(c) submits proposals to the Central Committee of the national-territorial organization;

(d) adopts viewpoints on the overall policy of the Party and its implementation in the representative organs.

Its members elect their own chairman and secretary.   [*44*]

(43) The Council of Elders is an advisory organ of the Central Committee of the national-territorial organization. It consists of Party members with good records and long experience of Party and public life.

Either on its own initiative or at the request of a Central Committee or its Presidium, the Council of Elders may express its opinion on particular issues concerning the political and organizational life of the national-territorial organization.   [–]

The Supreme Organs of the Czechoslovak Communist Party

(44) The Party organizations on the territory of the Czechoslovak Socialist Republic together form the single, bi-national Czechoslovak Communist Party.   [*45*]

(45) The supreme organ of the Czechoslovak Communist Party is the Party Congress. The Congress consists of delegates with full voting rights, elected at district conferences, and of delegates . . . [rest of para. NC]

A Party Congress is always convened by the Central Committee of the Czechoslovak Communist Party within four years.

The date and agenda are announced by the Central Committee at least six months beforehand.

The Congress of the Czechoslovak Communist Party

(a) NC

(b) NC

(c) NC

(d) elects the Central Committee and Central Control and Audit Commission;

hold joint meetings to consult on common problems and concert their approaches to them; or to draw up comparisons of viewpoint, or ideas and proposals, for the Central Committee of the Czechoslovak Communist Party. They will inform the latter of any intention to hold a joint meeting.

(*42*) The Presidium is the executive organ of the Central Committee of each national-territorial organization and in the periods between its sessions, with the help of its Commissions and working groups, it elaborates conceptual material, ensures the fulfilment of tasks arising from resolutions of the Committee or of a Congress, and carries out activities assigned to it by the Committee.

The Presidium is responsible to the Central Committee of each national-territorial organization and renders it regular accounts of its work.

(*43*) The Secretariat attends to the practical aspects of the fulfilment of tasks ensuing from resolutions of the Central Committee or its Presidium, and organizes and directs the day-to-day activity of the *apparat* and Party institutions.

The Secretariat is responsible to the Central Committee of each national-territorial organization and renders it regular accounts of its work.

(*44*) Communist Deputies in the Czech National Council and Slovak National Council constitute a communist Deputies' fraction, and this fraction works under the guidance of the Central Committee of the national-territorial organization and in accordance with its resolutions.

The Supreme Organs of the Czechoslovak Communist Party

(*45*) The national-territorial organizations together form the single, bi-national Czechoslovak Communist Party, which respects their equal rights and integrates the interests of the two nations, of the national minorities and of society as a whole.

(*46*) The supreme organ of the Czechoslovak Communist Party is the Party Congress. The Congress consists of delegates with full voting rights, elected by the Congresses of the national-territorial organizations, and of delegates with advisory voting rights, namely current members and alternate members of the Central Committee and members of the Central Control and Audit Commission, unless these were elected as full delegates.

The Congress of the Czechoslovak Communist Party

(*a*) approves the Party's programme and Statutes;

(*b*) evaluates progress in fulfilling the Party's programmatic aims and formulates its domestic and foreign policy concept and tactics;

(*c*) discusses the reports on the work of the Central Committee and of the Central Control and Audit Commission;

(*d*) elects the Party's Central Committee and Central Control and Audit

[No minimum length of membership was stipulated in this draft for membership of these bodies.]

(e) NC   [to here *46*]

An Extraordinary Congress can be convoked by the Central Committee of the Czechoslovak Communist Party

[now *cf. 47*]

(a) NC

(b) at the request of one-third of Party members, primary organizations, district committees or district conferences;

(c) NC

(d) at the request of one of the Central Committees of the national-territorial organizations.

NC

An Extraordinary Congress is held within three months of the fulfilment of conditions for holding it.

(46) NC [up to 'Party' (line 3). End sentence and continue:]

The Central Committee of the Czechoslovak Communist Party meets [pick up on p. 173, line 22]

(a) NC

(b) NC

(c) at the request of one-fifth of the members of the Central Committee;

(d) NC

(e) NC

The Central Committee of the Czechoslovak Communist Party [now return to *48*, line 4]

(a) NC [adopts viewpoints . . .]

(b) while respecting their autonomy, directs the lower Party organs and organizations, and supports their initiative;

(c) discusses the activity of the national-territorial organizations and helps them in their work;

(d) elects a Presidium, Secretariat, Chairman, Secretary-General and Secretaries of the Party Central Committee;

(e) NC

(f) elects a Council of Elders;

(g) publishes and answers for the central press organs of the Party, and elects their editors-in-chief;

(h) directs the Central Committee's enterprises and institutions and approves their directors or heads;

(i) approves the Party's budget, supervises income and expenditure and determines the size of membership dues.   [to here *48*]

Commission; only persons who have been members of the Party for at least five years may serve on either body;

(e) makes decisions on requests, complaints or appeals from Party members and organizations.

A Party Congress is convoked by the Central Committee of the Czechoslovak Communist Party within four years at the latest. The date and agenda are announced by the Central Committee at least six months beforehand.

(47) An Extraordinary Congress is convoked by the Central Committee of the Czechoslovak Communist Party

(a) by decision of a two-thirds majority of the members of the Central Committee;

(b) at the request of one-third of the members;

(c) at the request, supported by a four-fifths majority, of the Central Control and Audit Commission; or

(d) if asked for by a Congress of one of the national-territorial organizations.

Requests for the convocation of an Extraordinary Congress are submitted by members, primary organizations, district committees, district conferences, Central Committees or Congresses of the national-territorial organizations to the Central Committee of the Czechoslovak Communist Party and to the Central Control and Audit Commission. These organs are obliged to inform the membership at large of the number of requests submitted.

An Extraordinary Congress is held within not more than three months from the announcement of its convocation.

(48) The supreme organ of the Czechoslovak Communist Party in the periods between Congresses is the Central Committee of the Czechoslovak Communist Party, which

(a) adopts viewpoints on domestic and foreign policy and integrates the activity of the whole Party in support of the Congress's political line;

(b) lays down the procedure for dealing with political, economic, ideological, cultural and social problems on the basis of systematic information-gathering and in harmony with the Party's programme;

(c) directs the work of the national-territorial organizations and Party organs, and Party branches in institutions of a State-wide character which do not form part of either national-territorial organization, while respecting their rights and encouraging their initiative;

(d) elects the Presidium, Secretariat, Chairman and Secretaries of the Party's Central Committee;

(e) elects the Commissions of the Central Committee, and their chairmen;

[*add.*] In order to prevent either national-territorial organization of the Party from being outvoted, the following provisions are laid down:

(A) Problems concerning major issues and interests of one or another national-territorial organization will only be decided by the Central Committee of the Czechoslovak Communist Party after discussion and in the knowledge of the viewpoint of the Central Committee of the organization concerned.

(B) Resolutions on such questions become valid if approved by a four-fifths majority of members present in the Central Committee of the Czechoslovak Communist Party.

(C) In especially crucial cases these problems are dealt with at a joint session of the Central Committee of the Czechoslovak Communist Party together with one or both of the Central Committees of the national-territorial organizations. A joint session may be held on the initiative of the Central Committee of the Czechoslovak Communist Party or of one of the Central Committees of the national-territorial organizations.

(*f*) approves Party members as candidates for membership of the National Assembly and approves representatives of the Party for service in government and National Front organs. It co-operates systematically with communists in official, State and legislative organs and in organs of the National Front and social organizations, establishes conditions for their successful activity, makes use of their ideas and suggestions and discusses its decisions with them beforehand;

(*g*) renders accounts of its work to Congress and to lower organizations and organs;

(*h*) sets up and directs the Party's press publications and approves their editors-in-chief;

(*i*) establishes Central Committee enterprises and institutes and approves their directors;

(*j*) approves its own budget and that of its institutes and checks that they are adhered to; lays down principles for the Party's financial affairs, determines the amount of membership dues, and decides how funds for the Party's work should be built up and allocated.

The Central Committee and delegations appointed by it represent the Party in its contacts with the communist and workers' parties of other countries.

The Central Committee meets at least three times a year in accordance with requirements ensuing from the domestic and international situation and from the Party's tasks. A plenary session of the Central Committee summons the Presidium

(*a*) in pursuance of the Committee's working plan;

(*b*) by decision of the Committee's plenary session, or of the Presidium;

(*c*) at the request of one-third of the Committee's members;

(*d*) at the request of the Central Committee of one of the national-territorial organizations; or

(*e*) when asked to do so by the Central Control and Audit Commission.

(*49*) Decisions of the Central Committee of the Czechoslovak Communist Party on questions concerning the international communist movement, the work of communists in organs and institutions of a State-wide character, cadre matters in these organs and institutions, the Party's work in the armed forces including the People's Militia, the central press organs of the Czechoslovak Communist Party and the Central Party archives come within its exclusive competence and are dealt with in consonance with the principles of democratic centralism.

The Central Committee of the Czechoslovak Communist Party has access to all information on the work of the national-territorial organs and organizations.

173

(47) N C   [*50*]

(48) The Secretariat of the Central Committee ensures the practical aspects of the fulfilment of tasks ensuing from Central Committee resolutions and carries out other activity assigned to it by the Central Committee.
NC   [*51*]

(49) N C

[*add.*] The fraction

   (a) discusses and lays down the line to be taken by communist Deputies in the National Assembly;

   (b) helps to draft decisions of the Party's Central Committee on problems arising from the work of the representative and State organs, and submits its proposals and viewpoints to the Committee; the members of the fraction elect their own chairman and secretary. [*52*]

(50) The Council of Elders is an advisory organ of the Central Committee of the Czechoslovak Communist Party. It consists of public officials with good records and long political experience.

Either on its own initiative or at the request of the Central Committee of the Czechoslovak Communist Party, the Council of Elders may express its opinion on particular issues of Party policy.   [–]

The Control and Audit Commissions of the Czechoslovak Communist Party
(51) N C

The status and functions of these Commissions forbid any direct link with executive activity, nor can such activity be assigned to them by the directive organs. They cannot assume any of the responsibility of the directive or executive organs.   [*53*]

In all other matters, in so far as they concern survival, sovereignty or paramount national or territorial interests, a decision of the Central Committee of the Czechoslovak Communist Party is valid provided it is supported by the votes of over one-half of the representatives of both national-territorial organizations, voting separately. This method of voting will be applied to proposals supported by over half of the representatives of one or other of the national-territorial organizations.

The Central Committee of the Czechoslovak Communist Party approaches the discussion of such questions on the basis of its awareness of the viewpoint of the Central Committee of the national-territorial organization in question. It may convene a joint session of the Central Committees of both national-territorial organizations with a view to reaching political agreement on the solution of problems. Such joint sessions of the two Central Committees cannot pass binding resolutions.

(50) The Presidium is the executive organ of the Central Committee of the Czechoslovak Communist Party and in the periods between its sessions, with the help of its commissions and working groups, it elaborates conceptual material, ensures the fulfilment of tasks arising from resolutions of a Congress or of the Central Committee and carries out activities assigned to it by the Central Committee.

The Presidium is responsible to the Central Committee and renders it regular accounts of its work.

(51) The Secretariat ensures the practical aspects of the fulfilment of tasks ensuing from resolutions of the Central Committee and its Presidium, and organizes and directs the day-to-day activity of the *apparat* and Party institutions.

The Secretariat is responsible to the Central Committee and renders it regular accounts of its work.

(52) Communist Deputies in the National Assembly constitute a communist Deputies' fraction, and this fraction works under the guidance of the Central Committee of the Czechoslovak Communist Party and in accordance with its resolutions.

The Control and Audit Commissions of the Czechoslovak Communist Party

(53) The Control and Audit Commissions of the Czechoslovak Communist Party are impartial organs of control, independent of the organs of direction. Within the system of Party organs they constitute an autonomous element by which it exercises effective self-control; they are essential to the healthy functioning and development of the Party organism. They are elected by Congresses, conferences and plenary or annual general meetings, and it is only to these bodies that the Control and Audit Commissions are answerable for the performance of their functions. The prin-

(52) N C [but read in first two lines
      ... elects its own chairman, vice-chairman and secretaries, who . . .]
                                                                    [*54*]
(53) N C [but read in last two lines
      . . . incompatible with membership of any organ except a basic
      organization.]   [*55*]

ciples governing their activity are approved by the Congress of the Czechoslovak Communist Party.

The status and functions of these Commissions forbid any direct link with decision-making or executive activity, and no such duty can be assigned to them by the directive organs. They cannot assume any of the responsibility of the directive or executive organs nor give directions to Commissions at lower levels in the Party structure, though they co-operate with them for practical purposes.

(*54*) Each Control and Audit Commission elects its own chairman and vice-chairman, who are responsible to the Committee plenum for the performance of their day-to-day duties.

Through the Commission each plenum approves the establishment of its own executive *apparat* and the engagement or dismissal of its own officials; it approves its own budget and checks that it is adhered to.

(*55*) The Control and Audit Commissions perform the following main functions:

(*a*) a political control function, consisting of checking the creation, elaboration and fulfilment of the line laid down by Congress and by the resolutions of conferences and plenary sessions of Party organs, and the performance of executive organs and officials of the *apparat* in adhering to democratic principles in Party activity and in developing intra-Party relations; it includes also the investigation and evaluation of the standard and effectiveness of control work by Party organs;

(*b*) a confirmation and appeal function, whose purpose is to note whether Party organs and members are acting in accordance with Party Statutes, and in particular how far organs are establishing conditions favourable to the exercise by members of their own rights; to determine what use is made of ideas and recommendations and whether complaints submitted to the directive organs by Party members and non-members, by branches and by Party organs, are being duly processed; to deal with appeals by members, branches and organs against Party penalties and other decisions of the directive organs; through Party conciliation procedure to assess and settle disputes between members; to furnish effective protection to the rights of any member, Party organization or minority;

(*c*) an audit function, consisting in checking the proper expenditure of funds in accordance with political undertakings, the auditing of party accounts and ensuring of due order in the administration of organizations and their organs. At higher levels the Commissions are also concerned with the rational organization of administrative work and use of modern working methods and technology.

177

(54) NC [but end first para. at
    ... Commissions.]
  [Then read:]
  The Control and Audit Commissions provide one another with information; they are entitled fully to use the Party's information system and have access to all Party materials and documents necessary for their own work.

[*56*]

(55) NC [except in line 2 read
    ... or the vice-chairman or secretary, of . . .]
  NC [Joint sessions . . .]
  NC [Press organs . . .]

[*57*]

Party Organs and Organizations in the Armed Forces

(56) Party organs and organizations in the armed forces are guided in their activity by the Party Statutes. Through their work they exert the Party's influence in the armed forces. They are formed in accordance with the structural pattern of the armed forces.

  NC [Party work . . .]
  NC [Party organizations . . .]

[*58*]

The personnel and equipment of the Control and Audit Commissions need to be adequate for the fulfilment of these demanding tasks. Membership of a Control and Audit Commission is incompatible with membership of any directive or executive organ at the same level.

(56) The Control and Audit Commissions submit their findings, proposals and recommendations to the directive and executive organs, which are under obligation to consider them and state their viewpoints or decisions to the Commissions within three months at the latest.

The Control and Audit Commissions obtain the information they require independently and furnish one another with information; they are entitled fully to utilize the Party's information system and to have access to all Party material and documents.

(57) Plenary sessions of directive organs and meetings of executive organs are attended by the chairman, or the vice-chairmen, of a Control and Audit Commission. Other members of a Commission take part when instructed to by the plenum of the Commission. Control and Audit Commissions at all levels are entitled to ask for the convocation of a plenary session of a directive organ, or for an Extraordinary conference or Extraordinary Congress.

Joint sessions of directive organs and Control and Audit Commissions are held to discuss serious political and internal Party problems, or proposals and viewpoints which the Commission is submitting to the plenum. Each organ makes a separate decision on the resolutions under discussion. Should they fail to agree, the dispute is passed on for decision by a joint session of higher organs, or in the case of the supreme organs, by a Congress of the Czechoslovak Communist Party.

Press organs are under obligation to publish the full and unamended texts of viewpoints and resolutions of the plenum of any Control and Audit Commission which has decided in favour of such publication.

IV. PARTY ORGANIZATIONS AND ORGANS IN THE ARMY AND FEDERAL SECURITY BODIES

(58) Communists in the army and federal security bodies form Party organizations corresponding to the structure of the armed forces. They are guided in their activity by the programme and Statutes of the Party and by resolutions of higher Party organs. In the event of war they operate according to special instructions issued by the Central Committee of the Czechoslovak Communist Party.

Party work in the armed forces is directed by the Central Committee of the Czechoslovak Communist Party through the medium of democratically elected organs.

179

IV. PARTY INQUIRIES AND PENALTIES

(57) A Party inquiry or disciplinary proceedings can be instituted in the case of any Party member who fails to fulfil his duty, acts contrary to the Party Statutes or otherwise harms the public reputation of the Party. Party penalties have an educative purpose and are not imposed until other resources are exhausted, e.g. rebuke or severe rebuke by a Party organ, comradely criticism before a plenary meeting, an order to make amends, or public criticism. It is not permissible to impose Party penalties for differences of opinion, unless these are in fundamental conflict with the programme and Statutes of the Party. Decisions to award a Party penalty are taken by secret ballot. [60, 61]

(58) NC [59]

(59) Disciplinary proceedings may be instituted against a member on the basis of specific and proven irregularities or offences. In each case the organ in question sets up a special commission, to which the member is entitled to propose his own representative. The commission must discuss its findings in the member's presence. The results of disciplinary proceedings are debated and approved by a members' meeting or by the plenum of the appropriate organ.

The result of disciplinary proceedings must be a declaration of innocence, the imposition of corrective measures or the award of one of the following Party penalties: rebuke, severe rebuke, deprivation of Party office, severe rebuke with warning, expulsion from the Party. These decisions can be published in the Party press if the organ concerned deems it necessary. [60]

Dismissal from office . . . [and remainder of para. 2 of *62*]

(60) NC [Then *add.*]

The primary organization records the penalty on the member's card and reports it to the Party's district committee. [61]

(61) NC [from para. 1 of Article *62* except for last line reading '. . . the penalty (other than expulsion) in agreement with the primary organization'.]

[Then *add.*] [62]

The right to expel a member from the Party belongs to his primary organization. Should a primary organization, despite grave violation of the programme and Statutes, refuse to expel its member from the Party, this may be decided by the Central Committee of the Czechoslovak Communist Party after thorough investigation and a recommendation from the Central Control and Audit Commission. In exceptional cases higher Party organs may suggest to primary organizations that they institute disciplinary proceedings against a member, and ask for their viewpoints and conclusions. [62]

Party organizations and organs in the armed forces co-operate closely with the national-territorial Party organizations and their organs; they give support to their members in their public and political activity.

V. PARTY INQUIRIES AND PENALTIES

(*59*) Party organizations and organs are under obligation to consider any warnings and complaints, either from communists or other members of the public, about the actions and behaviour of their own members. For every such inquiry the organ in question sets up a special commission deputed to demonstrate the truth or falsity of the report received. A member has the right to propose a representative of his own to serve on such a commission. The commission must discuss its conclusions in the presence of the member. The inquiry is concluded at a general meeting or plenum of the organ either with a rejection of the charge made, or with the imposition of corrective measures (or, in more serious cases, institution of disciplinary proceedings).

(*60*) Disciplinary proceedings may be instituted against a member who fails to fulfil his duties, acts contrary to the Party's Statutes or otherwise harms the public reputation of the Party. If a charge is not proved, the proceedings are halted. If it is proved, then according to the seriousness of the case and with due regard to the person of the offending member a corrective measure may be applied, such as reproof, reprimand, order to make amends, comradely criticism at a general branch meeting or session of a Party organ, or public criticism. If such measures are inadequate, a Party penalty can be imposed, *viz.* rebuke, severe rebuke, deprivation of Party function, or severe rebuke with warning. If the offence was such that the member's continuance in the ranks of the Party would be exceptionally harmful to it, he is expelled by the Party collective. The conclusions of disciplinary proceedings must be discussed and approved by a general meeting or by the plenum of the appropriate organ.

It is not permissible to impose Party penalties for differences of opinion, where these do not imply activity on the member's part in conflict with the Party programme and Statutes.

(*61*) Decisions to impose Party penalties or expel members from the Party are made by secret vote at the general meeting of a basic organization. For the imposition of a Party penalty a simple majority of votes is required. Expulsion from the Party is valid if supported by a two-thirds vote of members present at a meeting. The expelled member is to hand over his membership book to the committee of his branch.

(*62*) Decisions to impose Party penalties on members and alternate members of district committees, Central Committees of national-territorial

(62) In cases where a Party member breaks the law and is prosecuted by the courts, his primary organization may suspend his Party membership and at the same time institute Party proceedings against him. The result of such proceedings may be renewal of his membership, a Party penalty, or expulsion. [*63*]

(63) N C [*64*]

(64) N C [*65*]

organizations and Control and Audit Commissions are made by primary organizations with the cognizance of the appropriate Party organ in all cases where the offence was committed in their area. Their decision is valid if confirmed by the organ to which the offender belongs. If, however, the occasion for the penalty arose in connection with the member's execution of his function in a higher organ, then the organ in question decides on the penalty in agreement with the primary organization.

Dismissal from office of a member or alternate member of a district committee, Central Committee of a national-territorial organization, or member of a Control and Audit Commission at one of these levels, may be ordered by the plenum of the appropriate organ on a two-thirds majority of members' votes. Such a decision requires confirmation by the appropriate conference or Congress.

Expulsion of a member of a higher Party organ from the Party is dealt with by primary organizations with the cognizance of such organs. The decision of a primary organization to expel a member from the Party is valid in such cases if confirmed by a two-thirds majority of the members of the Party organ to which the offender belongs. Where a primary organization refuses to expel one of its members from the Party despite his grave infringement of its programme and Statutes, then a higher Party organ may make the decision. In exceptional cases higher Party organs have the right to propose to lower organs and to primary organizations the institution of disciplinary proceedings against their members, and to require their viewpoints and conclusions.

(*63*) In cases where a Party member breaks the law and is prosecuted by the courts, the Party branch or organ to which he belongs may suspend his Party membership until the court's verdict is announced. Thereafter Party disciplinary proceedings may be instituted.

(*64*) A Party member who has been awarded a Party penalty or expelled from the Party, or whose request for the annulment of a Party penalty has been rejected, may appeal within one month of the decision to organs up to and including the Congress of the Czechoslovak Communist Party, which will make its own decision.

The same right of progressive appeal up to and including the Congress of the Czechoslovak Communist Party is enjoyed by any Party organization or organ whose decision has been changed by a higher organ.

A Party penalty remains in force until otherwise decided by a higher Party organ, which must give an answer to the member's request within two months.

When an unjustified penalty is annulled the Party organ in question must publish the fact in the Party press if the member concerned requests it.

(*65*) An organ which has imposed a penalty must assist the member to

(65) NC [*67*]
[No provision, as in *(66)*, for the dissolution of entire branches or organs.]

V. PARTY FINANCES

(66) NC [but without second sentence 'Party organs . . . expenditure'.] [*68*]

VI. FINAL PROVISIONS

(67) NC [but without last nine words 'after consultation . . . Commission'.] [*69*]
(68) NC [*70*]

overcome and make amends for his shortcomings and, according to the character and severity of the penalty, to evaluate the member's activity. If the reasons for which the penalty was imposed are found to have lapsed, or the member to have overcome his shortcomings, then the appropriate Party organ or general meeting can, at the member's request or of its own accord, decide by simple majority to annul the Party penalty.

(*66*) Where a branch or lower Party organ seriously infringes the programme or Statutes, the appropriate Central Committee of a national-territorial organization may in extreme cases dissolve that branch or organ and decide to what other branch the members affected shall be transferred. A decision to dissolve a branch or organ must be taken by a two-thirds majority.

(*67*) Detailed procedure for Party inquiries, disciplinary proceedings and imposition of Party penalties is laid down in instructions approved by the plenum of the Central Committee of the Czechoslovak Communist Party.

VI. PARTY FINANCES

(*68*) The Party derives its funds from members' dues, the profits of Party enterprises and other revenue. Party organs regularly inform the members of the Party's income and expenditure.

Party organizations, branches, institutions and enterprises may acquire rights in their own name and assume property obligations within the limits laid down in guidelines approved by the Central Committee of the Czechoslovak Communist Party.

VII. FINAL PROVISIONS

(*69*) The Statutes of the Czechoslovak Communist Party contain basic and binding regulations for the internal life of the Party. No instructions or resolutions of Party organizations or organs may be inconsistent with these Statutes.

The basis for interpreting the Statutes and their separate articles, in addition to the text itself, is the justificatory report approved by the Extraordinary Fourteenth Congress of the Czechoslovak Communist Party.

In case of dispute the valid interpretation is that given by the plenum of the Central Committee of the Czechoslovak Communist Party after consultation with the Central Control and Audit Commission.

(*70*) Alteration of the Party Statutes is the sole prerogative of the Congress of the Czechoslovak Communist Party.

[Published in *Rudé právo*, 10 August 1968.]

What needs to be done so that the Party can recover its health as speedily and certainly as possible? What is needed is that every Party member should begin, with complete calm and supreme care, to study, first, the points at issue, and secondly, the course of the struggle within the Party. Both things are necessary, for the points at issue develop and become clear and specific – and very often alter – in the course of the struggle, which passes through various phases and in each phase exhibits a different number and grouping of combatants, different positions of battle and so forth. One has to study both things and inexorably demand the most meticulous publication of documents and their availability for anyone who wants to check up on his facts. Anyone who accepts mere words is an incorrigible dolt and one can only wring one's hands over him.

V. I. Lenin, *Collected Works*, vol. 32, pp. 35-6

VII

Analysis of the Party's Record and of the Development of Society since the Thirteenth Congress; the Party's Main Tasks for the Immediate Future

(a rough outline)

The following text arose from the findings of working groups set up by decision of the Presidium of the Czechoslovak Communist Party's Central Committee, and composed as follows:

ANALYSIS OF DEVELOPMENTS SINCE THE THIRTEENTH CONGRESS:
    Comrades Sádovský (in charge), Slavík, Graca.

THE PARTY AND THE POLITICAL SYSTEM:
    Comrades Mlynář (in charge), Kašpar, Herchová, Erban, Colotka, Jičínský.

THE RELATION OF THE PARTY TO THE BASIC SOCIAL GROUPS AND INTERESTS:
    Comrades Lenárt (in charge), Kozel, Valenta, Václavů, Machonín, Vokrouhlický.

THE PARTY'S ECONOMIC POLICY:
    Comrades Kolder (in charge), Morkus, Kouba.

THE PARTY'S MAIN TASKS IN SCIENCE, CULTURE AND IDEOLOGY:
    Comrades Císař (in charge), Gellner, Kostroun, Hübl.

BASIC FEATURES OF THE PARTY'S LONG-TERM PROGRAMME:
    Comrade Richta (in charge).

BASIC QUESTIONS OF PARTY POLICY IN INTERNATIONAL RELATIONS AND THE INTERNATIONAL COMMUNIST MOVEMENT:
    Comrade Hájek (in charge).

The documents produced by these groups were collated by an editorial commission (to which Comrades Mlynář, Hájek, Kouba, Machonín, Provazník, Richta and Uher were appointed) and somewhat abridged into the following rough outline of theses, to some parts of which the commission has added its own remarks.

I Analysis of Past Developments

1. CHARACTERISTICS OF THE PRESENT SOCIAL CRISIS

The January plenum opened the way for an examination of the current state of our country. This examination made clear to every communist and to the whole public, over and above the individual difficulties we had been struggling with for years past, the much broader features of a profound crisis throughout society. This crisis touched almost every aspect of our life. The rigid and undemocratic system of the pre-January period offered no hope of fulfilling the just demands and needs of the various sectors of our society; gradually a state of affairs was created in which no sector at all was satisfied. The stagnation of the economy greatly reduced the chances of achieving economic equality for the Slovaks. Nor had the pre-January regime been capable of undertaking initiatives in the field of foreign policy which would have enabled it to cope with new issues abroad. Politics degenerated into practicism and, in ideology, empty pseudo-Marxist clichés concealed an eclecticism devoid of principle. In almost every sphere of life, the former leadership had practically no significant achievements to show for the past few years. The worst fault of the pre-January regime, however, was the incompetence with which it squandered the vast efforts, both of the Party's officials and rank-and-file, and of the other active elements of the public.

Whenever there were signs of discontent the bureaucratic machinery tried to cope with them either by authoritarian measures or by social and nationalistic demagogy. The various classes and groups in society who were drawn together by their resentment at the exercise of authority were thus split apart again and set against one another; quarrels between the workers, intelligentsia and farmers, or between the young and the old, were artificially fostered and kept alive. An atmosphere of distrust and suspicion was engendered among the Czechs toward the justifiable national demands of the Slovaks. Such manoeuvres, of course, could not prevent the gradual collapse of the political foundations of the pre-January regime. Dissatisfaction grew even in the most active parts of the Party – the primary organizations and the creative ideological element – and gradually found its way into the highest elected organs, leading to acute conflicts there. These were manifest signals for the onset of a profound Party crisis, itself the culmination of the chronic national crisis threatening the very basis of our socialist system. We cannot choose the right path for our future advance unless we critically assess our own past, the whole design for the construction of socialism in Czechoslovakia, and the assumptions from which that design arose.

2. POST-WAR DEVELOPMENTS: OPPORTUNITY AND REALITY

After 1945 Czechoslovakia faced quite new and peculiar tasks and problems. It was a country with a relatively advanced economic and social structure and a well-developed tradition of political life akin to that of the Western bourgeois democracies. In the course of, and after, its post-war economic renewal Czechoslovakia had the opportunity to embark on profound qualitative changes in the structure of its economy and its social relations and so to fit itself for participation in the scientific-technical revolution then spreading through the whole world. The unity of democratic anti-Fascist forces, welded during the Resistance, was creating new possibilities for socialism and also making new demands on it. The material and cultural context of Czechoslovakia afforded socialism plenty of scope to develop its asstes.

During the first post-war years the international situation was favourable, too. The country's position was secured by its alliance with the Soviet Union and by the emergence of a system of socialist States. Other advantageous factors were the continued co-operation amongst the members of the anti-Hitler coalition and the powerful influence of left-wing forces in Western Europe. However, these advantages were to a certain extent curtailed by the theory and practice of the communist movement at that time.

Such were the conditions under which the liberation was followed by a fundamental reconstruction of our country's constitutional and political pattern, with the Czechoslovak Communist Party as the main initiator of change and nationalization of the key sectors of the economy as its main result. Within the National Front, a multi-party political system was put into effect on the basis of a common programme.

The favourable international conditions, however, passed away. The anti-Hitler coalition fell to pieces and the Cold War shed a baneful influence even on domestic affairs. The political struggle was exacerbated, leading the National Front into an *impasse* and producing a conflict of authority which ended in February 1948 when the bourgeoisie was defeated and lost its share of political power. The February victory over reactionary forces made possible a faster advance toward socialism. The reconstruction of the Republic on socialist lines, though hampered by the complexity of the international situation, effected great economic, political and social changes whose profundity was equalled by the conflicting nature of their results.

After February 1948 there was a disproportionate concentration of political power in the top executive bodies of the Czechoslovak Communist Party. There was no place in this new power structure for any system of checks or for balancing opposed views. The Party virtually ceased to be a democratic organism and neither the rank-and-file nor the bulk of the officials at various levels had any serious influence on the Party's policy. Its further development was not absolutely pre-determined, but the practices evolved under the conditions of the Cold War, and of the theory of an ever-sharpening class struggle, prepared the ground for an arbitrary style of decision-making. The Party leaders failed to master this hazardous situation. Under the pressure of internal forces serious mistakes were made both in the political and economic fields.

The first Five-Year Plan was marked by considerable quantitative progress and by the liquidation of the bourgeoisie; but it also led to an economic imbalance, to a slower rise in the standard of living and, finally, to its stagnation. This situation bore especially hard on the farmers and small industrial producers.

The most tragic episode in this phase was the series of cases where socialist legality was criminally violated. A regime without checks or balances always contains the seeds of potential crisis. This, however, was kept at bay by the fairly broad social support which it enjoyed. For many years economic advancement, socialist ideology and socialist reforms ensured the unity of the Party and its popular backing. Yet as early as 1953 there were serious negative symptoms showing how urgent it was to reconsider the Party's whole policy.

3. MISSED OPPORTUNITIES FOR CHANGING THE PATTERN OF SOCIALISM

Soon after Stalin's death attempts at a change of direction were made in the socialist countries. In Czechoslovakia, however, the opportunity was made less use of than in several other countries. There were shifts in investment policy and the standard of living was improved, but all the changes that were made were superficial and failed to affect any of the essential features of the existing pattern of socialism. It was in the sphere of justice that least progress was registered. While in some of the socialist countries the first rehabilitations and amnesties began as early as 1954, in Czechoslovakia innocent people in that year were still being subjected to political trials and even receiving death sentences.

Another and much greater opportunity for improvement occurred after the Twentieth Congress of the Soviet Communist Party, but even this was not properly exploited. For it was impossible to find and implement a new design unless the existing leaders – Novotný, Zápotocký, Široký and others – admitted all the negative aspects of the past, which would have made their continuance in the leadership of the Party doubtful. The situation was made a good deal more difficult by the events in Hungary, from which the Czechoslovak Party leaders drew only one-sided conclusions. The 1956 reforms were accordingly half-hearted and inconsistent, only marginally affecting the basis of the system as created in Czechoslovakia. The theory of the ever-increasing class struggle was denounced and the worst excesses of illegality were put right. More attention was given to extending the democratic side of socialism, but the declarations made about the workers' share in management and in running the State remained largely on paper. Progress in implementing democratic methods within the Party was minimal. The labelling of revisionism as the 'main danger' became a weapon in the struggle against the progressive forces. These forces were still in the process of clarifying their main ideas. They did not yet constitute a live political factor and, in a situation where Party discipline was pretty firm and the economic situation fairly well in hand, with crisis factors kept in the background, it was possible to isolate them. In this period socialism had shown its undeniable merits by giving the public social justice and considerably reducing class differences. These facts, along with the rise in living standards, helped to neutralize the unsatisfactory aspects of the political system.

Toward the end of the nineteen-fifties there surged through the socialist countries a wave of unrealistic optimism which engulfed amongst others the Czechoslovak Party leaders. It arose from the apparent success of the expansion of the economy by extensive means, successes due to the tailing off of the first wave of investment. The Party leaders coined a series of unrealistic slogans and in 1960 proclaimed the 'victory of socialism'. A peculiar situation was thus brought about in which the evolution of the political system and development of socialist democracy lagged behind. There was no programme for improving social relations after the completion of the transitional period, and the political practices which had characterized it were perpetuated. On to these archaic features, however, there also began to be grafted hypothetical elements of a still unattained communist society.

Once the reserves which had made possible the economic expansion of the late fifties had been exhausted, the nation's economy, based on *dirigisme*, extensive methods, egalitarianism and a one-sided preference for the 'iron theory', started to enter a period of protracted depression. For a long time the leaders failed to grasp most of the reasons for the appalling accumulation of problems. The incipient social crisis, too, passed into a new phase. The expectations raised by the proclamation that socialism had arrived began to conflict in people's minds with the realities of life. The consequence was an increase in political apathy and a decline in enthusiasm for the Communist Party in all strata of society. The self-sacrificing efforts of officials and ordinary members alike could do little to remedy this state of affairs.

One very serious symptom of the growing crisis was the deterioration of relations between Czechs and Slovaks. The process of unification which had been going on since 1948 paid no regard to historical conditions or social structure in Slovakia, nor to the Slovaks' special political and psychological circumstances. The illegal acts of repression had in Slovakia, again, assumed the form of a struggle against alleged bourgeois nationalism, a charge brought against that whole group of the Slovak communist leadership associated with the wartime rising. The authority of the Slovak national organs of government was repeatedly cut down (lastly and most notably by the

1960 Constitution) and, under the leadership of Bacílek and David, the Central Committee of the Slovak Communist Party was converted into a body designed to side-track Slovak national interests as purely 'local' affairs. It was customary to set against all this the industrialization of Slovakia. But though this answered a genuine need, the way the political system developed and the position to which Slovak bodies were reduced meant that industrialization itself became dependent on the authoritarian and bureaucratic system of central management.

4. FROM THE THIRTEENTH CONGRESS TO THE JANUARY 1968 PLENUM

It was characteristic of the new phase in the crisis that the progressive forces in the Party manifested themselves on a much higher intellectual plane than in 1956. They became gradually convinced that the only way out of the crisis was to change the existing pattern of socialism, replacing it by one which fulfilled the requirement of participation in the scientific-technical revolution, which accepted the democratic and humanitarian content of socialism and which showed continuity with desirable values in the traditions of both our nations. Thus two trends began to merge in the Party: progressive and conservative. The greatest successes won by the progressive forces were a further stage in the rehabilitation process in 1963, and acceptance of the case for economic reform. Both were halted in midcourse, but they helped to enlarge the scope for critical examination of the past and for independent, original Marxist thought in various fields.

The Thirteenth Congress likewise illustrated the struggle between the two streams of thought and their relative strength. The Party officials responsible for drawing up the documents for the Congress managed to bring into them certain new ideas, such as the need for a *rapprochement* between social groups and classes, for greater scope for non-Party members, and for enhancing respect for special skills and understanding of scientific management methods – ideas which formed a springboard for the further fight for progress. But it was a very limited advance, for the old guard continued in power inside the Party and any criticism of them was limited to the mildest of hints.

Developments after the Thirteenth Congress continued to be marked by this struggle and in 1967 it became so acute as to produce a decisive showdown. The Writers' Congress and the Strahov incident not only highlighted the antagonism between the Novotný group, and the young generation and communist intellectuals; it also reflected the tension between the Party leaders and the broad masses of the people, including a large proportion of Party members. The country stood at the crossroads. Either the Party leaders would have to change their policy, or the gulf between them and the public would grow still deeper. This was the situation when Novotný introduced his 'hardline course', relying on coercion and authoritarian measures against all members and officials of the Party who disagreed with him.

From this soil sprang the conflict at the October Plenum between Novotný and his supporters on the one hand and a group of Central Committee members which, it soon became clear, included the overwhelming majority of the Slovaks. The Republic now stood on the brink of a serious State crisis, in the face of which the majority of the Central Committee's members realized the need to remove Novotný from the post of First Secretary of the Party. The latent rift in the Party's ranks thus became an open one. Although at the December and January plena the sole criterion for differentiation was still the issue of separating the supreme State and Party posts, most of the progressive spokesmen had by now pointed out the need to democratize Party and public life.

This democratization was to be the main content of the renascence made feasible by changes in the power structure brought about at the January plenum. The confrontation, though directly concerned only with the narrow question of separating Party from State leadership, was really a political struggle with far-ranging consequences. Cardinal issues affecting the whole direction of progress in our Party and country were at stake. The triumph of the progressives at the January Plenum was of historic importance, for it meant that the men who instigated the process of renewal and democratization and put themselves at the head of it were themselves communists. The leading role of the Party, hitherto enforced by administrative, bureaucratic methods which merely undermined the Party's real political prestige, now manifested itself for the first time in a new and healthy form.

5. SOCIAL AND POLITICAL DEVELOPMENTS AFTER JANUARY 1968

After the 5 January meeting of the Central Committee, Party life was marked by the initiative of the progressive forces and the resistance to it put up by the 'conservatives'. The conflict continued to discredit the old leaders of the Party more and more in the public's eyes, and it was consequently realized that there must be a complete break with those associated with the deformation of socialism. One result of this was the subsequent decision by the Central Committee, in May, to advance the date for an Extraordinary Congress of the Party to September 1968.

In the period immediately following 5 January, however, the tempo of movement in public opinion was slow. This was mainly due to the shortage of information, itself a consequence of the balance of forces within the Committee. Understanding of the real nature of events therefore matured first amongst people professionally concerned with the analysis of social affairs, but as soon as they were properly informed the workers and farmers started moving too.

The Central Committee outlined in its Action Programme a procedure for democratizing our society, i.e. for achieving a transition from revolutionary dictatorship to a democratic regime with legal guarantees. The Action Programme proclaimed a number of specific measures to promote the transition, but remained open-ended. It undoubtedly played a large part in post-January developments and will always be a unique document in the history of the international communist movement. Between its drafting and its publication, however, a longer period than necessary elapsed during which conservative and progressive forces came up sharply against each other. During this phase the censorship stopped working and freely-formed public opinion emerged. The Party leadership had to exert every effort in such a situation to keep pace with the tempo of change. The election and entry into office of the new members of the supreme Party executive bodies helped to consolidate the position, and in June the first laws were passed giving legal shape to points on the Action Programme, *viz.* the abolition of censorship, and rehabilitation.

The various differentiating processes introduced into our society an increased number of autonomous and pluralistic features, making it necessary to revive the National Front as a universal platform for all organized forces, social or political, especially the parties. There thus arose embryonic forms of political pluralism, subordinate to the National Front as the common political form and so excluding the possibility of any political struggle for power within the State. The Communist Party, however, has not yet learnt to think in pluralistic terms, in terms of the equality and autonomy of different parties and organizations. The greatest obstacle here is past history; old habits form a 'natural' bastion for the conservatives, enabling them to survive and recuperate. If the whole point of the Party's present efforts is to create a new model of socialism, then conservatism, meaning in fact the continuation of the old system we are trying to abandon, is a serious menace. During the period of fundamental revolutionary change anti-communist and anti-socialist forces have, of course, also raised their head. They have no great public backing. Anti-communist forces are nevertheless a considerable potential danger and could become a real one if the Party proves incapable of overcoming its conservative habits. The basic trend since January has remained, of course, a great enhancement of the Party's popular support.

6. CONTEMPORARY RELATIONS BETWEEN SOCIAL GROUPS

The overall significance of the historic changes our country has seen over the past twenty years has been the creation of a *new social structure*. Our society no longer has any room for capitalist exploitation and oppression, and this is a great achievement which the Czechs and Slovaks will never abandon. Relations of true socialist equality, however, do not yet predominate.

The pre-January system was marked by a wide and hierarchically graduated inequality between the narrow circle of men actually exercising power, the staffs of the various *apparat*, the corps of Party officials and, finally, the broad masses of the population, Party members and otherwise, who could play no serious role in running society. During the fifties, again, a fairly large category of people had arisen who were politically victimized for no good reason. The different extents to which people shared in exercising power often bore no relation, moreover, to their skill and knowledge. Many issues of vital importance were decided by bureaucrats whose lack of qualifications made them all the more fearful of losing their authority and willing to resort to undemocratic methods of wielding it.

The undemocratic political and ideological set-up meant at the same time that it was impossible to promote the real interests and needs of various social groups – workers, farmers, intellectual and other professional or common-interest groups, women, special age-groups, nations and nationalities – in an open and organized way on democratic lines. Under the cover of clichés about the moral and political unity of society and the leading roles of the working class and the Communist Party, top-level decisions were largely mere reactions to various random moods and pressures, often channelled through a variety of lobbies and bureaucratic cliques. The ruling groups also tried to prop up their positions by artificially widening the gaps between workers and intellectuals, workers and farmers, old and young and differing ethnic groups, even though the elimination of antagonistic classes from society should on the contrary have made it possible to secure better co-operation all round, and despite the fact that all groups had suffered to a greater or lesser extent from the same lack of democracy.

The very fact that the pre-January system ruled out genuine public assessment of weighty issues and genuine democratic decision-making, meant that all kinds of spontaneous pressures made themselves felt and the short-term needs of various groups were met in random fashion instead of fundamental solutions of benefit to the whole of society being put into effect. The upshot was that considerable social changes of an egalitarian kind were implemented in our country. Our wage policy, our policies in the field of social need and welfare, our cadre policy, our economic policy of extensive expansion of industry and subsidies for inefficient production techniques and other socially useless activities, as well as our ideological and educational practices militating on the whole toward conformity and mediocrity – all this led to the establishment in Czechoslovakia of egalitarian relations unparalleled in any country with similar conditions of production and culture. The socialist principle 'To each according to his labour' was quite forsaken.

Egalitarianism has little in common with true socialist equality and justice, especially if it amounts – as it did in our country – to egalitarian distribution of inadequate resources. Egalitarianism operates to the detriment of the well-qualified, the efficient, the assiduous and hard-working, of all those devoted to complex and demanding labour, whether mental or physical. It operates against the interests

197

of creative intellectuals and skilled workers, of those employed in efficient branches of production or in branches which could well prosper if conditions were normal. Egalitarianism is reflected in the low average qualification level of executive personnel in the public service and the economy, and in the low participation of competent persons in making and carrying out important decisions. Egalitarian and bureaucratic relations destroy people's interest in working or in gaining higher qualifications; they threaten labour discipline and morale. They ultimately contributed to technical and economic stagnation, to a freeze in the living standard and to a halt in the general dynamics of social progress. The peculiar combination of overall egalitarianism with bureaucratic methods of management also produced several symptoms of extreme social inequality. Incompetent and unqualified people in leading posts enjoyed the same, or greater, economic and social advantages as the competent and qualified. Some groups, on the other hand, find themselves at a relatively low social level and require urgent assistance, which our government is at present doing its best to grant them.

When the initiative undertaken by the Party's progressive forces made free expression possible for the needs and interests of the various social groups it became publicly clear that, for all its egalitarianism, there was not a single social group that was satisfied with the existing state of our system: neither the workers, farmers, intellectuals, women, the young, the old, nor the various constituent nations and minorities.

Once the artificial bonds of bureaucracy and ideology were loosened, the myth of an absolute 'ethico-political unity' of society finally collapsed. All the major social groups began to put forward their own needs, interests and demands.

During 1945 to 1948 it was the *working class* that formed the mainspring of revolutionary change. It continues heartily to support socialism and the positive values socialism brought with it. At the same time, its spokesmen have for years been criticizing bureaucratic methods of running society. Today, the workers are gradually realizing that the policy, pursued for many years, of randomly satisfying their most urgent short-term needs (particularly in wage-packet terms) and the false concept of economic expansion led to the continuation of outdated working and social conditions; to the downgrading of various efficient lines of production and the artificial preservation of inefficient ones which eat the bread out of our hands; and to egalitarianism, against the interests of qualified workers and so on. In these circumstances many different groups of workers have put forward their own wage demands. At the same time workers are beginning to see that their leading political role was often nullified in favour of decision-making by narrowly based groups, particularly by officials of the Party apparatus, while their own organization – the Revolutionary Trade Union Movement – had been drastically bureaucratized, was not defending the workers' differentiated interests adequately, and had no great influence on industrial management.

Events since January have enabled the working class – which is after all the most numerous and, in the last resort, powerful group in our society – to speak more and more audibly. The workers are showing decreasing confidence in the conservatives, who pay lip-service to the workers' interests but did nothing to promote them for many years. Apart from political issues the workers are demanding with especial emphasis the speedy drafting and implementation of an economic policy calculated to bring them prosperity and higher living standards.

The *collective farmers*, despite their unhappy experience of the sectarian practices current during the collectivization process, stood up as a socialist force after January. They stress their demand, however, for full economic and political equality as the basic condition for a thriving agriculture; and for the abolition of all injustices and regulations barring the collectives from independent economic operations and the farmers themselves from organized political activity and from full social equality.

Meanwhile non-collectivized farmers are also claiming their rights. They are putting forward guidelines for a new agrarian policy designed to protect agriculture and enable it to prosper.

The sharpest and clearest-cut criticisms of the pre-January policies have come from the *intelligentsia*, the great majority of whom, years ago in this country, supported the cause of socialism and revolution. People engaged in creative intellectual work have been the hardest hit of all by bureaucratic methods of running society and by the suppression of freedom. These have been particularly painful for those working in the humanities, for journalists, writers and social scientists. Egalitarianism has put qualified members of the intelligentsia at a disadvantage. Skilled technical and managerial personnel find it

199

hard to tolerate the lagging development of production potential and the ossified economic system. Teachers and university students deplore the policy of academic levelling and the decline in educational standards. This powerful criticism by the intelligentsia – a very numerous and growing social group whose work gives it a key role at the present time in tackling the weighty problems of consolidating and modernizing our society – constitutes a grave warning to the Party and challenges it to abandon the old model of socialism, and the policies of the conservatives, without further delay.

Another large social group, consisting of *administrative and economic officialdom* and workers in the *apparat* of the Party and mass organizations, the judiciary, police and armed services, is at present very sharply divided. The great majority of personnel in these fields undoubtedly favour the renewal process, hoping to perform their valuable and indispensable work honestly in the administration and protection of society. We must not forget, however, that in some parts of the managerial and executive *apparat* there are also people who oppose the renewal process for one reason or another.

Justified complaints that their work is insufficiently appreciated come from personnel in the *service industries*.

The *younger generation*, especially those with skills, were affected more than most by all the defects of the pre-January methods. Though the great majority of our young people take socialism in their lives more or less for granted, they particularly resent all its shortcomings and deformations and denounce these with the openness and vigour that come naturally to them. This is particularly true of representations made by students, both before and after January. In our country young people have found that it does not pay them to make the effort involved in acquiring qualifications, especially at the more advanced levels. This discovery, along with a certain qualitative decline in our educational system, which fails to prepare young people with sufficient specialization for particular jobs, has led to stagnation in the educational standards of the young. Yet these standards are a basic factor in integrating the young into society and enabling society to exert a useful educative effect on them. Young people with qualifications find it difficult to get into jobs appropriate to their skills and are in the main worse paid than they should be. The Party and other organizations have failed to adopt a sufficiently varied approach to the young, paying regard to differences in work, age and interest. The activities of the old political, social and interest-oriented organizations, including the once homogeneous Youth League, held insufficient appeal for the young. The result of this was that the young became largely apolitical in outlook and had no chance to acquire the necessary political and organizational habits. Youth was regarded as an object of political processes, rather than a subject capable of living its own independent life in society. The worst impact of the housing shortage was upon the young. Directly or indirectly, all these factors upset the relationship between the generations. The official world and its organizations became largely alien to the young, who accepted them as something external but did not and could not feel a sense of responsibility toward them. For most young people the Communist Party has ceased to be an attractive body. This jeopardizes the progress of society more than any other source of tension, for it seriously impedes the normal succession of generations upon which the forward movement of society depends.

The *aged sector* of the populace presents us with another serious problem, especially in the matter of providing social and economic security.

Women, who form over half the population, are critical of the contrast between the theoretical equality and practical inequality of the sexes in society. They ask for equal treatment in employment, wages and public life. They point to the unsolved conflict between woman's function in the labour force and public life on the one hand, and her job in the family on the other. They are dissatisfied with the availability of services and equipment for the household.

A profound discontent with the existing state of society is expressed in the *Slovak nation's* demand for federalization. A Czech national movement has also begun to stir recently. The problem of finding new constitutional forms has become the focus of a social tension which is the most acute in present-day Czechoslovakia. Rights are being claimed by national minorities and by the traditional territorial units of Moravia and Silesia.

In the period after January all significant social groups expressed their dissatisfaction with current trends. Leaving aside those extreme and over-impatient voices which gave absolute priority to their own specific needs and interests, all the demands raised were to a greater or less extent justified. Our social system is thus in a profound state of crisis brought about by previous political developments.

If we wish to overcome this crisis, the Party must offer all social groups
1. a new kind of social system acceptable to the overwhelming majority of the public; and
2. feasible paths for gradual transition to such a system.

The new developmental model for our society must stand in sharp contrast to the egalitarian-bureaucratic system. This, however, does not mean an utter rejection of our society's past values.

The peoples of our country embarked on the road to socialism of their own free will, through a spontaneous and profoundly popular social process. This is why the basic socialist tendency of our society has not been questioned in any serious, responsible social or political quarter even since January, when the past has been so much criticized. As the ruling Party, therefore, the Czechoslovak Communist Party must continue to defend with all its might the axiomatic socialist values of our society, which are at the same time genuinely national and popular values. This, again, is what enables our new developmental model to be a socialist one.

II A New Model of Socialist Development Consonant with Czechoslovak Conditions

The profundity of the social crisis into which our country has fallen in the past few years, and the trivialization of theory and disorientation of ideas that have gone with it, make it necessary to expound a whole concept of socialism and socialist development appropriate to our conditions and hard-won experience.

We must candidly state that the traditional version of socialism as applied more or less systematically in this country for the last two decades was in conflict with some of the basic ideas of Marxism and failed to match the level of development already reached by our two nations. Even the limited opportunities which it did open up were soon exhausted. The accumulation of internal contradictions in this system, its incompetence in every sphere of social life and the long years during which the creative energies of our people were squandered on a mass scale – these facts all show how impossible it is to base true socialism permanently upon bureaucratic power, a State-directed economy, perpetuation of extensive methods of industrialization and a policy of ignoring the human aspect in every sphere of life.

The denial and rejection of the bourgeois class structure is a precondition for socialist development. A truly new society and new relations between people, however, cannot be attained solely by such denial and rejection, but only by positive victory over capitalism, over its economic system, over its politico-cultural legacy and over its whole basis in industrial civilization. What is needed, then, is to create new and superior conditions for human life generally; that is, after the crushing of bourgeois class power to achieve a deeper and broader-based democracy with a greater measure of freedom for every working man. It is also necessary to abolish private ownership by an exploiting class in the sense of genuinely collectivizing production resources and of creating an economic system in which everyone is his own *entrepreneur*. This would likewise involve devising a new structure of production forces and a more dynamic application of material resources in place of extensive methods of expanding industry. Finally, a higher degree of civilization of manpower is needed, a degree unattainable under existing conditions where the individual is treated with indifference.

No socialism worthy of the name must be deficient in any of these respects; for without all of them it would perish or cease to be socialism.

We are in no way anxious to underestimate the achievements wrought by our people in twenty years of self-sacrificing effort. There are many fields in which sound foundations have been laid for socialist progress. Yet we should be deceiving ourselves if we closed our eyes to the necessity of asking once more, today, what model of socialism we want, with what purpose and what basic features. We must realize, too, that this desired model can work only as a complete whole with all its essential components, and that it cannot then be attained by partial or half-hearted modifications, by adding on this or that democratic slogan or humanitarian feature, but only by thoroughgoing reconstruction of the whole system as it now is. It must be candidly stressed, moreover, that the economic system cannot be changed without the requisite degree of democracy, nor democratization made permanent without a socialist economy in working order. And the same applies to the task of genuinely linking together all the essential characteristics of socialism.

Unless we make the basis of our general programme this complex effort to set up a new model of socialism appropriate to our own conditions, we shall never manage to rally around the Party all those cardinal social interests and groups whom the anti-socialist deformations of the past affected in various – and sometimes apparently opposed – ways. It is not the aim of our socialist endeavours to force upon society a pre-determined power structure or pattern of personal relations, nor to coerce citizens into particular ways of life. The essence and meaning of the changes that we are building into our model of a socialist society, in the belief that they are both indispensable and adequate for our country, is a continuous liberation of every member of society from those social, material and spiritual circumstances and situations that prevent a man from fulfilling his own creative humanity, which trim his freedom and thwart his initiative.

We take the view that socialist changes of this kind, if carried out as a whole, will gradually facilitate a favourable growth of human powers, skill and talent, of which there is no lack among our peoples. We are convinced that even at the level of general development now being achieved by our society, unsatisfactory as it is, this potential will in the end prove to be the decisive factor for progress and the basic resource of our age. For it is the cultivation of human power, on however modest and inconspicuous a scale at first, which finally provides the springboard for larger and faster transformations. This is the great and basic thought behind the programme of scientific socialism: it is to this that we must open our doors and on this alone, in the final reckoning, that we can rest our socialist ambitions. It is the humanitarian idea at the very bottom of socialism and never, in whatever sphere or project, must we allow ourselves to forget it.

We have every reason to assume that the conditions of our own country provide an ideal environment for the development of society along modern lines. The specific features of Czechoslovakia's case are that, as early as 1945, she embarked on a socialist path as an advanced industrial country with a large and highly-skilled working class, an influential working-class movement, a mature progressive culture, an unusually good level of education, deeply rooted democratic traditions and a lively awareness of all her past struggles for freedom of conscience, national individuality and State sovereignty. For the Czechs and Slovaks, traditionally intolerant of bureaucratic stupidity, of boorishness and bullying, of rigid hierarchies in the economic or political fields, socialism is acceptable only if it means a

system that encourages an efficient and rational economy, that re-
inforces democratic rights and defends human freedom, and which
is imbued throughout with a culture expressing the highest endeavours
and longings of the whole people.

Socialism can find its place in the subconsciousness of our people
only if it signifies a society free of class enmities, based on the rule of
law, advanced in its economy, technology and culture, just in its social
and national policies, democratically organized and competently
directed with the aid of scientific techniques, a society able from its
rich resources to offer a dignified way of life and comradely co-
operation amongst all, a society able to give free scope for the
expansion of the human personality.

A start was made towards creating just such a blueprint of socialism at the time when our Party was founded, and again when our
country was liberated – the concept of a Czechoslovak road to
socialism. It is to ideas of that kind that we now return, so as to
exploit all our past experience and the best traditions of the international socialist movement.

1. DEMOCRATIC SOCIALISM

The model of socialist development we are striving for requires first
and foremost a consistent application of democratic ideas implicit in
the very essence of the socialist system: the doors must be flung open
for free socialist activity by the public.

Within our country we have overcome the barriers of class antagonism, and the class struggle has ceased to be an important aspect of
society. But the bureacratic power system which grew up over the
same period proved unable to grasp the implications of this fact.
It has prevented socialist society from undertaking the gradual liquidation of the oppressive functions of the system's agents, so that they
shall not be directed against the public's own socialist activities. But
socialist progress is possible only in so far as society stops handing
down decisions from on high and gradually refrains from interference in matters where the instruments of power are out of place –
matters such as economics, science, culture and the like. Progress is
possible, then, only where society dismantles step by step the monopoly of decision-making and extends democratic rights and self-
determination for individuals and for nations alike.

To attain the progress we all wish to see, socialism needs not less but more civic freedom than capitalism: freedom of speech, publication, information, assembly, association, movement and foreign travel. It requires not fewer but more, and more meaningful, human rights: the right to a home and a job appropriate to one's ability; the right to education and development of skills; the right to personal property and democratic representation; the right to defend one's own interests and take a part in making decisions and running affairs. And it requires that such rights be accorded to everyone, without exception.

The socio-political system called socialism should, in our view, pass on and underwrite these fundamental rights and freedoms in the following ways: first, by means of representative democracy, notably through parliament; then, by refashioning this parliamentary system through association with a new and deeper form of direct democracy, i.e. self-government in all spheres of social life, but especially in those where it can make up for the weaknesses of formal parliamentary democracy and where conditions are ripe for genuinely free self-determination and for real participation by the citizen in decision-making.

We believe that such a development will lead to a far more democratic mode of settling the political line within the National Front on the basis of a confrontation of different ideas checking and balancing one another, with the various political parties appearing as proponents of different paths towards the same end – namely a modern, economically advanced, humanitarian and democratic socialism. And in due course the National Front can then be enlarged to include further organizations capable of proving their commitment to that end.

To fulfil its true purpose the socialist revolution requires, of course, a continual transformation of the socio-political scene. As the new social structure crystallizes, the socialist economy becomes well established and the civilizing process blossoms, the possibility will arise on the one hand of more and more open and uninhibited confrontations between different political approaches, while, on the other, the need will arise for further constraints to be placed on decision-making and acts of repression by the State authorities in sectors where their powers can be transferred to the organs of self-government, or where the field can be left free for direct personal initiative. Modern information and communication technology should make this process easier by bringing science into the decision-making process, enhancing people's familiarity with the alternatives between which they are choosing, and putting on an objective footing the selection of persons fitted by their abilities to determine the choice. We are entitled to hope that socialism will effectively combine the elements of democracy and of specialization in the management of human affairs.

2. SOCIALISM AS A ROAD TO SOCIAL AND ETHNIC JUSTICE

The abolition of class antagonisms, always considered one of the prime tasks of socialism, has altered the status and function of the various social groups but has not eliminated the distinctions either between the groups themselves – workers, farmers, intelligentsia and others – or between their respective interests. It has meant that the structure of socialist society became tied to a network of contrasting social functions related to people's different jobs, manner of life, position in the management system, and so forth. What is specifically characteristic of socialist society is its universalism: it has principles, that is, which apply generally and are not conditioned by class differences. The principle of performance is one such: reward based on the quantity, quality and importance of work done. The principle of equal opportunity for human self-fulfilment is another. These principles are the basis of a higher type of social justice, which does not enlarge social differences any more than the given degrees of poverty dictate and does not create permanent, immutable interest groups. They are principles which acknowledge the growing variety of people's needs, interests and aspirations and refrain from smothering their initiative and ability under an egalitarian blanket. They do not, in short, sacrifice achieved liberties on the altar of formal equality.

Socialism has always proclaimed the universal right to work as one of its cardinal values. But if it is to remain true to this pledge it cannot interpret it as meaning the right to continue in any given activity performed in the past, regardless of its economic utility and social importance – which would only bring economic and social progress to a halt. On the contrary, it must interpret it as an assured opportunity given to all, as a guarantee of social fulfilment in rapidly

207

changing conditions, a safe prospect of going over to other work and other qualifications, and so on.

Socialism has always proclaimed the universal principle of performance, the right to a reward in accordance with work done. If it is to be true to its aims it must consistently apply the principle of the worker's stake in the results of his work, while interpreting this in a new and broader context so as to include not only rewards for individual performance, but rewards for the fruits of collective production efforts too.

Socialism has always proclaimed the universal right to human dignity and, if it is not to forsake its principles, it must guarantee truly dignified living conditions even to those whom age or ill-health prevents from working, to those who stand in need of social or human assistance.

For a long time to come socialist society must accept a *de facto* inequality between the social group for whom simple, useful work does not provide an adequate means of self-realization (and who are particularly anxious for an outlet in the form of consumption) and those groups whose activity possesses some, albeit limited, features of true human satisfaction. This is a social distinction which no longer has a class character. It makes it possible to reconcile the basic interest of all social groups, as soon as the necessary mobility is available. For on the one hand socialist society is seen to rely on the positive interest of those whose skilled and partly managerial activity gives them scope to use their strength and ability during a period of transformation of their entire culture. And on the other hand it uses all available means to mobilize the interest of people in the second category, people who are seeking an escape from the limitations imposed by the level of their work and their consumption, and can only hope to find it in a revolutionary transformation of the whole social and cultural basis of life.

The reconciliation of these interests constitutes the social basis of socialist dynamics. Their assessment and utilization involves creating institutions and mechanisms through which the interests of social groups can be expressed, set in confrontation with one another, influenced and satisfied in harmony with the requirements of social development on progressive lines.

Importance attaches in this connection to the position of our two nations and various minorities, whom our model of socialism must provide with every opportunity to develop their lives in complete equality with no constraint whatever (according to the 'right of self-determination to the point of secession'), and on the basis of deep understanding and mutual internationalist assistance.

3. SOCIALISM WITH A DYNAMIC ECONOMIC SYSTEM

According to the model of socialist development which we have in mind, democracy and social justice can be attained only with the support of an independently functioning, socialist-orientated economy.

We have eliminated capitalist ownership and transferred the means of production to the hands of the State. By doing this we destroyed the stimuli to economic development operating under capitalism without finding sufficiently effective substitutes for them. Attempts to direct socialist society like one huge enterprise, and to replace economic processes by State directives prescribing production programmes down to the last detail, merely took the decision-making function away from the actual site of activity, vastly expanded the economic *apparat* at the centre of power, and turned the State from an instrument of the people's will to the people's sole employer: it bureaucratized the whole system.

Scientific socialism, however, envisages not a formal and superficial collectivization but a meaningful one, i.e. the creation of positive economic devices to ensure that the country's whole wealth, its whole reproductive process, truly serves the interest of the working man.

The old doctrinaire notion of a single form of State ownership must therefore give way to a whole spectrum of social ownership making use, according to the attained level of the production forces and the content and purpose of an enterprise's activity, of a wide variety of forms from large State combines and national and co-operative enterprises down to small-scale individual businesses. Thus it should be possible to mobilize the workers' whole entrepreneurial initiative in different shapes: one way in modern-style large-scale industry, another way in agriculture, and another again in the service industries.

What emerges as the basic link in the socialist economic system is therefore the enterprise as an independent economic subject, separated from the State, operating under market conditions, exposed to the pressure of economic competition and combining optimal productive efficiency with optimal sensitivity to individual and social needs. In such a situation each enterprise can survive only if it is able to apply all the abilities of its staff to its operations, to select the most competent managers and the most efficient methods and to combine professional direction with democratic and socialist self-management. It may be assisted to these ends by various types of self-management – workers' councils with a mission to further the immediate interests of the workers and to link them with the interests of society. It is these bodies which can provide a stable but dynamic forum for the views of skilled and – both technically and organizationally – advanced management.

The central economic authorities will not then intervene in the process in order to make up for the absence of other economic stimuli, but in order to create, by means of economic rules and instruments including the National Plan, a general framework within which enterprises can reach decisions, and to produce conditions under which the interests of producers will redound to the benefit of all; conditions favourable to the movement of such economic resources as our country happens to possess and to those economic activities which are by world standards most progressive; conditions, finally, calculated to promote economic efforts which the market alone would not suffice to stimulate, i.e. where priority needs to be given to social or human considerations, as in decisions affecting the environment, culture, and so on.

Socialism will never stand completely on its own feet in our country until it works out its own economic system, welding together the interests of the workers both as producers and as consumers, and as genuine owners as well, controlling and managing the production of everything that makes up their own lives. Socialism cannot take root until it encourages a universal spirit of enterprise, opening up the field of human interests to new stimuli as culture and civilization progress.

4. SOCIALISM WITH THE AMENITIES OF MODERN CIVILIZATION

Socialism cannot exist in its truly democratic and humanitarian form without the basic material amenities of civilization – amenities measuring up to the expectations of socialist living in respect of the character and volume of human labour expended and the standard of material and intellectual resources made available; amenities, moreover, conducive to the emergence of social interests which themselves, without any external pressure and thanks to the sheer free activity of the public, ensure the mobility of a socialist society.

In its historic origins socialism had no such amenities at its command; it had to create them in the course of industrialization. In itself, of course, industrialization was not one of the chosen tasks of socialism but was rather in conflict with them. For inasmuch as society expands production at the cost of decreasing consumption among the majority of the population, or extends the forces of production by simply multiplying the number of menial tasks in industry, or introduces scientific management by denying most people a share in management, or creates an artificially civilized environment at the price of devastating people's living conditions and forcing culture out on to the fringes of life – then overall development is only being achieved by limiting the development of most of the working class and there is little chance that the end of exploitation will bring any truly socialist character into human relations.

The model of socialism we have in mind can function only when society achieves such a level of industrial advancement that the next stage in the process of creating civilization sees a switch from extensive industrialization (which put the main stress on industrializing the face of the country and often made this an end in itself) over to intensive growth of production forces (which shifts the accent to the exploitation and improvement of the existing industrial basis and to expansion of services and pre-production areas, where again conditions are created for more intensive growth).

Experience has shown that the tasks of extensive industrialization have already been fulfilled in our country, and its potential exhausted. To perpetuate this traditional mode of expansion holds the country back technologically, produces a disastrous decline in services, increases the sum of human worry, wastes energy on outdated working methods, under-exploits science and squanders the intellectual resources which under modern conditions, and especially in our country, could be the decisive source of new wealth. A model of socialism suited to our conditions is therefore tied up on all sides with the need for gradual changes in the amenities of our civilization and with the need for sufficient dynamism in our productive forces to harness the vast potential of modern science (as the most pervasive production factor of all) with a view to extending by degrees the vital horizon of all our working people and so to changing the manner and measure of human work, the scope and content of consumption, and indeed the whole outline of human existence. Each success in enlarging human power and skill will then in turn accelerate the changes in the structure and energy-pattern of the production forces. To achieve all this means simply to gain access to that scientific-technical revolution which is beginning to take place in this world of ours.

A democratic, humanitarian socialism obviously cannot be grafted on to industrialization of the traditional sort. For democratization would then by-pass the essence of that unfreedom which most people encounter in their work – the unfreedom of menial, monotonous and purely executive activity. And humanitarianism in these terms would ignore the poverty experienced by many workers in their limited consumer power and in their life after working hours altogether; it would rather tend toward an equal distribution of shortage.

The socialism we want must gradually overcome the limits set by traditional industrial practice. On the one hand it must humanize existing forms of work by rational organization, by enlarging the workers' role in decision-making, by raising the cultural level of the work itself and of the working environment, by compensating for time lost over intermittent jobs, by combining work with education, and so forth. On the other hand it must progressively reduce working hours; eliminate unnecessary, inefficient, old-fashioned and unskilled operations by exploiting modern scientific and technological advances; shift the human effort into the pre-production stages; and gradually bring it closer to the realm of free creative activity.

The kind of socialism we want is equally impossible without the liberation of man from his daily concern over making a living, and without the creation by stages of such an abundance as would on the one hand allow consumption to reach levels appropriate to modern civilization, with ample and uninterrupted satisfaction of present human needs, and on the other hand would permit the creation of new and higher demands, the refinement of people's interests, and an end to those self-justifying pressures that make the consumer society.

It must be evident that unless our country abandons the path of extensive industrialization and finds its way to that higher stage in the development of productive forces, the scientific-technical revolution, socialism will not be able to fulfil its basic human mission here.

5. SOCIALISM WITH A MATURE CULTURE

One final component of socialist existence is of course cultural advancement, understood in the widest sense as the cultivation of the whole living environment as well as of the individual. The source of culture in this sense is man's creative work and the use made of its fruits, be they material or spiritual.

In the phase of extensive industrialization, State *dirigisme* and bureaucratic power culture manifested itself as a sphere on its own, sharply distinguished from the material aspect of civilization where boorish utilitarian attitudes prevailed. It was treated as broadly irrelevant to social progress, which concentrated on the amassing of tangible wealth. There was thus ample scope in everyday life for ridiculing the values of cultural achievement, for insensitivity toward disturbances of the environment, for ruthless attitudes to Nature, for indifference to human effort and to the daily travails of other beings. Culture was pushed out to the fringes of life as the speciality of a small minority, and subordinated to the general control of the authorities. But this undermined the whole social significance of creative work and stemmed the interflow between the results of material effort and the first signs of a new advance in civilization – an interflow which can be encouraged only by the refinement of human powers, and which is the very breath of life for socialism. Without it, the relatively rich resources of science and education in our country have remained almost without effect on the actual development of society.

If we want our new model of socialism to be in line with the modern trend of civilization, *viz.* with the scientific and technical revolution, we must put our faith in the type of man with high intellectual attainments, well-developed sensually and emotionally, possessed of a dynamic will and sensitive to the human significance of things. We must open our doors wide to everyone able to create this kind of wealth and pass it on to others.

We must rely on the free, autonomous and perfectly untrammelled progress of science and research, confident that the relation between science and the working-class movement is one neither of subordination nor of compromise. The more forthrightly science marches ahead, free from all pre-conception, the closer it harmonizes with society's interests. A scientifically managed society, where scientific insights are brought to bear at every point that is decisive for the future – only such a society deserves to be called socialist.

We must rely, too, on a native blossoming of art, nourished from springs of free creativity and protected by the autonomy of culture – by complete freedom of artistic creation, that is, and a universal right of access to things of cultural value. Only that society can be called socialist which appreciates the role of art and defends it both from bureaucratic interference and from commercial narrow-mindedness.

We must rely on a flourishing and expanding educational system calculated to bring out the talents of every member of society and to remain at his disposal all his life. This should assure us, as a socialist country, of an enormous advantage through the quantity and quality of school training we can provide.

Finally, we must look in our socialist endeavours for paths that will open up the whole stage of life to cultural influence: our work-sites and our homes, our places of recreation and means of transport, our social life and our personal relations, our thoughts and our behaviour, every aspect of our existence where it is possible to achieve some success, however slight, in the inward and outward liberation of man.

6. THE ROLE OF THE COMMUNIST PARTY IN THE MODEL OF DEMOCRATIC SOCIALISM

In bringing a democratic, humanitarian model of socialism into being an indispensable mission awaits that Marxist-Leninist party which is able to establish and develop the model on scientific lines and to rally the majority of society in support of it. We do not hesitate to say that we shall try and ensure that our own Party plays such a role and wins the trust and recognition of the whole country for its efforts. To do this, of course, our Party must undergo a profound rebirth. Its outward image and its internal activities must be purged of all bureaucratic lees. It must re-emerge as a movement striving before the eyes of society toward ends universally agreed upon. It must cease to be an institution of power, dictating every step taken by every member of society.

At its very inaugural congress our Party wrote into its programme the aim of being not merely a political party in the traditional sense, but 'the vanguard of a new life'. Though originally it claimed to represent only one social class, our Party is transforming itself, in accordance with the changes taking place in the structure of society, into the *avant-garde* of modern progress, into an alliance of all those creative forces in society which support the socialist and communist programme and are able to contribute to its fulfilment. Yet the Communist Party does not for one moment cease to be the defender of the working man's essential interests.

As the pioneer of democratic socialism our Party strives unceasingly to maintain a position in our political system which will enable the exercise of power to be controlled by a system of partnership and balance, of competition between ideas and personalities, and which at the same time affords the best guarantee against any throwback to reactionary policies. In addition to its traditional political activity the Party is also a pioneer in furthering self-government by democratic institutions whose private activity must no longer be bound by Party regulations.

In this concept of socialism the Party's status is based on the assumption that there will be an investigation into the principles of the Party's expansion and methods as they developed in an age where the Party was a tightly-knit body struggling for power against its class opponent. First of all, a thoroughgoing democratization of the Party will be needed: conditions must be created for genuine exchange of views within the Party; members must have the right to hold and defend their own opinions; a minority must have the right to try, before the eyes of the whole Party, to become a majority; and there must be a democratic selection of senior officials, who should not be permanent professional functionaries but men commissioned by the communist movement, taking turns in office, and chosen from the ranks of able members enjoying moral credit and maximum public prestige. Secondly, the Party must acquire a scientific attitude to modern discoveries; its information network must be turned into an up-to-date instrument used by the Party in coming to its decisions. The *apparat* must not make decisions itself but be a professional staff engaged in skilled executive work.

If the Party is to undergo constant self-renewal, so as to provide a continuous stimulus toward socialist advance, it must overcome its traditional programmatic weaknesses and formulate aims and perspectives transcending the horizons of the present and the immediate future. It must offer society a long-term programme, tying the new model of socialism to the insights of modern science and to the totality of experience won by the worldwide socialist movement, putting it into a broad communist context and presenting the public with a humane variant of contemporary civilization.

Despite some promising starts made at the beginning of its existence and then again in the thirties and after the liberation, our Party has never had a programme of its own. This fact must be seen as an anomaly, liable to introduce arbitrary elements into public life as well as into the work of the Party itself. It tends to conserve old-fashioned notions of socialism, to blind members' eyes to what is really socialist, what arose from the exigencies of the age, and what is a distortion of socialist thinking.

The elaboration of a new Party programme must therefore be seen as an integral part of the rebirth of socialism and of the renewal of the Party. We should not, however, dictate a ready-made blueprint for society to follow, but simply initiate the public creation of a new programme on the basis of the Party's suggestions and of competition between different ideas. We propose that, once a draft has been prepared in co-operation with the scientific and cultural communities at large, a long period of discussion should follow inside the Party and among the general public with a view to approving a new programme by the fifteenth Party Congress. (Even this, however, should not be considered a closed concept, for further debate and consideration of any necessary additions and amendments ought to feature prominently on the agenda of every subsequent Congress.)

*

In trying to outline a model of socialism appropriate to our own conditions we have started from the assumption that in Czechoslovakia socialism can be strong and attractive only if both our nations find in it a means of self-fulfilment, a continuation of their own traditions and a sound answer to the problems which impinge on contemporary man everywhere and provoke such uneasiness and ferment in the world.

At the same time we must realize how exposed and difficult our position is in the heart of Europe, at the crossing of diverse historic and cultural paths, amidst the struggle between opposing political and social systems, between capitalism and socialism. We regard it as our paramount duty in the spirit of internationalism to establish socialism firmly and ineradicably in this country, making it a true fatherland for every patriot and an attractive picture of modern society for every working man, every man of culture in the world. For all that, we do not regard this model of socialism as an example to put before other nations for imitation. If there is anything of general value in the special conditions and historic traditions of our people, anything analogous to the conditions and traditions of other nations, those nations will discover it for themselves without our instruction or advice.

III The Party's Main Political Tasks in the Immediate Future

1. THE UNITY OF SOCIAL GROUPS IN CZECHOSLOVAKIA

The new model of socialism which the Party is starting to work on is not a mere abstract reversal of the deformed and bureaucratic pre-January model. Nor is it a mere application to our context of trends observed elsewhere. In all fundamental issues it is a response to the clearly expressed interests and needs of our people and of the various social groups.

At present, however, these interests conflict with one another. The development of society since January has naturally emphasized criticism and exposure of past mistakes from the standpoint of the various groups' needs and interests. The declaration of heterogeneous and scattered interests predominates, and this at a time when the economy is in very severe straits and there is in practice no way of satisfying these multifarious interests except by partial repayment of the greatest debts.

What political attitude should the Party adopt in such a situation? As the ruling party, the Czechoslovak Communist Party feels a multiple responsibility for the present state of affairs and for the future progress of society. Together with other elements in the National Front it intends to promote further development by securing the elimination of bureaucratic control of society through regulations, the thorough democratization of our political set-up and the involvement of every citizen in the democratic solution of public

H 217

issues, both economic and political. At the same time it will endeavour to see that the most urgent needs of various groups are gradually met in proportion as we achieve economic results. But it is a precondition for this that instead of the present welter of disparate interests a will to negotiate and unify should in time emerge, a willingness for mutual agreements and compromises so as to facilitate the creation of a plan for the progressive satisfaction of the most pressing requirements. (This indeed is the social *raison d'être* of the National Front as a political organization adapted for coping with the confrontation of special interests and the search for adequate overall solutions.)

We must expect the implementation of the economic reforms and the introduction of a system of enterprise self-management to have particularly profound effects on social relationships. A certain separation of economics from politics, inevitable when the production sphere, and to a certain extent the individual enterprises, are being made autonomous; the transformation of enterprises into large social units with their own independent life; all these things will raise serious problems for the organization of society, methods of social integration and so on.

When we set about democratizing our economic and social life we shall also have to reckon with a certain reasonable expansion of private economic activity, especially in the area of services, crafts and retail shops, and we shall obviously allow private farming to continue wherever it has survived.

Progress in the social field should also be linked with the elimination on principle of egalitarianism and incompetent management in favour of personal stakes in the success of an enterprise and efficient management. Economic problems should be tackled in such a way as gradually to overcome those social barriers that keep the system from progressing, and to attain a level of prosperity that will guarantee more rapid and more lasting satisfaction of public needs. In a democratic system this can be done only by setting the whole issue before the public and before the National Front, and working out an economic and social policy for the whole nation and the whole State that will systematically get rid of the evil legacy of previous egalitarian policies.

The key to solving all our major social problems lies in our efforts to achieve a synthesis of democratic and of rational, specialist management, both for the economy and for society in general.

These guidelines of Party policy, if they are accepted by the National Front and supported by the public both through elections and in daily practice, could in the course of a few years gradually ensure the satisfaction of the most urgent needs of the main social groups, who in a democratic system will in any case possess the instruments for defending their interests directly.

The *workers*, as the most numerous force in society, will gain through democratization the decisive say in the fashioning of our society, to which they are entitled as producers of the bulk of our material goods. Freedom of speech, assembly and association will enable them to familiarize themselves objectively with the complex issues of modern life and to add their weight to the right side of the scales. Freed from bureaucracy, the trade unions will be a powerful weapon for the defence of workers' rights, making gradual wage improvements possible in the hardest-hit categories and facilitating genuine improvement of the conditions they work and live in. Workers' councils will give qualified spokesmen of their class an opportunity really to influence the progress of their enterprises. A reasonable economic policy, supported by communists and carried out by the government, can improve the status of qualified workers and all staff engaged in efficient production. At the same time, communists in the government, in the enterprises and in the National Committees will see to it that employment is assured and that labour tied down in inefficient production is enabled to transfer smoothly to other places of work.

The *farmers* are already creating within the National Front a professional and political organization which will enhance their impact on public life. Measures are under way which will give equal status and equal security to farmers and to industrial workers. Our Party members will win acceptance for an integrated agricultural policy designed gradually to make farming a prosperous and attractive economic activity.

What the *intelligentsia* will particularly gain from the new policy is a proper measure of political freedom. The Party is giving up for good the practice of issuing directives in the fields of science, technology and the arts. It is abandoning promotion ceilings for noncommunists in specialist and managerial posts. It expects to see a considerable increase in the proportion of qualified people in responsible jobs. The large degree of autonomy to be accorded to economic and cultural institutions will enable specialists and managerial personnel to display more initiative. The incomes policy we are pursuing will in the first place eliminate the most crass of the remaining cases of discrimination against particular sections of the intelligentsia and ensure a more rapid alignment of pay rises in the centrally-determined salary sector with pay rises in industry, and then proceed toward a genuine differentiation in favour of skilled and complicated work. The Party will pay special attention to finding favourable solutions for the problems of teachers, university students and the schools. All this will give gradual expression to the Party's correct attitude to the intelligentsia as a numerous section of the public entitled to fair treatment and critically important for the progress of the country.

The Party will afford full support to qualified and conscientious personnel in the administrative and economic fields in the Party *apparat*, National Committees and mass organizations, and likewise to the judiciary, security and armed forces. It will make it its task to explain to all workers the significance of their work. It will favour the democratic and legally executed removal from their ranks of all those who have committed grave wrongs in the past. In cases where it may be necessary to dispense with employees who are insufficiently qualified or have become redundant in the course of trimming down overstaffed areas, the Party will urge that this be done in a humane manner with minimal disruption and with the same social protection for those concerned as in the case of other workers who change their jobs.

In its economic policy the Party envisages a rapid expansion in the spheres of health and welfare services, retail trade, catering, the tourist industry and all material and cultural *services*. This will require the provision of suitable working and social conditions in all these branches. In craft production, catering and service trades the Party will favour the expansion of communal, co-operative and small-scale individual enterprise.

The Party will actively support democratic solutions for problems of Czech-Slovak *national relations*, based on the federal principle of free mutual agreement on rules of co-existence that respect the interests of both sides. It will also promote constitutional guarantees for the free development of the minorities and for due consideration of the specific problems of Moravia and Silesia within the Czech part of the Federation.

In conjunction with the *youth* organizations the Party hopes to stimulate the drafting and acceptance of a basic complex plan for integrating the young into society in ways appropriate to them. The key concept here is that of youth as an active legal subject, endowed with full rights, and already playing a part in transforming society according to its own ideas. As well as dealing with organizational issues (a differentiated youth organization; co-operation with, and representation in, the National Front; parliamentary representation for the young, and so on) we shall also have to create an infrastructure covering, for example, a State programme of social and financial aid for the young; reform of the school system so as to give the young better and more differentiated vocational training; economic and organizational guarantees that qualifications will not be wasted; suitable conditions for sports, tourism and cultural activity; and opportunities for experience abroad. The basic pre-condition for youth's lasting support for socialism and the Party is, of course, the Party's whole advance to a new, up-to-date, democratic and humane model of socialism, which young people will certainly want to support.

In the spirit of the Action Programme the Party hopes gradually to tackle the oppressive economic and social problems of the *aged sector* of the population.

The Party endorses the demands of *womenfolk* as expressed in the Women's League Action Programme. As in the case of young people's interests, here too the Party will support the drafting and implementation of a complex programme for ensuring women equal rights in employment, in wage apportionment, in public life, in the expansion of services and in production for the household.

These new directions in the Party's policy require a newly formulated attitude to the revision of the political system and to economic and cultural policy.

2. EVOLUTION OF THE POLITICAL SYSTEM

(i) After the January plenum of the Central Committee and the acceptance of the Action Programme there began what was virtually a qualitative reform of the political system. The previous system by which monopolistic centres of political power were formed through the fusion of Party and State organs has been rocked to its foundations. This is in general accord with the needs of society, for under the old system there was a very inadequate impact on the decision-making process of the various interests, needs and opinions of different groups, even though the structure of society was already socialist; and scientific and professional analyses of problems earned equally short shrift. Indeed, the old system led to arbitrary decisions and to a progressive accumulation of unsolved disputes – economic, social and political – between groups. If we are to avoid a return to that state of affairs, a prospect which would provoke domestic political conflict in itself, we must evolve a qualitatively new political system.

(ii) From the standpoint of *practical* political developments we must regard the first two or three years, say from 1968 to 1970, as a period of *transition* to the new system. (A broad theoretical design has been outlined above in the passages dealing with Czechoslovakia's specific model of socialism.)

It is possible for this transition to have the character of a political *reform*, not of a mere destruction of all the institutions and organic links of the previous system. Briefly, the object of this reform is to bring about a political system that suits our conditions by combining the principles of *formal* democracy (i.e. equal political rights and freedom for all, representative machinery, more than one party, power divided and controlled, legal guarantees for civic freedoms and constraints upon the authorities, etc.) with the principle of subjecting policy to the influence of the largest social group. (This latter will mean granting influence over the State to the organizations of the principal interest groups – the Farmers' Union, Youth League, Women's League, etc. – instead of giving the political parties the sole right to represent them. It also involves various forms of enterprise self-management and of self-government at local and district level, and so on.)

The intention is that the system should in this way ensure a hearing for the wishes of social minorities (wishes which may, as when they concern, for example, scientific progress and educational levels, be of long-term importance for the whole country) while also ensuring that no political decision, especially one affecting the power-structure, is made against the wishes of the largest section of society, *viz.* the industrial, agricultural and other groups of the 'working masses'.

(iii) Political reform as described above would have to go through several stages.

– 1 –The *first stage*, based on implementation of the Action Programme, has in practice taken up the whole period until the Fourteenth Congress. It can be summarized as follows:

(*a*) Express *condemnation* of the main features of the old political system, with monopoly of power invested in a State-Party centre, and stating of the demand for a *qualitative* reconstruction of the whole set-up.

(*b*) Formulation in politically binding terms of the principle of *non-substitution of Party bodies for State and social bodies*.

(*c*) Establishment of the National Front as the forum where policy is formed by *agreement* between the various interests, which are able through the Front (including its political parties) to express themselves in institutional form.

(*d*) Formulation of the demand for elimination of old illegalities and creation of *legal safeguards* for democracy: freedom of expression (and abolition of preliminary censorship); freedom of association and assembly; decentralization, division and control of power, involving the reorganization of the security and other departments of the Ministry of the Interior, banning of any private 'political police', ensuring independence of the courts, establishment of control over government and parliament, acceptance of the principle that State organs derive their authority from the electors, and so on.

(*e*) Formulation of the demand for *democratic administration of socialist enterprises* as an element of self-management outside the mechanisms of political democracy proper.

(*f*) Formulation of the demand for a *political role for the trade unions* under socialist conditions.

Despite some shortcomings, arguments and inconsistencies, the *implementation* of the Party's Action Programme has created a new political reality in this country within six months. The idea of a qualitative reconstruction of the political system, under such labels as 'democratic socialism' or 'the process of renewal', has seized the imagination of the public at large, making impossible any return to the pre-January state of affairs without a profound political and social crisis.

The following facts illustrate the changes in *political reality* that have occurred to date:

(*a*) Discredited representatives of the old system have been *re-*

moved from key positions of political authority and have no immediate hope of returning to the political stage.

(*b*) Legal norms have been promulgated for rehabilitation inside and outside the courts, and the Party is completing its total dissociation from the deformations in question (including the involvement of former Party leaders).

(*c*) *The National Front is beginning to function genuinely* as a platform for democratic statement and for the confrontation and mutual opposition of interests in the course of making political decisions; this has involved reactivating the political parties in the Front, and the main organizations representing political interest-groups. (In saying this we have of course assumed that the Statutes of the National Front will be drafted by September and that these will permit the component bodies in the Front to play a practical role in politics.) The interest-group organizations are already starting to act independently.

(*d*) Freedom of expression in the press and on radio and television already exists and is serving as an instrument by which public opinion influences political life and vice versa. The state of political lethargy has given way to one where the most varied sectional interests are politically active and exert pressures which are often disorganized and are all the more powerful for representing a reaction against the past.

(*e*) Freedom of association and assembly has been legalized (i.e. will be by the date of the Fourteenth Congress) in accordance with the principles of political democracy (with the sole restriction on political rights of conformity to the National Front platform).

(*f*) Certain measures for the decentralization of power in the executive organs of the State have already been carried out, especially with regard to the repressive powers of the police. (In this field, however, developments have not yet even reached the stage envisaged by the Action Programme with regard to institutions or to personnel replacement, and the same applies to the judiciary.)

Furthermore, four changes of cardinal importance have become political realities without, so far, any legal underpinning:

(1) The Party in practice no longer uses the methods of retaining loyalty familiar from the old command system, at least not in

fields critically important for fulfilling the Action Programme in the respects mentioned above.

(2) The question of a federal settlement of Czech-Slovak relations has been settled for political purposes beyond question.

(3) It is politically accepted that *elections*, whether for parliament or within non-State organizations including the Communist Party, must not be a mere formality concealing the appointment to office of persons really selected outside the electoral process.

(4) In the socialist enterprises a system of democratic organs of management, the workers' councils, is being inaugurated in an orderly manner, while the trade unions are becoming an independent political force: i.e. elements of self-government are being evolved which go beyond the classic framework of formal democracy in the sphere of collective work. The continuation of this process is already guaranteed by government measures.

After six months, then, the implementation of the Party's Action Programme is completely satisfactory as regards the qualitative reform of the political system. It is accompanied also by certain undesirable tendencies, of which the principal ones are these:

(*a*) The loosening of the ideological keystone of the old system of centralized, *dirigiste* decision-making in politics is not yet matched by sufficiently rapid growth of a new concept. Thus we find sectarian-dogmatist reactions to developments that follow the spirit of the Action Programme, and at the same time tendencies to *idealize* purely formal democracy such as even bourgeois societies are familiar with; to seek solutions to problems in the mere transfer of loyalties by formal democratic procedure; to ignore in such cases the real interrelations of social interests, and so forth. There are also signs of ideological conflict within the Party.

(*b*) The inability of some local units in the system to conduct policy in the new fashion leads to situations where old loyalties have ceased to be effective before new loyalties are created. (This applies in the Party, in the machinery of State, in the National Front, in the mass organizations, and so on.) Hence, for example, a certain haphazardness in the expression of various socio-political and group interests and in attempts to institutionalize them; hence also scepticism and apathy in the attitudes of certain groups whose interests are at odds with any realistic prospects for the development of an independent political system, or run ahead of such prospects. This transitional state of affairs also provides fertile ground for the possible growth of disintegrative tendencies which may then be exploited in anti-communist or anti-socialist directions.

(*c*) Implementation of the Action Programme's political targets, however thorough, cannot alone satisfy social and economic demands to the extent, or at the speed, necessary for resolving all the accumulated conflicts of the past. This again gives scope to disintegrative tendencies both from the 'Left' and the 'Right'. But such tendencies cannot be countered by a mere return to the *status quo*, only by the further extension of effectively functioning relations in a *qualitatively new* political system.

(*d*) With the very rapid tempo of development so far, it is not possible adequately to foresee *which* social groups, with their own political interests, will emerge from the restructuring of the old system as permanent forces, what permanent weight they will carry and what long-term interests will accordingly exert pressure on political events. Opening the door to a *possible plurality* of political subjects produces a state of affairs where the class composition and economic background of some of these subjects cannot be quite precisely gauged. Hence a growing atmosphere of *nervousness* arises whenever ill-defined interest-groups and political pressures show themselves, especially if they bear some relation to pre-1948 conflicts which belong to a past era but could still be resurrected in favourable conditions.

These generally formulated facts about our political life since January (or April) 1968 take dozens of different forms in everyday reality. Thus we may find the composition of some elected body preventing it from fulfilling its new function. We may find the press frequently acting, not as the 'seventh Great Power' but as the only one, as a kind of shadow cabinet. We find Party organs and officials, for all their general acceptance of the new policy, succumbing to nervousness in certain questions. Doubt arises over the policies and long-term backing of the non-communist parties in the National Front. We see organizations like the KAN [Club for Committed Non-party Men] coming into being. Inside the Communist Party disagreements continually crop up between opposing groups over a variety of topics. The communist intelligentsia shows a tendency to extremism, including idealization of bourgeois political forms, while the working class feels a certain mistrust toward the prospects of financial security. And so forth.

In the *international* field, the Action Programme policy comes up against a complex situation, especially in relations with those socialist countries which have acute domestic problems of their own (often of a kind similar to those we experienced before January 1968) and where the 'Czechoslovak events' accordingly arouse certain fears as a factor that might influence their development on lines not envisaged by their own Party and State leaders. There are also justified fears in such quarters lest those unfavourable factors which are really to be found in our case might not acquire such strength as to produce developments like Hungary's in 1956. *The importance of paying attention to international reactions on these lines is a characteristic feature of the political facts of life today.*

Nevertheless we are now, as the Fourteenth Congress opens, at a stage where *the qualitative reconstruction of the political system is on the whole proceeding successfully,* and the political reality that surrounds us is different from that which we knew in January 1968. The line laid down in the Action Programme is being pursued, and it is up to the Fourteenth Congress to extend it into an integrated concept of political reform capable of being completed in the course of some two years and then anchored in a new Constitution.

- 2 –The *second stage* of development should start after the Fourteenth Congress and should exhibit the following stages.

(a) Acceptance in September 1968 of the Constitutional Law on the National Front, giving it the legal status of an organization outside which no political parties, or organizations fulfilling the functions of political parties, may arise or continue.

(b) Renewal by the end of 1968, through special congresses, creation of federal integrating bodies etc., of the principal political *components* of the National Front – trade unions; organizations of collective farmers, intelligentsia, youth, women; political parties, and so on.

(c) Definite establishment on this basis by the end of the year of the National Front as an *inwardly pluralistic* forum for the creation of a political line *outwardly monopolistic* in accordance with the Constitutional Law. Securing of a definite mandate from the whole country for a National Front established in this way, e.g. by a referendum to entrust the National Front with the task of organizing elections to the new representative bodies, etc.

(*d*) Acceptance of a Constitutional Law on the Federalization of the Republic by 28 October, either in its entirety or at least complete in its main clauses.

(*e*) Completion of elections to the new, federalized, representative bodies at parliamentary and National Committee level in the spring of 1969.

(*f*) Declaration for political purposes of an entire period – perhaps 1969–71 – as 'constitution-forming' (and application of the same term to the new Federal Assembly, assuming that there will be only a single Constitution) so as to preserve the idea of *transition and experiment* while lending to this period at the same time the necessary character of *stability and legality*.

(*g*) By late 1970 or early 1971 a new *Czechoslovak Constitution*, anchoring the new political system with a reasonable prospect of stability over fifteen to twenty years.

(*h*) Holding of the Fifteenth Congress of the Party at the same time with a view to agreeing on its programme for the same period of fifteen to twenty years.

The main practical problems to be expected in this political phase following the Fourteenth Congress can be summarized as follows. (We leave on one side the questions concerning federation, which will be the subject of special treatment in the Congress documents and will be considered in general terms after a joint session of the Presidia of the Central Committees of the Czechoslovak Communist Party and the Slovak Communist Party respectively.)

(*A*) *Status and development of the Communist Party within the political system*

The composition of the Party, its relations with the various social groups, and so on, are today still under the direct influence of the old command system. It can be briefly stated that the Party is *ageing* (nearly 25 per cent of its members are retired) and is not attracting into its ranks enough of the *intelligentsia*, especially of the scientific and technological intelligentsia. It is poorly represented in collective agriculture, where as many as 4 per cent of Party members are pensioners.

The links between State and Party under the old system have produced, moreover, a situation where the Party's working methods, structure, etc., are ill-adapted to political work outside itself, i.e. *vis-à-vis* the mass of non-communists; instead, the Party is tied to the use of organs of administrative power with a tradition of simply 'handing down' the Party line, so that even in present conditions it is still too obsessed with its internal affairs. The existence of groups within the Party representing different viewpoints and, to some extent, different social interests is a plain fact, and progress with the new political system promotes confrontation between these groups. (These groups are not necessarily fractions in the strict sense; a group only becomes a fraction when it adopts its own tactics, discipline and organization.)

The Fourteenth Congress must therefore make a start on solving these outstanding problems of practical politics:

(1) The Party must in the first place face the problem of integrating its own highly-qualified minority, i.e. the Party intelligentsia, into the whole Party mechanism. There are two aspects here: bringing this minority into the process of deciding the Party line, and employing it adequately in Party offices, particularly at the highest level such as Central Committee membership.

Maintenance of the Party's unity will depend to a considerable extent on finding a solution to this problem, and an incorrect choice could in the present situation greatly increase the danger of a split.

This serious state of affairs results from incorrect Party policies pursued above all during the period 1956 to 1968, when certain groups of the Party intelligentsia and certain age groups were relegated to the periphery of Party life. The inner leadership of the Party represented an extreme example of the Party's fundamental 'generation problem', i.e. its ageing character. The Party's intelligentsia was largely made use of as an ancillary *aktif* which offered its thoughts and conclusions as raw material for the decision-making process, but was excluded from the process itself, where decisions were then reached arbitrarily and undemocratically. This is why a part of the communist intelligentsia even today feels radical distrust toward the Party machine and its leading officials, including those at Central Committee level.

The Fourteenth Congress must approach this problem along two lines. First, it must formulate general principles of Party policy on this issue, stating the problem and outlining its solution. But, secondly, the Congress must in itself constitute a beginning in the integration of the Party intelligentsia into the process of carrying out Party policy. In other words it is essential that adequate representation both of the intelligentsia and of the younger generation groups within the Party should be assured on those bodies which are to be elected at this Congress.

If the Congress were to fail to produce a satisfactory solution there would be an inevitable continuation of the process by which the Party intelligentsia and young members find a stronger community of interests with fellow-members of their own respective social groups outside the Party than with the Party as a political organism *in toto*. There would be a danger of the ageing process going further, and of the composition of the Party continuing to fall behind the long-term needs of society in its proportion of highly-qualified personnel.

(2) The Congress must issue guidelines for the development of the Party's corps of officials at all levels so that they will be fit to take part in a political system in which administrative management by command has ceased to be the main method of deciding things. This applies to future relations between the Party's central *apparat* and its branch officials, to relations between State and economic officials and self-management bodies such as workers' councils, and to relations with the trade unions and other mass organizations.

A special complex of problems is presented by the concept of the National Front. The existence within it of non-communist parties makes it urgently necessary that the Communist Party, too, should become an independently functioning one on the classical model. This of course runs counter in general to the Marxist working hypothesis that the Party can be progressively transformed from the classical type of political group to the point where it fades away amid a socialist society. It is clearly impossible for the Congress to deal with these issues in depth; that will perhaps have to await the drafting of the Party programme. For practical purposes, however, throughout the whole period in which a plurality of parties operates within the National Front, we shall have to assume that the Communist Party will exhibit a number of features characteristic of classical parties and that it will be necessary to improve intra-party relationships and methods of political operation, to create the Party's own political strategy and tactics, and so on.

This epoch-making fact of life in our own special political development must be taken into account in applying the principle of 'opening the Party's windows to the public'. It will clearly lead to a number of specific problems alien to political systems of the Soviet or, for example, Yugoslav type. The Congress should draw attention to this question and give direct instructions for its theoretical and political examination in depth.

(3) A related issue is the need to ensure the *dominant political influence of the Party* under the new system in two ways. The first is by impressing society through the attractive, militant and persuasive nature of the Party programme with its various practical proposals and political ideas. But secondly the Party's leading role must be secured institutionally. This would be simpler if there were no other political parties. Since, however, there are, it must be assumed even in the longer run (i.e. including the period of validity of a new Constitution) that the loss by the Communist Party of its majority positions in State bodies and the National Front would in effect mean their passing to another party, so that there would be a revolution in the power structure. In theory such a state of affairs need not necessarily jeopardize the development of socialism and communism. But no responsible observer could regard this as a realistic speculation for the foreseeable period of five years or so. It will therefore be necessary to ensure by a complex of well thought-out measures that relations within the National Front, and the system of elections, continue to guarantee the hegemony and privileges of the Communist Party so that the Party shall not find itself in a minority position in the National Front or in the representative assemblies, i.e. the Federal and National parliaments (though this need not apply to local National Committees).

(*B*) *The concept of the National Front*

For reasons already discussed, the politically realistic concept of the National Front is that of an organization outside which no political party can operate, while at the same time it includes the main political-interest organizations as components with the same rights as the political parties proper.

The law of association would of course also allow the formation of

231

open clubs and interest-group organizations of a non-political character and purpose *outside* the National Front.

The fundamental political issue which has to be decisively settled at the Fourteenth Congress is whether the new political system in Czechoslovakia can, or cannot, be a so-called 'open' one, allowing the 'free play' of political forces.

For the transitional period up to the passing of the new Constitution the answer is clearly that it cannot. Without the assured monopoly of the National Front it would be impossible to rule out the danger of a conflict over political power aimed against the hegemony of the Communist Party. In fact such a conflict would seem highly probable.

It is only on the basis of practical experience in 1969 and 1970 that it will be possible to judge whether the above concept of the National Front must necessarily be incorporated in a constitutional solution intended to be viable for ten or fifteen years. The decision must largely depend on the following alternatives.

(*a*) If the system of several political parties within the framework of a National Front were to 'catch on' in such a way that the non-communist parties formed a practical alternative to the communist hegemony, then the concept of the National Front outlined above would have to continue in force.

(*b*) If on the other hand developments proceeded not in that direction but towards according a greater influence to the political interest-group organizations and to the self-management principle, then it would be possible to entertain an alternative constitutional solution. (This might be the inclusion in the Constitution of criteria for the existence of a party, and the creation and dissolution of parties could be decreed by a constitutional court.)

It is in any case essential to regard the National Front as an open-ended organization, that is, to make an expansion of the structure of political organizations possible while integrating them on a common platform. On this view the National Front must be able to exclude an organization (including a political party) from its ranks if it consistently deviated from the common platform, violated the internal order of the Front or otherwise acted against the political purpose of this institution.

The problems attending the development, structure and practical political functions of the National Front can only achieve definitive theoretical solution after some experience has been gained during the transition period of the next year or two, and the same applies to the operation of the political interest-group organizations included in it. There will be many developmental changes in its internal structure – processes of decentralization, differentiation of interests and also new cases of integration, as in the new federal organizations of young people, intellectuals, etc. It should be the policy of the Communist Party to create room for experiment and then to press in good time for the overall concept of the National Front as a force for political integration.

(C) The problems of representative democracy

Apart from those questions of socialist parliamentary life already raised in the Action Programme, such as the independence of representative bodies and their control function over the executive organs of government, it will be necessary at the Fourteenth Congress to deal with certain further practical issues. (That of federalization, as already said, will not be covered here.)

(1) Both federal and national parliaments are organs of political representation. It is therefore necessary to define the ways in which various interests can be reflected in these fora, where the creation of the *State's political line* takes place.

Parliament's function in a new political system based on the concept of pluralism restricted by the National Front framework is reflected in the presence on its benches of spokesmen of the main political organizations, both parties and political interest-group organizations.

For the transitional period, however, it remains to decide whether the system of representation should give priority to (or help to keep alive) the plurality of political parties and organizations in the first place, or whether it should limit its importance by introducing in some suitable form the direct representation of *social professions.*

The general need to combine the principles of parliamentary democracy and of the direct political impact of social interests would be institutionally served by a structure of federal and national representative bodies based on the *multi-cameral* system.

Parliament itself would possess all legislative and control powers.

233

But it might be partially restricted in the exercise of these powers by an obligation to respect the views of special 'ancillary' chambers corresponding to the main social divisions of labour and consisting of representatives chosen not in territorial constituencies but in their *places of work*.

Federal and national parliaments might include three such chambers:

- an Industrial Chamber elected by factories, industrial and trading enterprises, etc.;
- an Agricultural Chamber elected by the socialist agricultural units (collective and State farms); and
- a Social Services Chamber, elected by institutions concerned with public health, education, culture, etc.

These chambers would have special powers, e.g. to send back draft bills on subjects in their own field for further discussion, or to exercise surveillance over State and economic administration in their own spheres. The 'work-site' method of election would ensure observance of the principle that those who decide State policy in the direction of this or that sphere of activity will be drawn from the ranks of men engaged in such activity, will be responsible to them, are subject to their control and can be dismissed from office by their votes. This would introduce into the work of the representative bodies an element linking democracy with the principle of 'having an expert at the wheel'. It would also forge an embryonic link between the parliaments and the self-management bodies on the work-sites, especially in socialist enterprises.

[NOTE: Doubt was thrown on this idea during working discussions because of the difficulty of applying it simultaneously with federalization; federalization is in itself a very hard task and might be made much more complex still by the introduction of this untried factor. It was also suggested that a well-developed and functioning system of self-management must first be shown to exist 'at shop-floor level' before experiments could be made in applying it in the supreme organs of state. Against this it was urged that this idea too should be 'tried out' before things were finally settled by a new Constitution, i.e. *during* the great federal reorganization and simultaneously with the enterprise self-management experiment.]

(2) The *electoral system* must be sufficiently settled for the Party to be able to come forward with a clear concept immediately after the

Fourteenth Congress. The formalization of elections under the old system cannot be maintained and is incompatible both with the changes already effected in the political system and with present public opinion in Czechoslovakia. The Party's line on this issue should

- embody the existing constitutional formula of universal and equal suffrage, and of direct and secret balloting (secrecy being treated not as a right but as a duty of every elector); and
- revise the procedure for electoral preparations in clear legal terms, clarifying especially who is entitled to propose candidates (at present this might well be the National Front as described above, i.e. its component organizations); who is entitled to make the final selection of candidates whose names will be included on the voting slips (this might be done, perhaps, at National Front 'primaries', but in any case the present system of reaching 'agreement' on a single candidate at an electors' meeting must be abandoned); and how the actual allocation of mandates is to be carried out (i.e. the whole complex of technical problems concerning elections).

In many advanced capitalist countries the universal character of elections comes into conflict with the practical impossibility of achieving universality under the existing political constellation of powers. The electoral system, as part of the political behaviour of society, then tends more or less to maintain or reinforce the constellation ruling at the time.

In a socialist society, too, the electoral system is clearly part of the existing political pattern. Not even socialist conditions allow for the existence of an ideal system. But it is perfectly possible to work out an electoral model satisfying certain requirements under certain conditions, e.g. a given distribution of political strength, a given political situation, a given distribution of votes by various criteria, etc. These assumptions represent the dynamic element in the elections, on the basis of which the static factors can be determined. Of course, any notable deviation from the original assumptions may lead to a disfunction of the electoral system, i.e. to a result that diverges from the original intentions.

Any consideration of the electoral system in a socialist democracy must, then, have regard to the particular social and political conditions of the country involved. In discussing an electoral model for

Czechoslovakia we must start from consideration of the possible distribution of political strength and the existing political and State structure. We must also realize that there is no such thing as an ideal electoral system, but only an acceptable one.

The art of election-designing is to find a democratic balance between differentiation and integration. The existing system of single-mandate electoral districts can, of course, be democratized in various ways. But if we consider the characteristics of single-mandate districts we shall see that the present requirements of our society are better met by large districts voting for several Deputies at once.

Under present conditions in our country there can be no satisfactory electoral technique as long as the dogma of the absolute majority in its traditional, personal, form is retained as the cardinal principle. This Stalinist tradition is an anachronism in our present political structure and is incompatible with the ideas of socialist democracy. Yet while the process of democratization makes the old principle of absolute majority untenable, considerations of the political structure of the country and of the particular character of the present phase of democratization make the principle of relative majority unacceptable without manipulation.

If our electoral system is to express today's socialist democracy while maintaining a proper degree of integrating and consolidating influence over the political structure, then what has to be considered under present circumstances is a *combination of proportional representation and personal selection*.

This would mean in practical terms the following:

(*a*) The single list of National Front candidates would be retained.

(*b*) The list would enumerate candidates representing the various components of the Front – both parties and the main political organizations (trade unions, collective farmers, youth league, women's league).

(*c*) The elector would be obliged to make two choices:
  – the choice of a particular component as such, with all its candidates on the list; and
  – the choice of a fixed number of candidates (say for 25 per cent of the seats to be filled) by name as individuals, regardless of the chosen component.

(*d*) Candidates obtaining the requisite majority of votes as individuals are automatically elected.

(*e*) The remaining seats would be allocated in proportion to the votes received among the various components and the candidates put forward by them.

Such a system would in principle benefit whichever party or other National Front component was able to win most votes for its representatives as personalities, and also had its members included on the lists of candidates of the mass organizations. It would considerably favour such a party even if that party did not, as such, win an absolute majority in the constituency. If for example, the Communist Party as such secured only 30 to 35 per cent of votes, but also won say 3 out of a total of 15 mandates for communist candidates as individuals and also among the candidates standing for the mass organizations, then some 55 to 60 per cent of Deputies elected for the constituency would inevitably be communists.

One might also consider allowing 'independent' candidates, that is, granting the right to stand to anyone obtaining some minimum number of signatures of electors (say, 2,000) in support of his candidature. This, of course, would have to be considered in the light of contemporary political facts. (An asset might be seen in the possible splitting up of the anti-communist 'opposition', a defect in that such an institution could be exploited in an organized fashion by forces outside the National Front.)

[NOTE: Owing to the short time available for preparation, the following issues are ignored here which would have to be treated in any final draft: 1. Basic questions of the construction and activity of executive organs of the State and of the State administration, from the federal government down to district level. 2. Conceptual questions on the future of the National Committees, e.g. the effect of federation, the abolition of committees at regional level and the self-governing aspect of committees at town and village level.]

(*D*) *Principles of the creation of public opinion and its effect on political life*

A precondition for the active and democratic involvement of the whole country in solving social and political questions is a high availability of information, the confrontation of opinions, the open expression of views and their mutual communication. Without these a socialist democracy is unthinkable. Press, radio and television have the arduous task of providing one guarantee for the free development of a socialist society. Concern for the inalienable rights and duties of the mass-communication media is at the same time concern for the rights of the public. They are not and must not be restricted by open or covert censorship, but only by a sense of responsibility toward society and one's fellow-citizens, and by the activity of impartial courts in applying valid laws for the protection of the socialist and democratic basis of the State, its alliances and most essential secrets, and also for the protection of the individual's inviolability.

The mass-communication media both influence and reflect public opinion; they are a tribune for expressing attitudes and an institution specifically suited to exercise social control over the government and State authorities. In its broad sense an information system is complex, covering both the sources of information and its communication and distribution, facilities for access to it and its effect in society. Any tampering with one part of the information cycle, any reluctance to offer information, subjective interference with its communication or inattention to its public repercussions is a threat to the function of the media.

A differentiated press facilitates the formation of opinion and the defence of the interests of non-antagonistic social groups. The communist press has an exceptionally important role in the Party's political work. It has the function, in consonance with the Party Statutes, of implementing the principles of intra-Party democracy, of aiding public discussion of political issues and of actively influencing the Party's work in promoting a socialist society. As an integrating force the Party uses the press to make a differentiated appeal to different social groups. It supports the growth of the regional and local press, whose purpose is to activate the political life of the provinces, towns and villages.

The Party press is the tribune of the whole Party, and the Statutes define the responsibility of the editors to whom the immediate management of the press has been entrusted.

The television, radio and press agency are national institutions, and it follows from their monopolistic character that they should be run as such. They render due service to all sections of the community and so it is natural that their activities should be supervised by the bodies that represent the whole people.

Mass-communication media are immune from any censorship but subject to control by society. Their personnel take on a high moral responsibility, which the laws define only in general terms. In modern society the media exercise a highly effective form of influence. Freedom of expression is a universal civic right, and a sense of responsibility is part of the professional code of journalists and publicists.

Since the abolition of directive interference by the authorities with the prerogatives of the press, radio and television it has become increasingly important to ensure the continuous improvement of the media and of the work of those who look after them. It is up to political, economic and other public servants, as well as of the population at large, to learn to make the fullest use of the media.

(E) *Additions to the legal code*

In regard to legal policy the Fourteenth Congress should in general follow the line of the Action Programme and make quite clear the Party's attitude to the main legal reforms. The Party should

- urgently demand acceptance of the Law on Association and Assembly;
- urgently demand complete revision of the Press Law;
- take legal measures such as would together provide a genuine system of guarantees of the legality and constitutionality of all regulations having the force of law, and of the whole institutional aspect of the changing political system (including control by the courts of the State administration, and the establishment of a constitutional court);
- take legal measures appropriate to the concentration of authority in a single judicial branch, and designed to guarantee the *independence of the courts*. (Relations between the Public Prosecutor's Office and the courts should be defined with this aim.)

[NOTE: For questions concerning organs of self-government on work-sites (workers' councils in the enterprises) see the section on economic policy and control of the economy.]

[NOTE: The material dealing with the development of the political system is not, like the other sections, formulated as a draft resolution but as a series of theses for internal Party debate, especially with regard to the *Party's tactics*. After discussion in the Political Commission, then, the text will be amended in such a way that the approved alternatives can be effectively defended and expressed in a form suitable as a document for Congress delegates and as a draft resolution.]

3. OUTLINE OF THE PARTY'S ECONOMIC POLICY

Ultimate success for the new political line depends on success in the economic field – on our ability to elaborate and put into practice a new economic policy, ensuring adequate employment, a due measure of prosperity and fundamental social security for every citizen.

It is well known, from all the evidence about the present state and movement of our economy, that we are not managing to catch up with the more advanced European countries whose circumstances are comparable to ours. During the first half of this decade, in particular, we were unable even to keep pace with their rate of expansion of production forces and with their rising standard of living. The inappropriate structure of our production and of our new construction, with its disproportionate emphasis on increasing the production of capital goods, our antiquated system of administrative *dirigisme* and our inadequate efforts to stimulate the growth of socialist enterprise made it impossible for us to avoid falling behind.

The old management system also had a bad effect on relations between Czechs and Slovaks. For all the efforts made, we did not achieve our basic aims in the economic and social development of Slovakia and definite 'deformations' of socialism were to be found in this field too.

It nevertheless remains true that we have considerably increased our economic base and this will serve as a valuable reserve in our further growth, so that improved performance can finally have some effect.

Attempts to solve the economic situation by partial reforms, leaving intact the old social, political, and economic system with all its deformations, have proved vain. But the democratization process is capable of producing conditions basically more favourable, giving back to the human individual his role as the main productive force, rehabilitating an actively functional economic policy and expanding the ideas behind the individual reforms into a new, integrated concept.

Linking on, then, to the progressive economic ideas already developed during the pre-January period, the Communist Party proposes to draft in conjunction with the other parties and components of the National Front, and consistently to implement, a new economic policy based on the following aims:

1. Creation of a more bracing economic climate both for enterprises and for fund allocators, so as to stimulate faster and more efficient economic expansion.

2. Promotion of structural changes in harmony with the trends of the scientific and technological revolution and with the need effectively to integrate our economy into the worldwide economic complex as well as to exploit Czechoslovakia's own natural economic conditions.

3. Stabilization of the currency, renewal of the economic function of cash on the home and foreign markets, gradual achievement of convertibility for the *koruna* and expansion of markets, *viz.*:
   - the home and foreign currency market with a view to renewing the basis for objective economic calculation;
   - the investment and exchange market;
   - the consumer goods market by overcoming bottlenecks and ensuring the supply not only of basic consumer items but of housing, services and private cars;
   - the labour market as an instrument for changing the structure of wages, abolishing egalitarianism and transferring workers to desirable and efficient branches of production.

   In parallel with these efforts we should seek to revive the economic function of price with regard to world price levels and to introduce an effective price policy that takes account of desirable structural and scientific-technological changes in our economy.

4. Support for the efficient expansion of both our national economies under the conditions of federalization. In Slovakia we should seek to restructure the economy and increase its profitability by exploiting untapped resources and continue the process of economic equalization by fuller use of available labour, especially skilled labour.

5. Development of international economic and financial links; encouragement of commercializing, liberalizing and integrating efforts between enterprises in the various socialist countries, including capital transactions; strong encouragement of commercial relations with advanced industry in the capitalist countries, with emphasis on expansion of co-operation in the production, trade, financial and other fields including licensing arrangements (where we should play both active and passive roles).

6. Introduction of elements of democratization at both enterprise and national levels into the running of the economy, and preservation of distinct forms of enterprise under State, self-managing, communal, co-operative and small-scale private aegis.

7. Encouragement of socialist initiative and support for expertise, including that of qualified managerial and other senior personnel, as well as for greater variety and freedom of socialist enterprise.

8. Association of enterprises and employees with common interests in interest-groups, which should be given maximum scope for self-fulfilment.

9. Correct demarcation of relations between politics and economics, so that political organs do not interfere in specific economic decisions (especially at enterprise level). Creation of a favourable economic and socio-political atmosphere for socialist enterprise and for the effective functioning of the economic system.

10. Establishment of basic aims and priorities for a selective economic policy so that increased efficiency and consequent improvement of material and cultural levels become the paramount ends of economic policy; regard for the basic social security of the citizen even where structural changes are inevitable; and, in line with the policy of enhancing the employee's economic stake in his enterprise, furtherance of a wages policy which encourages the movement away from egalitarianism and seeks to reflect the individual's qualifications, performance and skill, as well as the standard of goods produced and the market demand for them.

*

What the Party stresses above all is the need to create political conditions favourable to a new economic policy. It will lend its support primarily to economic measures consonant with the permanent interests of the public and its various sections, though immediate needs are by no means to be ignored. However, our resources are not unlimited. The Party will work for scientific direction of the economy and oppose arbitrary methods both in theory and practice.

The State in its economic dealings will respect all the features of the new political system and create conditions favourable for integrating and co-operative processes within the federal framework. Leading positions in our economic life will be filled by experts without regard to nationality or political affiliation. Monopolistic tendencies, whether on the part of political parties, organizations or other groups, are quite alien to the democratic purpose of our new economic policy. There will be no constraints on the movement of labour.

The difficulty of shaping and implementing a new economic policy arises, of course, from the considerable economic imbalance which gives rise to inflationary pressures and is in turn exacerbated by social pressures and demands. We must embark on a realistic policy corresponding to the realities of the economic situation.

At the present time (1968) the economy is full of contradictions. On the one hand a moderately high growth-rate of production for consumers is being maintained, but incomes are rising at above-average rates. On the other hand the instruments of the New Economic System are not functioning completely and the uncompetitive climate on the production side is not helping greatly to intensify the utilization of production factors. Yet wage, investment and social pressures continue to rise. It is possibly true that with a stable investment flow and at least reasonable success in foreign trade the growth of non-production consumption may not lag behind that of national income. This last is not negligible (estimated figure for 1968, 5 to 6 per cent), but one cannot call it more than that and it is quite inadequate, of course, to satisfy the great backlog of demand for all kinds of goods.

Such is the complexity of the situation, and hence the need for different instruments to support the New Economic System in the government's economic guidelines. The connection is obvious: the better the enterprises cope with the demand for greater efficiency, the more there will be for the consumer to buy. Both economically and politically it is more correct and more acceptable to exert pressure on the producer than on the consumer. In either case there will be no lack of friction.

The success of the new economic policy depends on our ability to utilize the democratization process and its component elements so as to create the sort of political climate where the virtues of the policy can be applied to the restoration of economic balance, the encouragement of growth factors and the reorientation of the economy on to the road of dynamic expansion and prosperity. This, in the long run, will determine the success of the political path we have embarked upon and the final victory of the progressive forces.

[NOTE: The Editorial Commission considers that this section on the economic system and policy needs considerable revision and expansion. It is not the job of the Fourteenth Congress to formulate a long-term economic programme. Work on an integral concept of economic policy will proceed after the Congress. But what the Congress should do is adopt a view on some of the immediate problems of the present economic situation and prospects, of the further extension of the New Economic System, and of the bearing of economic policy on the interests of various social groups. The results of introducing the new system have so far failed to match the expectations of the economists. We have not yet seen a turn for the better in the achievement of economic efficiency, and the creation of economic control instruments alongside the general methods of centralist management is leaving the faults in the structure of production unaffected. The switch to a planned socialist market economy requires solution of the following problems in particular: the economic content of federalization; the designing of a socialist enterprise, and in particular of its collective organs, on lines appropriate to a regulated socialist market economy and compatible with democratic socialism; the relationship between the organs of enterprises and those of the central authorities; the main trends of economic policy; the scope for satisfying the immediate demands and interests of various sections of the public; and the preconditions for an improvement in material standards and the socialist way of life.

The economic part of the Congress documentation will also include a section on agricultural policy and the Party's attitude toward the farmers.]

4. MAIN TASKS IN THE FURTHERANCE OF SCIENCE, EDUCATION, CULTURE AND IDEOLOGY

In the present age we have to link the growth of society far more than before with the progress and exploitation of science, education and culture. In the past, the one-sided subjection of these fields to narrowly utilitarian principles of ideology led to a harmful underestimation of the special nature of creative work, to the hampering of cultural development and to a serious political crisis. This is why the Party acknowledges and guarantees freedom of thought, research, expression, creation and access to cultural values. The social status of science rises markedly in proportion as its application in every sphere of life becomes a basic prerequisite of social progress. The Party therefore deems it a task of high priority to create ever-increasing scope for creative scientific work and for the more timely and effective application of its significant results in society.

Opportunities for the expansion and utilization of scientific work were greatly restricted in the past by incorrect *dirigiste* methods of management. Warned by this experience, the Party wishes in future to accord to science a genuinely autonomous and special position and to reject any authoritarian interference which could produce new deformations in this field. *Science is the equal partner of politics, and at the same time a valuable co-creator of policy*. Science and politics should mutually influence and inspire each other; there must be no relationship of superior to inferior. The Party is anxious to co-operate with the largest possible corps of scientists, to entrust them with functions in the representative assemblies and other organs of social management and to create conditions guaranteeing a consistent flow of scientific information into the Party's organs both during the process of making decisions and during that of implementing them and checking their correctness. The Party resolutely rejects any attempt to downgrade science, especially the social sciences, to the function of an instrument for the defence and imposition of particular political notions and assumptions.

The Party will strive to secure a radical improvement in the financing of research so as to enable it to continue at an international level in key fields; it will support functional specialization related to Czechoslovak conditions and linked with international co-operation.

The Party sees it as an important task to *overcome all barriers separating science from its social application*. We shall favour greater incentives for the utilization of science in production and other social contexts and aim for an improved qualification structure both in production and research.

The Party will urge the State authorities to review the existing principles and pattern of organization and direction in science and research in the light of the foregoing. It will recommend the drafting of a new law for the Academy of Science, implementing the new constitutional arrangement, giving full autonomy to both national academies and establishing their relation to the universities on a footing of complete equality. This law should also settle the internal structure and activity of both Academies on a basis of completely democratic self-management.

*

In the field of *education* the Party envisages the creation of a profoundly democratic school system, free from administrative authoritarian interference, imbued with respect for our progressive traditions and for the standards of the modern age, and able to bring the highest rungs of the educational ladder within the reach of everyone according to his talents.

In order to get rid of past deformations the Party will exert its political influence to secure the drafting and acceptance in 1969 of a new school law acknowledging Czechoslovakia as a special case and ensuring the uniformity of the school system, its institutions and concepts, according to the principle of internal differentiation and well-considered interrelations between the different types of school and educational levels.

The Party will also urge that a law is drafted at the same time to acknowledge on democratic lines the special nature of the universities as independent institutions for teaching and research, to establish the participation of students in the direction and administration of the universities and to increase the universities' share in scientific research.

In the context of federalization and territorial reorganization the Party considers it essential that the school system should acquire a status in the new system of management proportionate to its importance and calculated to protect both schools and school-teachers from disruptive interference. The problem of schools for national minorities must also be solved at the same time.

The Party appreciates the self-sacrificing labours of our school-teachers in the past. It sees the need to create in the schools an atmosphere conducive to free and creative activity, combined with a sense of social responsibility for the socialist upbringing of the young, to enable every teacher to evolve his own personality as an educator, and to support his social status with adequate material rewards.

The Party expects those of its members who are teachers or educational officers to stand in the forefront of progressive efforts, to display initiative in the moulding of the Party's educational policy and to try and win over all other teachers and officers in its support. The Party regards the intellectual potential of the teaching community as a valuable asset which can not only assist the development of the school system, but further the spread of socialist democracy and humanism throughout our society.

*

In our new approach to the construction of socialism it will be necessary for us in the *cultural* field to do all we can in the coming period to erase from the mind of the Party, the State authorities and the general public that narrow and false view of the social and human purpose of culture which overrates its ideological and political roles and underrates its basic and broadly aesthetic function in the transformation of man and his world. We must do everything we can to eradicate artificially fostered prejudices against the intelligentsia and against education in general. It is necessary to review very critically not only the principle of a narrowly ideological management of culture and one-sided subordination of culture to ideology and politics, but also the whole body of currently valid Party resolutions concerning culture and the measures which brought about this treatment of culture at the hands of State bodies. This is the only way of ensuring objective reconsideration of the present state of culture and of existing tendencies in our society. It is the only way of responsibly preparing the ground for specific organizational and legislative measures designed to terminate the rigid centralism of the past and to promote the growth of cultural autonomy and self-management in the sense of a pluralism of ideas, nationalities and regions. The pre-conditions and effect of self-management are the same, namely that genuine experts, widely trusted by the cultural community, will be the men to direct and administer cultural activity. It will be necessary on the same basis to tackle the complex of cultural-economic problems, so as to stabilize planned investments in this field and, as they increase in proportion to the growing national income, to concentrate the funds in the organs which actually perform cultural administration. Resources must be used in such a way as functionally to extend and modernize the material infrastructure of culture while preserving cultural monuments for our nations.

[NOTE: The Editorial Commission feels that the foregoing passage needs to go deeper. It should concentrate on the principles of the Party's modern cultural policy.]

*

The concept of *ideological* work in the Party, and especially of its practical application, has been arbitrarily narrowed down and considerably perverted during the last few years. The contradiction between words and deeds which was intensified after the Thirteenth

Congress represented something which the Party's ideological front was unable to bury or to explain away satisfactorily. The crisis in the Party's policy and the fall in its prestige were bound to injure the prestige of its ideological work, and vice versa. The main ideological task today is to assist in the rapid birth of a *new ideological concept* of society, and in the cleansing and stabilization of ideological values.

Today's crisis of values – an accompaniment and consequence of the long-term crisis in the whole country – exacerbates in turn the contradictions of contemporary evolution. This leads to numerous disagreements within the Party and outside it, and provokes feelings of uncertainty and chaos. Values have been discredited which only a few years ago seemed incontrovertible, and new values have yet to take their place in people's minds. Conflicts of interest between different social groups are projected into the ideological dimension. One finds in strange juxtaposition ossified notions of socialism warped by the practice and propaganda of the past – egalitarian, sectarian and dogmatic views derived from Stalinist ideas of socialism; conservative and retrograde opinions about social security and justice; and so on – alongside thoughts evolved through idealization of certain aspects of bourgeois society. The individual suffers from an insufficient sense of identity in society.

It is our ideological work which must play a large role in overcoming this crisis as part of the implementation of the new line. It must point out the sequence of changes in the system of values, the reasons why socialist values became deformed and the meaning of their revival, which is to be the starting point for an ideological re-examination of socialist society. It must urgently seek new approaches to the political and intellectual training of communists with a view to overcoming dogmatism in thought and sectarianism in political behaviour. The democratic model of socialism and the Party's new policy must necessarily change the very concept of ideological activity as well. Its function will be to help implement the new policy, to inspire and stimulate creative thought, to reconcile different social interests. The ideologist cannot be a mere 'defender' of policy, a mere warrior against 'incorrect tendencies' and guardian of doctrinal purity. Ideology has to combat quite a number of its own myths and to achieve a new synthesis with the social sciences if it is to pass muster as an integrating force in society. This cannot happen unless there is free sociological research, democratic discussion and a balancing-out of views.

The new role of ideology requires changes in the status and effectiveness of ideological work in the Party. Standards are not yet sufficiently high and the methods of organizing and directing it do not yet meet the needs of the new policy. It is also essential that we should formulate a new concept of Party educational work, propaganda and agitation in conformity with the Party's position in the new political system. We must work out an open-ended system of political education inside the Party and concentrate it upon the targets described.

5. OUTLINE OF A FOREIGN POLICY CONCEPT FOR THE PARTY

As a social phenomenon the process of rebirth in Czechoslovakia also has its impact abroad. There it provokes various reactions, sometimes understanding and sometimes fear.

The Communist Party is engaged in explaining the process. Summary of this activity from the Dresden meeting up to the present Congress.

The choice of one's own road to socialism is not in conflict with the aims of world socialism. The socialist character of the State determines our place in the revolutionary process and conditions our foreign policy.

The need to reconcile our country's national and international interests is leading to a change of attitude towards some aspects of foreign policy, e.g. a new understanding of the unity of the socialist countries, an active European policy and co-operation with world centres of science and technology.

We shall follow on where results have been favourable in past years. At the same time we must overcome deformations, analysis of which has shown that failure to consider specific local conditions in the construction of socialism reduces the possibility of affecting social and political events in the outside world.

In our foreign policy we shall observe Marx's words on respect for the laws of morality and justice. We shall support the deeply democratic nature of this policy, *viz.* the broad participation of the various National Front components by means of parliament and government, and the fulfilment of the interests of both our two nations.*

*

* *Translator's Note:* This paragraph appears irrelevant to the rest of the section, which is itself evidently a rough series of jottings.

Changes in the world over the past few years. Tendency to universalization; greater mutual dependence and at the same time intensification of differences between living conditions in one area and another.

Principal opposing forces in the world and their difficulty in adapting to the new conditions of world-wide social and economic change. Urgent need to support a policy of peaceful co-existence.

Policies of ruling circles in the US and other capitalist countries. Aggression in Vietnam.

The socialist countries as a factor limiting the scope of imperialist policy and as a component in the balance of power and preservation of peace.

Czechoslovakia accepts the reality of military threats and a wide spectrum of instruments of policy such as various forms of pressure, ideological influence, etc. But we refuse to admit that the exacerbation of international tension cannot be reversed or a new world war avoided. Practical possibility of a broad coalition of progressive and realistic forces in the capitalist world in alliance with ourselves against world reaction.

The developing countries as a significant element in world policy. Complex and contradictory processes going on in these areas. Attitude of Czechoslovakia to these issues.

*

Friendship, alliance and co-operation with the Soviet Union and other socialist countries is a basic feature of the foreign policy of our Party and State. The solidity of friendship depends on observance in practice of the principle of mutual respect, sovereignty and equality, on acknowledgement of each country's specific conditions. The growth of friendship requires the growth of progressive forms of co-operation, complete openness, extensive and truthful publicity about developments in the socialist countries, numerous contacts and sincere confrontation of ideas.

The foreign policy of our Party and State also reflects the common interests of all the socialist countries. A key question: the unity of national and international interests. To find the optimal relation between national and international interests is not only the prerogative of each communist party, but its duty *vis-à-vis* the international revolutionary movement, just as it is in duty bound to strive for open discussion between the various communist parties so as to reach the most objective possible conclusions and hence the broadest possible unity of opinion.

We regard the active share of Czechoslovakia in forming and carrying out a joint strategy as a positive contribution to the formation of correct views, though also as an expression of reservations towards steps of whose justification we are unconvinced.

Different views on certain questions are nothing abnormal. One must understand the other man's opinion. Necessity of scientific appraisal of foreign policy problems which are central to our interests and which we want to help solve.

*

The main field of Czechoslovak foreign policy is Europe. We can play an important role as part of the community of socialist countries. The central problem is security. The need to reinforce unity of action among the democratic and peace-loving elements of European society.

Close connection between internal stability and external security. Sole responsibility of the Czechoslovak people for the fate of socialism in our land.

The role of Czechoslovakia in creating the foundations of European security. Recognition of the post-war settlement a pre-condition. Main Czechoslovak contribution in Central Europe. Purpose: to secure recognition of the existence of two German States. The German question has two poles for us: we shall continue to support East Germany, but this does not prevent us from formulating our own ideas on the German question. In our policy toward West Germany we realize the conflicting developments in that country. We shall support the position of the democratic forces. Conditions for normalization of relations with the Federal Republic.

Efforts to procure acceptance of peaceful co-existence as a principle of international relations. How we conceive peaceful co-existence.

*

In our relations with the underdeveloped countries we shall aim at a realistic policy. We shall reinforce our ties with national liberation movements, support progressive forces and exploit the positive aspects of the policy of non-alignment. We should like to develop mutually beneficial trade and economic co-operation.

*

The Czechoslovak Communist Party as a component of the international communist movement. Its efforts to promote dynamic development in the movement.

Past deformations: misunderstanding of the principle of proletarian internationalism and of the unity of communist parties. (Attitude to the Yugoslav League of Communists, etc.)

A complex process under way in the international communist movement. Main aspects of it: (*a*) formulation of a new concept of unity;
(*b*) defeat of sectarian tendencies;
(*c*) efforts toward a scientific Marxist analysis.

Active involvement of the Czechoslovak Communist Party in the process; it considers this to be its contribution to the preparation of an international consultation.

Through its domestic achievements the Czechoslovak Communist Party is sharing in the world-wide confrontation of socialism with capitalism.

The criterion of internationalism is not mechanical uniformity but the ability to see and use specific opportunities to make one's own contribution to the joint efforts of the socialist progressive forces throughout the world.

Opportunities for co-operation between the Czechoslovak Communist Party and peaceful and democratic non-communist forces in the capitalist and developing countries.

Efforts by the Czechoslovak Party to intensify scientific analysis of new developments and achieve a confrontation of ideas within the international communist movement.

*

[NOTE: In addition to the questions raised in this part of the theses, the final version will also include lengthier treatment of some other issues in respect of contemporary events, and this will affect the structure of the whole material.

In the section on foreign policy an important passage would be devoted to the Czechoslovak Communist Party's position and role as part of the international communist movement, as a link in the struggle for the socialist transformation of the world. This passage would include an explanation of our concept of proletarian internationalism and the unity of communist and workers' parties, and of the relation between national and international interests. The starting point here will be that the determination of the optimal relation within the policy of each communist party is that party's inalienable right and responsibility, which naturally presupposes respect for the specific aspects of every party's policy. It is only unity based on this attitude, unity in diversity, that constitutes the pre-condition for progress toward a socialist revolution, whereas efforts to subject communist parties and socialist countries to a single schematic model and struggles against the specific features of their policies only disrupt the communist movement and ruin its prospects of useful development.

This general introduction will lead on to the Party's foreign policy views considered in two contexts, *viz.*:

(1) in the international communist movement, where the Czecho-slovak Communist Party is the political agent, and

(2) in the field of international relations, where the Party presents its ideas to the nation in its capacity as the leading force in our society.

In regard to (1) the report will concentrate on the problems of the World Conference of Communist Parties so that the Congress resolution can emerge as a mandate for the Czechoslovak Communist Party's stand at the Conference.

This part will include our ideas on methods of strengthening the socialist system, and an expression of resolute rejection of any denial of the right of each socialist country to go its own way – a denial which must lead in practice to the break-up of the socialist system.]

VIII
Statements Relating to the Fourteenth Congress

*Communiqué Issued After the Opening Session of the Newly
Elected Central Committee of the Czechoslovak
Communist Party**

1. The Central Committee of the Czechoslovak Communist Party
   elected at its Extraordinary Fourteenth Congress met for its opening session in the late hours of 22 August 1968 in the presence of the
   Central Control and Audit Commission and elected a Presidium
   composed of the following Comrades:

Dubček, A.	Šik, O.	Litera, J.	Zrak, J.
Smrkovský, J.	Šilhan, V.	Goldstücker, V.	Ťažký, A.
Černík, O.	Slavík, V.	Vojáček, B.	Sádovský, S.
Špaček, J.	Hrdinová, L.	Hübl, M.	Colotka, P.
Kriegel, F. .	Matjříček, V.	Moc, Z.	Turček, J.
Šimon, B.	Kabrna, B.	Šimeček, V.	Pavlenda, V.
Císař, Č.	Hejzlar, Z.	Husák, G.	Zamek, A.

2. The plenum of the Central Committee unanimously elected Comrade A. Dubček as its First Secretary.
3. The plenum elected Presidium member Comrade Věnek Šilhan as
   a Secretary of the Central Committee and entrusted him with the
   management of the Presidium's business during the absence of
   First Secretary Comrade Dubček.
4. The plenum decided upon short-term political and organizational
   measures to cope with the serious political situation in the country.
5. As the sole rightful leading organ of the Party during the period
   between sessions of Congress, the plenum calls upon all subordinate Party organs to conduct their activity exclusively in accordance
   with the instructions of this legal Central Committee and its
   Presidium.

* From *Rudé právo*, 24 August 1968, p. 1.

Statement by the Slovak Delegates to the Congress*

After considerable difficulty, further duly elected delegates of Slovak regional Party organizations to the Extraordinary Fourteenth Congress reached Prague in the early hours of Friday. After receiving basic information and conferring with members of the new Central Committee, they issued the following signed statement:

The undersigned duly elected delegates to the Extraordinary Fourteenth Congress, whose arrival was delayed by transport difficulties, have been informed by Presidium-member Comrade J. Litera of the course of the Congress and wish to be regarded as full and present participants of the Congress:

Eng. Otto Pezlar (Svidnik)	Požgay (Detva)
J. Gula (Spišská Nová Ves)	Eng. Viktor Roth
Eng. Karol Járek (Nové Zámky)	(Michalovce)
Choma (Košice)	Medel (Zvolen)
Lupták (Zvolen)	Ján Marejka (Čadca)
Tamás (Košice)	Štefan Chovanec (Čadca)

Letter from the National Assembly to the Newly Elected Central Committee of the Czechoslovak Communist Party†

Prague, 23 August 1968

Dear Comrades,

We have received with genuine pleasure the report of the Fourteenth Congress session. Its delegates come from the ranks of those elected and authorized representatives of Party organizations whose decisions constitute valid Party documents. The National Assembly, with its Deputies from all parties in the National Front, stands fully behind the political declarations of the Fourteenth Congress. We see in them a continuation of the political line of the January plenum of the Communist Party's Central Committee, enhanced with all the positive features of democratic socialism, and reflecting the democratic and humane traditions of the nations of our socialist fatherland in accordance with the Communist Party's Action Programme. We wholly agree with your assessment of the current situation. We reject the gross violation of our State sovereignty by

---

* From *Rudé právo*, 24 August 1968, p. 1.

† Document No. 12 in the volume of *National Assembly Documents, 21-8 August, 1968* compiled from National Assembly archives on the instructions of its Presidium.

the entry of occupation troops. We demand their immediate withdrawal and complete freedom of operation for all the legal agencies of the State.

We welcome you as the Communist Party's new Central Committee and recognize you as the supreme organ of that Party.

We are convinced that your activity will further promote the democratic character of our socialist society, that it will rely on close co-operation with all the parties and social organizations comprising the National Front, and that by its daily exercise of socialist policies it will win over all the citizens of this country and ensure that socialism here has a human face. This is the only way in which the Communist Party – as we all sincerely hope, regardless of our particular affiliations – can play a leading role in the future.

The Czechoslovak National Assembly is ready to lend the new Central Committee all support in its power to help reinforce socialist legality, give reality to civic rights and freedoms, and create conditions in which the public can work peacefully and live happily. We hope that under the leadership of the new Communist Party Central Committee all the best elements in the country will unite to produce a general burgeoning.

We wish you every success, Comrades, in your highly responsible task. Long live free, independent, sovereign, democratic, socialist Czechoslovakia!

The National Assembly of the Czechoslovak Socialist Republic

The text of this letter was discussed at the August 23 session of the National Assembly's Presidium and approved by the Assembly itself on the same day.

Statement by the Trade Unions on the Congress*

The following 'Statement by the executives of the Central Trade Union Council and of the Central Committee of the Trade Union Associations' was issued on the morning of 23 August 1968:

The executives of the Central Trade Union Council and of the Central Committee of the Trade Union Associations, being in constant touch with constitutional bodies, with President Svoboda, the National Assembly and the government of this Republic, give support in the name of the $5\frac{1}{2}$

* From *Seven Days in Prague,* the 'Black Book' on the invasion published in September 1968 by the Historical Institute of the Academy of Sciences, p. 174.

million trade union members to the measures agreed at the Czechoslovak Communist Party's Extraordinary Fourteenth Congress and to the Central Committee there elected, with its Presidium headed by Alexander Dubček.

We fully concur in the Fourteenth Congress's appeal to all citizens to join in a one-hour general strike at midday today as a sign of protest against the presence of the armies of occupation of the five Warsaw Pact States on the Republic's territory. By means of this symbolic one-hour strike we shall assure the legal government and the National Assembly of our backing and we demand the release of leading representatives of the people – Comrades Dubček, Černík, Smrkovský, Kriegel and all others – so that they can perform the functions entrusted to them. We shall never recognize a government or executive body of any kind composed of impostors and we refuse all collaboration with occupation authorities and military units.

We call upon all trade union bodies and strike committees to ensure the peaceful conclusion of today's strike and subsequent resumption of work. We ask employees of the health service and other essential sectors to make their protests in token fashion. We urge all trade union organs and strike committees to remain alert and ready to carry out further instructions.

*Appeal by the Communist Party's Central Committee to the Population**

At 12.30 hrs on 23 August 1968 Věnek Šilhan, a Secretary of the Communist Party's Central Committee, read out the following appeal to the public over Prague radio:

Dear Fellow-citizens, I turn to you, the whole people of our Republic, in the name of the Communist Party's Central Committee that was elected yesterday at the Extraordinary Fourteenth Congress of our Party. As you already know, we elected Comrade Dubček, the existing Central Committee Secretary, to the leading position on the Committee. But since he is at present illegally deprived of his personal freedom and of his capacity to work, I have been assigned the task of informing you of the Committee's attitude to the latest serious events.

I must begin by expressing the thanks of the whole Party, and of everyone in the country, to those Prague factories which played a decisive part in the holding of the Party Congress. Similar thanks go to the People's Militia, which took an active and self-sacrificing part in ensuring the personal safety of the delegates and thus, in most trying circumstances,

* From a roneoed leaflet issued by the Central Committee Secretariat.

became once more one of the foremost, and most dependable, defenders of the interests of Party and people. The course of events has been a lesson to all of us and taught us at the same time that the People's Militia is again well aware of its rightful place. It proved this yesterday in extremely difficult conditions and we all, accordingly, owe it a debt of gratitude.

Today we are faced with a new and extraordinarily serious matter. A delegation of State and Party representatives, led by General Ludvík Svoboda, President of the Republic, has left by air for Moscow to take part in direct negotiations. We learnt this from President Svoboda's radio address today. I should like to make a statement on this in the name of the Central Committee Presidium.

General Ludvík Svoboda, President of the Republic, enjoys our full confidence and support, as do the other delegation members who were voted into office at the Party Congress, *viz.* Comrades Husák and Dzúr. As to the other members of the delegation, our attitude to them will be guided by their attitude, in these highly important negotiations, to the decisions of the Extraordinary Fourteenth Congress as the supreme organ of the Party.

The resolutions of the Extraordinary Congress demanded above all things the immediate withdrawal of occupation troops from the soil of the Republic. We admit of no compromise in this matter, however realistic we remain and open to reasonable agreements, as we have been throughout the post-January developments. We insist unequivocally on the restoration of the full sovereignty of our State.

It is to be hoped that our delegates are able to make some progress in connection with the normalization of the Republic's internal life and foreign relations alike. The Party's Central Committee has made a start in this direction on the basis of earlier resolutions.

The gross violation of our State sovereignty has done serious damage to the basic values and certainties upon which our international position rests. It is not therefore surprising that the demand should have been raised in various parts of the country for the President to declare our country neutral. The Presidium of the Party's Central Committee feels it necessary to make its position clear on this. There cannot be a moment's doubt who is to blame for the creation of our country's highly abnormal situation. It was not our State and political organs who trod underfoot the concept of our alliance with the Soviet Union and the other Warsaw Pact countries. Our whole post-January policy, on the contrary, stemmed from the assumption that the existing obligations of alliance, purged of everything that obstructed their full and healthy development, would continue to form the basis of Czechoslovakia's foreign policy.

The Extraordinary Fourteenth Congress noted in its turn, then, that

Czechoslovakia, which has violated none of its alliance obligations to date, would likewise in future have not the slightest interest in maintaining hostile relations with the other socialist States and their peoples – not even with those whose governments are at present adopting a hostile stance towards us. The Central Committee Presidium therefore expresses its conviction that the sad experience of 21 August 1968 must be the occasion for a thoroughgoing renewal of relations between the socialist countries on the principle of genuine internationalism. The democratic nature of internationalism was long ago expressed in the axiom that no nation can be free which denies freedom to others. This is an ideal which socialists have always cherished.

The aims which consequently guide Czechoslovakia in her choice of direction as a nation and as a State within the larger community of European countries, and particularly within the community of socialist countries, cannot be adequately stated or achieved in terms of a demand for neutrality alone. We are aware, moreover, that neutrality does not in itself guarantee national or State sovereignty. Sovereignty demands tireless efforts and a reinforcement of all the elements of international security, as well as peace and quiet inside Europe. This pre-supposes an unrelenting determination to counter everything that might disturb the political balance and create new foci of international tension.

That in turn requires that Czechoslovakia should tread the path of reinforcement of democratic international relations amongst all States and peoples, above all amongst those which have already set forth on the road to socialism. We are aware that the success of such a policy depends on the good will of all of us. We know only too well that it does not only depend on the restoration of those certainties and values which are at present being spurned. However, we consider it our paramount duty to let slip no opportunity of promoting movement in this direction, both in European policy and in that of the socialist countries.

Dear Comrades, dear Citizens: the first sixty hours of the occupation have brought us, besides an avalanche of sufferings and disappointments, one basic insight. The moral strength of our peoples, the inner unity of ideas, the civic courage and maturity of our two nations have been manifested during these past days in a manner more convincing and unmistakable, perhaps, than ever before in our history. The surprising energy and inventiveness of vast numbers of simple folk, the constant endeavour on all sides to contribute in some small way at least to the difficult common effort – all this has become an essential part of our lives which can never again be forgotten.

Allow me, dear friends, particularly in this connection to express the sincere gratitude of communists toward all those citizens who, often at the cost of supreme effort, gave their support to yesterday's Party Congress. These are the links which we have sorely missed in previous years, but which have now been forged in the direst times of our life. These links, this evident inner unity, demonstrated by deeds under conditions of great hardship, have become a treasure belonging to the whole nation – one which we hold in common and must add to in future. For it is this which, in happier days to come, will have decisive value for our joint progress.

At this moment and in this context, you may be glad to learn that the Presidium of our Party has today already begun its work and confirmed its status, and that the new Secretariat is functioning. Under highly abnormal conditions, then, the activity of the Party's central organs is achieving normality. In a day or two the Slovak Communist Party will be holding its Extraordinary Congress. The Presidium of the Czechoslovak Party's Central Committee will send to that meeting a delegation composed of the following: Libuše Hrdinová, Štefan Sádovský, Josef Borůvka, František Vodsloň and Josef Zuda. We wish our delegation, and the fraternal party's Extraordinary Congress in Slovakia, the best possible conditions for their deliberations, and may they achieve good results.

Finally, allow me in the name of our Central Committee and its Presidium to address the district and regional committees of the Party. Maintain the highest measure of legality in your work! You are working in and for your own country. Do not succumb to the psychosis of the underground, or resort to illegal methods of work without serious reason. But if circumstances make this unavoidable, then use all means to ensure the operational capability of our Party, for which we are answerable to every citizen in the land. What you have shown, dear citizens, in the past two-and-a-half days will be assessed by history as a unique demonstration of the moral strength and unity of two small nations in one small country. By all pulling together, each to his best ability, we shall strengthen the permanent foundations of that inner security which will lead us past the rocks and into happier times for our common socialist Republic.

New Editor-in-Chief for Rudé právo*

Oldřich Švestka Dismissed

The Presidium of the Czechoslovak Communist Party's Central Committee has decided to relieve Oldřich Švestka of the post of Editor-in-Chief of *Rudé právo* and to appoint in his place the First Deputy Editor-in-Chief, Comrade Jiří Sekera. Comrades Emil Šíp and Zdislav Šulc have been appointed Deputy Editors-in-Chief. Comrades Sekera,

* From *Rudé právo*, 24 August 1968, p. 1.

Šulc and Šíp have at the same time been instructed to ensure the continuation of editorial work and the publication of *Rudé právo* as the central printed organ of the Party.

The Presidium has decided to take over the independent transmitter of the Prague City organization as a publicity organ of the Party's Central Committee.

*Letter from Čestmír Císař to the Fourteenth Congress**

I welcome and greatly esteem the decisions and resolutions of your Congress, and I thank you for the confidence you have shown in me by electing me to the Central Committee of the Party. I am ready to perform any tasks entrusted to me. For the present, I am unable to do anything. I was detained on August 21 but managed to escape and am now staying with good communists and Czech patriots. I ask your assistance in protecting the activity of the Czech National Council. Even under the present difficult conditions we must fulfil all the duties that arise from the new constitutional arrangement. I assume that it will be possible for me to take part in the work of the new Central Committee and its Presidium. I expect that the efforts of the Party, the National Front and the public at large under the leadership of the new Central Committee and the constitutional organs of the Republic will combine to secure the withdrawal of all occupation troops, the restoration of complete sovereignty and the creation of conditions for normal life in our fatherland. I send you militant greetings and wish you success in your labours. *Au revoir*, Comrades!

Čestmír Císař

What Communists Must Do Today: Statement by the Central Committee Presidium†

To all members and officials of the Czechoslovak Communist Party!

Send your resolution both to the Central Committee and to the Soviet Embassy. We are fighting for the vital interests of the whole people.

---

* From *Rudé právo*, 24 August 1968, p. 1.

† Reprinted from *Rudé právo* of 25 August 1968 in *Seven Days in Prague*, *op. cit.*

Last January, Comrades, our Party acquired after many years a new leadership with Dubček at its head, approved its Action Programme and began to carry out a policy supported by the overwhelming majority of the people. We have begun to strive for a socialism really made for the people's benefit and wearing, as Comrade Dubček often said, a truly human face.

Now our fatherland has been occupied by the troops of several Warsaw Pact armies. The blood of Czechs and Slovaks has been wantonly spilt. The road by which we hoped to strengthen socialism and increase confidence in the Communist Party, and hence to ensure its growing political influence in the country, has been torn up by tank-tracks.

What must communists do today, in order to be able in the future to implement the policy they have embarked upon?

We know from our Party's history that the worst thing that happened in past years was for the Party to be dominated by men who enjoyed the trust neither of Party members nor of the other workers and the public at large. These people violated the principles of intra-Party democracy and turned the nearly 2 million members of the Party into an instrument of their arbitrary will, depriving them of their own free will and of the right to think and act as they thought best.

Judge for yourselves! It must not happen again that communists in the primary, district and regional organizations become the tools of people who do not enjoy the Party's confidence. Hold meetings immediately in the primary and district organizations and decide for yourselves which road you wish to take.

The Extraordinary Fourteenth Congress was made up of delegates chosen by the whole Party by democratic procedure according to its Statutes. It elected in turn a new Central Committee headed by comrades who in the post-January developments won the trust of Party and people. The new Central Committee included in its Presidium those comrades who are prevented from exercising their functions because they have been interned by Soviet troops against their own will and the will of the constitutional organs of the State: Comrades A. Dubček, O. Černík, J. Smrkovský, J. Špaček, F. Kriegel, B. Šimon.

Decide for yourselves in each Party organization whether you recognize this Central Committee, duly elected at the Fourteenth Congress, as the Party's supreme body, or are prepared to see people speaking on your behalf who have nothing in common with this Committee!

Make speedy, legal and democratic decisions in all Party organizations, plenary meetings and committees as to whom you recognize! Act consistently with your decisions, publish your resolutions in the press and radio! Ask for assistance from local radio stations, National Committees and factory radio systems.

Send your resolutions not only to the Central Committee's address in Prague, but also to the Soviet Union's Prague Embassy with the request that they be communicated to the Soviet Party's Central Committee and published in the Soviet press as the views of Czechoslovak communists.

Certain people who were not re-elected to senior functions by the Extraordinary Fourteenth Congress are claiming nevertheless to speak in your name. Make your protests against this and point out that you can speak for yourselves!

Communist members of the People's Militia! Do not accept orders from those who have silently accepted the internment of your Commandant, Comrade Dubček, in a place unknown and for reasons unknown, contrary to the laws of this State, to the wishes of the Party Congress and the People's Militia! Follow the Prague People's Militia in recognizing the Party's duly elected Central Committee and accept instructions only from its Presidium or plenary collective.

Communists in the security service and armed forces! Obey only commands given by Czechoslovak constitutional agencies: the National Assembly, the Government and the President of the Republic.

Communists in the trade unions! Take the initiative in active political work within these bodies. Give full support to the strongest organization of the proletariat and other working people, our Revolutionary Trade Union Movement. The workers, communist and non-communist, are today in complete agreement that our people in the factories are defending their interests and can settle matters themselves without intervention from abroad.

Our factories and enterprises, our working class, have sufficient strength for this task. May the Revolutionary Trade Union Movement prove a powerful weapon for the defence of all the working people's political interests in the extraordinary situation of today. The trade unions are a legal organization which belongs to us all. Let us all make use of the trade unions and turn them into a mighty instrument of the workers and all the labouring classes, an instrument no one will dare suspect of harbouring anti-socialist or anti-proletarian aims. Let us all work in the trade unions on democratic lines, manifesting the power of their millions of members and mobilizing it in the interest of our country and of our nations.

Only those who have won confidence can give leadership. All Communist Party officials are responsible to the members – to communists in the factories, the villages and the towns. Keep permanently in contact with the Party's regional committees and do not allow anyone to try and lead your regional organization other than those comrades in whom you have expressed your trust at regional conferences. Do the same at district and municipal level. In all cases where Party Secretariats are occupied by foreign troops, Party officials and bodies are in duty bound to continue operating from other premises – local National Committee rooms, factory offices, and so on.

The new Central Committee as chosen at the Extraordinary Fourteenth Congress is not afraid to rely on your will and on your decisions as formed in the primary organizations of the Party, for it is sure that your thinking is the same as the thinking of the Congress delegates you yourselves elected. The Committee trusts you and needs your initiative, independence and determination; it relies on your own communist sense of responsibility.

We are convinced that the Party's unanimity represents a real access of strength for the principles of the post-January policy.

Do not be provoked into leaving the Party. Even if the worst should happen and the Party's organs, duly elected at the Congress, should be forced into silence, do not abandon the Party! To weaken or liquidate the Party's ranks would only help those who might be prepared to set up a handful of unscrupulous and spineless individuals once more as spokesmen for the Communists of Czechoslovakia.

Tanks and machine-guns can, of course, achieve a great deal. But it is hardly possible for the activities of the Communist Party to be banned by those who say they have come to help strengthen its leading role.

Reinforce the Party, enrol new members – workers, peasants, intellectuals, youth, and all who are willing and able to fight for the Party's Action Programme and for the demands of the Extraordinary Fourteenth Congress. It is incumbent on communists not only to acknowledge in full the patriotism, energy and courage of the young, but to give them the benefit of their own political experience and tact and to

264

put before them a clear programme for genuine socialist democracy. Accept young workers and students as Party members and give an opening in our Party to the voice and will of the younger socialist generation.

The Extraordinary Fourteenth Congress has fully endorsed the statement put out by the last regular session of the Presidium on 21 August 1968, condemning the fact that our Republic was occupied militarily without the knowledge of the President of the Republic, the Speaker of the National Assembly, the Prime Minister, the First Secretary of the Party's Central Committee or any other responsible agent.

Give your support everywhere to appeals for calm and moderation. The withdrawal of foreign troops, though a basic pre-condition of any independent creative policy for our Party, is something we cannot secure by force of arms but only by our morale and by the force of justice. Do not be afraid to demand legal measures of any kind. Give your backing only to the legal and constitutionally appointed government, and to Party, State and National Front officials chosen under valid Czechoslovak laws and regulations.

We call upon all Party members to take an active and forceful part in curbing any attempts by anti-socialist elements to exacerbate the situation by provocation. We are in a position to cope with unaided anti-socialist elements. Do not allow their activation to be used as a pretext for military intervention in our country.

Today, Comrades, let us discard everything that divides us and leave petty quarrels on one side. The only possible guideline for each of us is his sincere assent to the Party's new post-January policy, coupled with his own inflexible resolution. Let us concentrate the joint efforts of all our members upon the following key problems:

1. Let us demand that Comrades A. Dubček, O. Černík, J. Smrkovský, F. Kriegel, J. Špaček and B. Šimon are all, without exception, enabled immediately to resume their functions in the government, Party and National Front.
2. Let us withhold recognition from any Party spokesmen who have received no democratic mandate to represent it, *viz.* from all members of the Party's central bodies who have not received their mandate from the Extraordinary Fourteenth Congress.
3. Let us demand the complete withdrawal of foreign military formations of the Warsaw Pact countries, since the presence of these

troops at this moment on the territory of Czechoslovakia, a member State, is in clear contradiction to the Pact.

4. Let us warn against any provocative or thoughtless action. The blood of our people is the most precious possession we have and anything that might lead to needless bloodshed must be avoided. Effective steps must be taken to avert this danger.

5. Even in the worst case, even if everything guaranteed by the Constitution, the country's laws and the Party's Statutes should be brutally suppressed, do not abandon the Party's ranks. Let as many honest people as possible – workers and others – remain in the Party, for if its ranks remain strong it will be able in the course of time once more to produce competent political leaders and guide our nations out of the plight into which they have been brought by *force majeure*.

If all we communists strive together along these lines, Comrades, it is not for our Party alone that we shall be fighting! We are fighting for the vital interests of our two nations, of the whole population of our country. Everyone who distrusts the people and is ready to trample underfoot those values our people have struggled and suffered for, will in the last resort be judged by his own kin. The Czechoslovak Communist Party has never acted and will never act in this fashion, for it does not regard it as its mission to become a dominant political clique, but to serve the interests of socialism in this country so that the socialist system can provide our own people with a real home.

We see this, moreover, as our international duty in the deepest sense. The alliance of socialist countries and the unity of the communist and progressive movement throughout the world cannot be achieved by force, but only by trust, co-operation and mutual help – the kind of mutual help, that is, which every socialist country or communist Party truly desires in the common interest. This is the way in which the Party's leaders, appointed by the Extraordinary Fourteenth Congress, also interpret all the basic documents of the international working-class movement, including the joint Bratislava Declaration by the six Parties on 4 August 1968. The armed intervention undertaken against this country by the five other signatories of that Declaration stands in blatant contradiction to its text.

We communists represent the leading political force in the country. Let us now prove this by our deeds; let us trust our people, to whom we are fully answerable for our policies.

It is a tragedy that on the pretext of 'aid' for our Party a situation should have been created which threatens to destroy confidence in socialism, in the Soviet Union and in the ideals of the communist movement. Let us defend ourselves in the name of that movement and its ideals. Let us do everything, everywhere, to retain the people's trust, that socialism may continue to be the objective of our millions of working people in their voluntary effort and initiative, the objective of every Czech and Slovak patriot.

The Central Committee Presidium of the KSČ

Parliament, Party and Government Adjure the President of the Republic*

Prague, 25 August 1968

To the President of the Czechoslovak Republic,
Ludvík Svoboda,
Moscow.
Esteemed Comrade President!

Our whole land and its people trustfully await the outcome of your negotiations in Moscow with feelings of excitement and impatience.

We now feel it needful to inform you of the situation in this country since your departure as we see it and assess it.

In complete and solid unity, and in accordance with the views of the new Party Central Committee elected at the legal Extraordinary Fourteenth Congress and with the views of the National Assembly and the government, our public rejects the occupation as illegal, unconstitutional and unjustified and demands the withdrawal of occupation troops. The State security forces, army and People's Militia stand unanimously on the side of the people.

The National Assembly and the government are in permanent session under difficult conditions. They entirely endorse the demands and attitudes of the public. The Party's Extraordinary Fourteenth Congress has duly elected a new Central Committee and Presidium, expressing, in the process, full confidence in Comrades Dubček, Smrkovský, Černík, Kriegel, Špaček, Šimon, and others. The Congress's resolutions enjoy the full support of the entire Party and public, as the symbolic one-hour strike throughout the land on August 23 also demonstrated.

All these agencies have so far managed to maintain relative calm in the country with the help of the mass media, though the latter's work is being

* Document No. 15 in the volume of *National Assembly Documents, 21-28 August, 1968, op. cit.*

systematically obstructed and foreign troops are occupying radio and television buildings as well as newspaper offices and printing shops. Personnel appointed by the government to take charge of the mass media are having with great difficulty to seek alternative facilities. Two attempts have already been made to occupy the Foreign Ministry's radio transmitter, which is our only link with the National Assembly and likewise with you.

Such is the situation our people are facing on the fifth day of the occupation. Tension is continually rising because of loss of life and property. In Prague alone some thirty dead were counted up to Saturday, and over three hundred injured. In Slovakia casualties appear to have been still higher. These losses refer to our own side. The area around the Radio building in Prague shows considerable destruction. Only with great effort can order be maintained and clashes prevented. The work of elected bodies is continually hampered and civil rights and freedoms curtailed. Arrests are taking place and no day or night passes without shots being fired in the streets of Prague. Any excuse is used for opening fire. Foreign troops carried out searches last night in all central offices, confiscating in some cases weapons belonging to the People's Militia; weapons were used in the Transport Ministry building.

The occupation authorities have not yet succeeded in obtaining the slightest support or co-operation from the public. This is making them all the more nervous. The National Assembly and other agencies in the country have evidence of acts of violence. We must stress that we cannot regard it as normal that no adequate channel of information about the negotiations exists between our delegates in Moscow and ourselves. The economy is suffering and there is a growing danger of a hold-up in supplies for the public. In Prague it is in practice impossible to be out on the streets after 10 p.m., so that public transport has ceased functioning. Rail transport is interrupted and there are no air flights. Imports and exports are suffering. Coal supplies are dropping to a bare minimum. And all this is the outcome of the occupation regime.

A dangerous factor is the increasing fatigue and nervous exhaustion of the occupation troops and of our people alike. Tension on both sides has now risen because of the unpredictable prolongation of your own absence from the Republic, as well as other factors.

The overwhelming majority of communist and working-class parties, as well as public opinion throughout the progressive regions of the world, unambiguously deplores the occupation as an act of force. In the Security Council's discussions the Soviet Union was completely isolated.

In the realization, esteemed Comrade President, that any written report is inadequate to describe, above all, the atmosphere of our cities and the spirit of our men and women, and that the Soviet authorities are being unobjectively and quite wrongly informed on the basis of TASS reports, we consider it indispensable for the further progress of your negotiations that you should be fully and more accurately apprised of the true state of things. We therefore recommend that you should consider the possibility of receiving such information from a special advisory group made up of Central Committee, National Assembly and government representatives, whose arrival in Moscow you may think fit urgently to demand.

We also suggest that you might consider a temporary, brief interruption of negotiations to enable you to return to Prague with Comrades Dubček, Smrkovský and Černík. You could use this short pause to make a closer study of the situation and consult with the appropriate organs.

We send you, esteemed Comrade President, our sincere greetings and assurances of our full confidence.

For the Presidium of the National Assembly: J. Való
For the Government of the Czechoslovak Socialist Republic:
L. Štrougal
For the Presidium of the KSČ Central Committee: V. Šilhan

The text of this letter was approved at a plenary session of the National Assembly on 25 August 1968.

The National Assembly Appeals to the Population*

To the Czech and Slovak nations, to the whole population of Czechoslovakia!

On the eve of the Slovak Rising anniversary we recall with especial clarity that national freedom and independence can only be achieved by a struggle of the entire people. Freedom cannot be won by begging on one's knees. In the course of our historic development the freedom, independence and sovereignty of the Czechoslovak Socialist Republic, together with the hope of a truly humane and worthy life for Czechs and Slovaks and the whole population of Czechoslovakia, have twice in this century been created amidst a struggle against foreign domination. After we set out in January 1968 on the path of correcting the deformations that marred our previous socialist development, the path of building socialism with a human face, and had begun to reap the first successes in that effort, the peaceful work of our country's people was disturbed. Our hearts tremble in anxiety for the future of our State and for the road we set out on, of our own free decision, after January. The attempt is being made from outside to compel us by brute force to sink on our knees and submit to an alien will.

* Document No. 17, *ibid.*

269

The anniversary of the Slovak Rising reminds us, Czechs and Slovaks, that the freedom of our two peoples is the main pillar of Czechoslovak sovereignty. We remember the lines of Jan Kollár:

Sám svobody kdo hoden
*Svobodu zná vážiti každou.**

Czechs, Slovaks and all people of the Czechoslovak Socialist Republic! The Deputies whom you have elected to the National Assembly solemnly declare in this fateful testing-time to which history has subjected us:
We shall strive resolutely to ensure
- that the foreign armies leave the soil of this Republic;
- that the constitutional agencies of the Republic and their representatives who have been elected by the people's will and enjoy its full confidence are enabled to discharge their functions in a free and independent manner;
- that our whole people shall live in a sovereign State and conduct its affairs according to its own wishes;
- that socialism shall grow in this country out of the free striving of workers, peasants and intellectuals; that it shall be a humane socialism consonant with the democratic, progressive traditions of the peoples and minorities of our land; that it shall be a kind of socialism that puts into practice the principles of the Action Programme and of the Extraordinary Fourteenth Congress of the Czechoslovak Communist Party;
- that a Constitutional Law for the federalization of the Republic will be prepared in time for the fifteenth jubilee of the creation of the Czechoslovak Republic, in close co-operation with the Czech National Council, the Slovak National Council and all constituent organizations of the National Front.

Czechs, Slovaks and all people of the Czechoslovak Socialist Republic! In this fateful test we adjure and warn you:
Remain in brotherly unity and solidarity, deal worthily and resolutely! Do not bow your heads before the occupier! Stay true to the ideals of freedom, democracy, socialism and truly proletarian internationalism! Be true to the President of the Republic, Ludvík Svoboda; to the Černík government; to Smrkovský's National Assembly; to Kriegel's National Front; to the Dubček leadership of the Communist Party elected at the Extraordinary Fourteenth Congress!

Prague, 26 August 1968
The National Assembly of the Czechoslovak Socialist Republic

* None be to freedom's spirit true
Who seek it not for others too.

The text of this appeal was discussed in the Presidium of the National Assembly at its session of 26 August 1968 and approved by the Assembly's evening session on the same day.

*National Assembly Statement to the Population**

During seven days of occupation the National Assembly has acted in full consciousness of its responsibility and in consonance with the will of the Czechoslovak people.

It adheres to its views of the violent and illegal attack launched against our country.

The National Assembly supports the organs legally elected at the Fourteenth Congress of the Czechoslovak Communist Party and acknowledges them in all respects.

The National Assembly has today received a first partial report from its Speaker, Comrade Josef Smrkovský, whom it heartily welcomes back in its midst. It continues to extend him complete confidence.

The National Assembly, in accordance with the Constitution and in full awareness of its responsibilities, reserves the right to adopt such attitudes towards the report and proposals of the government as may guarantee the sovereignty and freedom of the land and procure the further democratic development of our socialist Republic.

The National Assembly has resolved to suspend its session until the government submits its report and makes the necessary proposals. At the same time it calls upon the government to conduct the necessary operations in awareness of their extraordinary importance for the future of our country and for the life of all its people, and to do so with a supreme sense of responsibility.

The National Assembly charges its Presidium to continue its work and carry out the required consultations. At the same time it calls upon its Constitutional, Foreign Affairs and Defence Committees to prepare analyses of all appropriate questions.

The National Assembly appeals urgently to all citizens once more to give no pretext for any exacerbation of the situation.

We trust you. Trust us!

Prague, 27 August 1968
The National Assembly of the Czechoslovak Socialist Republic

The text of this appeal to the population was approved by the plenum of the National Assembly at its session of 27 August 1968.

* Document No. 19, *ibid.*

*Statement by the Central Committee Elected at the Congress**

The public has heard the communiqué on our representatives' negotiations in Moscow with bitterness and a sense of disappointment. We share these feelings and are fully aware of the gravity of this moment. We are yielding to superior force, but we shall never abandon our claim to sovereignty and freedom. We understand the difficult conditions in which Comrade Dubček and the other comrades, long separated from us, have been working in Moscow.

Comrades, Brothers, Friends!

Do not despair. This is not yet the end of all things. To achieve socialism with a human face is still the mission of our nation. It has proved impossible to overthrow our legal government, to destroy our political system or to subject our fatherland to permanent occupation. Your heroic behaviour during the last seven days has enabled much to be preserved for times to come.

In the name of that unity which has bound us together in these last heavy days we appeal to you to maintain calm, pride and caution.

The Central Committee is considering and discussing the new situation. We shall do everything in our power to help find a way out, and to create conditions for the future existence of our people.

Trust us, be with us! We are with you.

* From a leaflet put out by the new Committee.

IX

Conclusion

A study of the records of the Czechoslovak Communist Party's Extraordinary Fourteenth Congress, of the documents submitted to it and the resolutions that it passed, must suggest several important conclusions. It must also raise many questions in the mind of anyone interested in changing contemporary society in a socialist direction, and of anyone who has for that reason followed events in Czechoslovakia through 1968 up to the military intervention by the Warsaw Pact forces and the developments that followed.

Since the Fourteenth Congress managed to start its work and to do what was needful and practicable under occupation conditions, but not to go any further, it posed more questions than it provided answers. They are questions to which we can only slowly seek a solution, and answers which for Marxists must seem unconventional or even, at first glance, heretical. Unconventional – because they arose from a situation the Marxist classics never reckoned with: occupation of one socialist country by another. Heretical – since all newly-discovered truths are thought so at first, however obvious they come to appear later on.

A few conclusions can be drawn without further ado:

1. It is apparent from all the Congress records and from the resolutions previously passed by Party bodies that the *Extraordinary Fourteenth Congress was a legal, paramount forum of the Party and an authentic expression of its policies*. It was convened under the Party's current Statutes by a plenary session of the Central Committee. Its delegates had been duly elected by the democratic method of secret ballot at meetings of primary Party organizations and at district and regional conferences.

The fact that the Congress met on 22 August instead of the date originally planned, 9 September, and that some delegates, especially from Slovakia, were unable to attend, merely resulted from the abnormal situation of a military occupation which could not, of course, have been foreseen. The holding of the Congress was nevertheless perfectly in order, for over two-thirds of all delegates took part. The Congress, moreover, showed great political prudence and resolved that, in view of the absence of some of the Slovak delegates, their representation in the central bodies of the Party should be considered again as soon as the Congress was able to meet normally.

The mere fact of the Fourteenth Congress being held at all was a great moral blow to the occupying power and an obstacle to its political aims. Hence the declaration in the 'Moscow Protocols' that the Congress was invalid, and the attempts even today to discredit it by every possible means. The thought of a Fourteenth Congress being convened with properly elected delegates is still an alarming one for the Russians. With increasing frequency, therefore, we hear that elections of delegates to the Extraordinary Congress took place in an atmosphere of 'moral blackmail', that their results did not reflect the social composition of the Party, that 'extremists' were chosen. All this is intended to pave the way for an annulment of the elections of delegates and then, by a familiar process, for the holding of new elections in an atmosphere of intimidation, demagogy and strict control by the Party *apparat*, just as in the old days. The fact is, of course, that throughout the whole history of the Czechoslovak Communist Party since 1945, preparations for a Congress, the election of delegates and selection of candidates for a new Central Committee had never been conducted so democratically before, never involved the active participation of so many Party members, and never exhibited such efforts to choose the best representatives both for the Congress itself and on Party bodies thereafter. In 1968, for the first time, the list of candidates for Central Committee membership, instead of being drawn up beforehand by the top leaders and the appropriate departments of the *apparat*, represented a free choice by primary Party branches and by district and regional conferences.

All this, indeed, is borne out by Party documents of the time. These documents were approved by the Presidium and by the whole Central Committee, including men who today take the opposite line. The Presidium's reply of 17 July 1968 to the Warsaw Letter from the Five Parties (a reply endorsed two days later by the entire Central Committee) states, for example: 'The standard of delegates elected to attend the Congress guarantees that the Party's future policies will be determined not by any extremists, but by the democratically chosen, healthy, progressive core of the Party.'

Further confirmation comes from the very report prepared by the

Central Committee's Information Collating Unit for the Presidium meeting of 20 August 1968. (This report was reproduced on 2 July of the following year by *Rudé právo* as a source of 'reliable information' for Party members on what was actually going on before the invasion.) In analysing the spectrum of opinions among the delegates, it concluded that 'some 10 per cent will be coming to the Congress with very clear-cut views [i.e. conservative and dogmatic ones] about the policies of the last six months . . . about 10 per cent with very radical, often extreme attitudes . . . [while] almost 80 per cent of the delegates belong to the category which holds objective, progressive, but at the same time realistic ideas on current events, Party policy and future prospects'.

All this only goes to support our first conclusion, that *the Extraordinary Congress was a genuine reflection of the views of Czechoslovak communists and of most of the public*. The communists had become true spokesmen of the nation and their Party had become its leading force, not imposing its decisions on the other partners and treating them like 'transmission belts', but obtaining their voluntary consent by putting forward correct and intelligible policies. The Fourteenth Extraordinary Congress was intended to stabilize, and had every prospect of stabilizing, what had at first been an unpredictable surge forward to a renewed socialism. It was intended to reinforce the role of the Communist Party. The very fact that the renewal of socialism, and the renewal of the Party, were proceeding so democratically, inviting initiatives from the broad masses and increasing their involvement in the formation of the Party's policies and the running of the country – it was this which seemed so dangerous to people who stood for a bureaucratic version of socialism, and it was this that made it necessary in their eyes to call the process to a halt.

It was because the Extraordinary Congress of the Czechoslovak Communist Party was the most democratic gathering in the history of that Party and of the country, and because it was calculated to confirm Czechoslovakia's success in seeking 'socialism with a human face', that an army of half a million men with thousands of tanks and aircraft was sent to prevent it from taking place.

2. The records of the Congress, with the documents submitted to it and the resolutions passed by it, show that *what was happening in Czechoslovakia from January to 20 August 1968 was beyond doubt a process of a socialist nature*. This may be self-evident to anyone who

experienced the developments in question or even followed them from a distance. But it is necessary to repeat the fact, in view of the claim by the five Warsaw Pact countries that their intervention was motivated by 'fears for the fate of socialism', and of attempts by native Stalinists to justify abandonment of the January line by the bogey of 'a grave right-wing threat to socialism'.

It is true that the beginning of the renewal process was marked by criticism of past errors and distortions rather than by a detailed and positive programme for the future. This was an inevitable outcome of the regime of personal power exercised by Antonín Novotný, who had led the country into that profound political, economic and moral crisis which culminated in December 1967 and January 1968. In the conditions prevailing under this regime it was impossible to elaborate any positive programme of reform, for every attempt in that direction was denounced as factional activity and mercilessly suppressed. The principal way in which people could show their awareness of the crisis was therefore through criticism of particular weaknesses in the behaviour of individual Party officials. Even this criticism of past mistakes, of course, had a clearly socialist character; it was aimed primarily against 'deformations' which implied a departure from Marxism and at mistakes which had the effect of weakening socialism. Anyone who reads the welter of articles and speeches dating from this period will see that the originators of criticism were for the most part communists whose aim was to restore the Party's authority and to make socialism more appealing.

The dogmatists are fond of quoting Lenin's assertion that the Communist Party differs from bourgeois parties in being unafraid to confess its own errors. Yet in fact every radical criticism of mistakes made in the communist movement provokes among dogmatists a degree of shock and horror far greater than bourgeois politicians ever experience. Since the onset of Stalinism, self-criticism has been replaced by pompous trumpetings of 'victory', while criticism of past actions, or even tentatively critical analyses of developments, are instantly decried as 'denigration of successful results', 'nihilism', 'minimization of achievements', 'slandering of our glorious progress', and the like.

The sincerity of those who quote Lenin on self-criticism can be easily tested by looking at the pronouncements of the Soviet Party's own Central Committee over the last ten years. One may search in vain for any admission of error in important issues of programme or tactics, apart from a few attempts, regrettably superficial, made after the Twentieth Congress and now deliberately consigned to oblivion. To judge by the Central Committee's statements, the policies of the Soviet Party leaders have been invariably 'correct', 'confirmed by life itself', and 'the sole valid platform'. At most there has been some admission of shortcomings in the management of agriculture, industrial production or services, always attributed however to 'faulty implementation of the correct line by subordinate Party and State bodies'.

This attitude has deprived communists in the socialist countries of the ability, and the opportunity, to assess their own efforts critically and to take the initiative in looking for new ways ahead for socialist society. A development like that in Czechoslovakia after January 1968, which broke through this ossification and opened the way for critical inspection of the past, was therefore bound to cause panic among those bureaucratic and dogmatic communists who at present exert decisive influence in the Soviet Party and in those of four other socialist countries: Poland, Bulgaria, East Germany and Hungary. Let us consider, however, what they regarded as a 'threat to socialism' in Czechoslovakia.

No alteration occurred after January 1968 in the country's economic or social structure, nor was any such demand put forward. In contrast to Poland after 1956, and to Hungary, not a single agricultural collective was dissolved – and this in a country where 90 per cent of the land is collectivized. There was no single case of a nationalized factory, craft co-operative or shop returning to private ownership. (In contrast to Poland, East Germany and Hungary, Czechoslovakia knows only public ownership of the means of production throughout industry and in retail trade and services.) Czechoslovakia's trade with Western countries has never reached as large a proportion of her total foreign trade as in the cases of East Germany, Poland or Romania. She was solidly integrated in the Warsaw Pact and her army, police and people's militia were under the firm control of the Communist Party. The same Party had an absolute majority in parliament, in the organs of local government and in the principal mass organizations.

If we examine the Warsaw Letter from the five Communist Parties, along with press articles and public speeches from these countries before and after 20 August 1968, we can see that by the expression 'a threat to socialism' they chiefly meant the following:

- the fact that other political forces had become active beside the Communist Party (e.g. the social organizations and above all the trade unions) and were beginning to play a part in elaborating and implementing the Party and State programme, not just as 'transmission belts' but as independent factors in public life. This new situation, however, did not mean that the Party's leading role was being reduced; it meant on the contrary an enhancement of the Party's prestige, thanks to correct policies;
- the abolition of censorship and the introduction of genuine freedom of expression and information as the first pre-condition for every citizen to play his maximum part in public affairs;
- thoroughgoing implementation of economic reform involving not only a change in planning methods and economic instruments, but above all initiative on the part of workers and technicians, the establishment of self-administration in industry and the opening up of avenues toward dynamic advances in the technico-scientific revolution;
- the rehabilitation of people wrongly sentenced and the creation of guarantees in the judicial and police sectors against further violations of legality and personal liberty.

It would be wrong to deny, nor did progressive communists ever try to deny, that the process of renewal, especially the greater freedom of speech, brought to the surface a number of genuinely anti-socialist statements and trends, not to say false ideas and illusions, for example, about the nature of capitalism. All these things had existed before January 1968; they were not publicly displayed, but they enjoyed all the more backing because it was impossible to argue against them. With the new policy, however, they no longer had any appeal, or in so far as they found an audience, especially among the young, they would soon have lost it in open debate. Anyone, incidentally, who knows the true facts of life in East Germany, say, or in Poland, is aware that anti-socialist trends are far stronger in those countries than they were in Czechoslovakia, and that they are still growing.

In its reply of 17 July 1968 to the letter from the Five, the Czechoslovak Party's Central Committee wrote:

But if we ask whether such symptoms are to be correctly interpreted as meaning the extinction of the Party's leading role under the pressure of reactionary and counter-revolutionary forces, then we must answer in the negative. For all these things are but a part of contemporary political reality in our country. This reality has, however, a second side to it, which is in our view the important side, namely the growing prestige of the Party's new democratic policies amongst the broadest masses of the working class, the growing political activity of the great majority of the population. The great majority of our citizens of all classes and social strata favour the abolition of censorship and favour free speech. The Czechoslovak Communist Party is seeking to demonstrate that it can exert political leadership and control by methods other than the discredited ones of bureaucracy and police rule; that it can do so above all through the strength of its Marxist-Leninist ideas, through the appeal of its programme, of its correct and universally endorsed policies.

It is clear, then, that the advocates of 'bureaucracy and police rule' were not in the slightest interested in what new ideas were brewing in Czechoslovakia, nor in the fact that the Communist Party there was enjoying, and still continuing to acquire, more authority than ever; that the overwhelming majority of the people were spontaneously uniting around it; and that there was such a surge of revolutionary activity and patriotic sacrificial zeal that socialism was being strengthened and developed. They were alarmed and indignant, in fact, that Czechoslovakia should be abandoning those bureaucratic and police methods which, they felt, had proved so effective in their own countries and without which they could no longer conceive of socialism existing at all. Had they not thought on these lines, they must long since have perceived the threat to socialism constituted by the Novotný regime. But *that* had been perfectly acceptable to them; indeed, they had consistently praised it as an example and held its leader up as their 'closest ally'.

It was the men who put pressure on Czechoslovakia, and finally occupied her, who were most scared of free speech, the abolition of censorship, independence for the trade unions and mass organizations, workers' self-management, the rehabilitation of victims of Stalinist illegalities, and the defence of civic freedoms.

What these men were concerned with was not defending socialism, but defending bureaucratic police methods and the Stalinist model of iron-handed socialism.

3. *The Central Committee* chosen by the Extraordinary Congress *was one that expressed the changes in the Party and society since January 1968 and was calculated to give the Party a leadership with the*

backing both of the whole Party and of the public at large, a leadership capable of continuing on the January course and of developing it further as a creative socialist platform.

The question of a change of leadership which would naturally reinforce the position of Alexander Dubček and his colleagues was one of the key issues between January and August 1968. The Soviet leaders were much exercised over it and put great pressure on Dubček in this connection.

It must be recalled that the renewal process began in January with the decision to separate the functions of First Secretary of the Party and President of the Republic. The Central Committee that made this decision had been chosen in 1966 at the Party's Thirteenth Congress under the direct control of Novotný, who exercised a substantial influence over the selection of members and took care to prevent too many 'liberals' and independent-minded people from joining it. The majority of this Central Committee consisted of Party and State officials, many of whom had been involved in the perversions of the past and were therefore interested in maintaining the *status quo* or allowing at most minor reforms in political practice. There were rather deep and complex reasons why even such a Central Committee as this should finally turn against Novotný. There was discontent over the general situation in the country and over Novotný's arbitrary handing down of decisions; 'inter-generation' conflicts between the old guard and the rising middle-generation officials who did not find themselves exercising the authority they had expected; the failure to solve the nationality question, which made the Slovaks on the Central Committee dissatisfied. Only a small number of members tried to bring about basic changes and reforms in the political and economic system. Although most of the Central Committee, then, were able to join together in fighting for the separation of functions and the consequent limitation of Novotný's monopolistic powers, its ranks broke up as soon as new policies had to be worked out and new paths embarked on. The Committee now split up into the old guard (who constituted the majority), the wavering centrists and the progressives: these had to fight hard for fundamental reforms and were forced into continual compromises. As the democratization process went on in the primary Party organizations and throughout public life – especially at Party conferences – a large proportion of hard-line members of the Central Committee were forced to resign from posts in the Party or in other organizations. Thus by May 1968 about half of the members were in fact jobless; they spoke for nobody and were the subject of votes of non-confidence.

In this way the Central Committee had lost its authority as a Party organ with the rank and file, who ever more insistently demanded the convocation of Congress and the holding of fresh elections. For the longer the current Central Committee remained in power, the harder it made things for the Party and the more it played into the hands of various right-wing groups, quite apart from the fact that it hampered Dubček and his supporters. At first Dubček hesitated to convene a Congress and tried to solve the problem by asking the most discredited members of the Central Committee to resign. Only after the majority of them had refused to comply did he accept the call for an Extra-ordinary Congress to be held in September 1968.

In the course of preparations for this Congress it became clear that the Party wanted radical changes carried out in its leading bodies, and particularly that it wanted to see the backs of the men responsible for the current crisis and for the past 'deformations'. The above-men-tioned report of the Information Collating Unit, submitted on 20 August 1968, points out:

A particularly remarkable feature of developments in the Czechoslovak Party is the way in which a period of less than six months has seen the replacement not just of a part of the higher echelons of the Party, but of virtually the whole leadership. Whereas in other Communist Parties changes have normally affected only a few individuals while the rest of the Central Committee has remained intact, the opposite tendency has been manifested in the Czechoslovak case: almost the entire Central Committee is being exchanged except for a small fraction of the inner core of Party leaders. Another important feature is that the new people who will be coming into leading Party positions are for the most part politically unknown factors, people who have been involved in politics only for a brief period.

The report goes on to say that, according to provisional findings, a maximum of 30 per cent of the old Central Committee would be re-elected into the new one and that in the case of secret balloting a third of these in turn might fall by the wayside. This assessment looks like an attempt to frighten the Party's current leaders with the prospect of not being re-elected themselves. However, in its 25 July resolution the Presidium had evaluated the Party election campaign in very different terms, saying, for example:

The commission entrusted by the Presidium with the personnel aspect of preparations for the Congress has so far received 935 proposals reflecting the views of Party members on the desirable composition of the new Central Committee. The majority of these proposals put forward the names of the *most able** communists, men who have been gaining the confidence of the rank and file of the Party and of the public at large and who carry authority with them.

This leads us to the further conclusion that *military intervention in Czechoslovakia was intended to prevent the holding of the Fourteenth Congress and so, amongst other things, to forestall the election of a new Central Committee reflecting the views and hopes of Party members*. It was evident to the Soviet leaders that the new body would not contain people willing to ride roughshod over popular wishes. To the bureaucratic mind it was out of the question that a new Central Committee should be chosen democratically, by secret ballot, from among the 935 names put forward, and hence enjoy real authority. It accorded with the hard-liners' ideas and habits that the Central Committee should be selected from above and be bound by an oath of obedience, for they expected it to do nothing but approve the 'leadership's' decisions and see that they were carried out. The idea that the leadership should have to answer to the Central Committee and that the Central Committee should expect to check up on the leaders' activities and criticize them filled the dogmatic Stalinists with boundless horror and pious indignation.

What most frightened the self-styled defenders of socialism and of the working class was, paradoxically, the prospect of a Central Committee containing 80 per cent of 'new people', i.e. of those very industrial workers and technicians who were in a position to reflect real working-class opinion. With such a Committee they would have lost, for good and all, any chance of plotting or executing an internal Party take-over whenever they felt their interests to be jeopardized. They realized that as long as they kept the old Central Committee they could hold Dubček and the other reformers in check; they could even blackmail them and if need be liquidate them in the Committee's name. A new Central Committee would bar this road to them. They therefore selected a date for the military intervention so as to prevent any Congress being held at which a new Committee could be chosen. When the Congress nevertheless *did* take place and a new Committee

* Editor's emphasis.

was elected, they forced the imprisoned leaders of the Party to promise to declare the Congress invalid.

From this a moral can be drawn of great importance for the international workers' movement and in particular for the present socialist countries. *Whenever the Soviet leaders lose complete control of the upper echelons of any Communist Party anywhere, they will seek to replace them by a take-over inside the Party with the help of elements loyal to them within the Central Committee – elements often under some obligation to the Soviets and corrupted by them. If they fail, they will not hesitate to embark on a military policing action.*

4. The organizers of the military action against Czechoslovakia justified their decision both before, and especially after, 20 August by reference to the onset of 'counter-revolution'. Even though the Dubček team had very convincingly refuted this claim in their reply to the Warsaw Letter from the five States and again in several speeches and documents after the invasion, when they were subject to the grossest pressure, the Soviet leaders are still trying to reconstruct the 'counter-revolutionary danger' in retrospect out of various public manifestations of hostility to the occupation, sundry 'secret reports' to the pre-invasion Ministry of the Interior now published, and other pieces of evidence constructed in the familiar way. For this campaign they have even won over some of the present Czechoslovak communist leaders who need the 'counter-revolutionary danger' as a justification for their own hard-line policies and so have come to acknowledge – or were forced to accept – the correctness of that 'fraternal aid' rendered by the socialist countries on the night of 20 August 1968.

Was there really a counter-revolutionary danger? As we have said, the progressive members of the Party were the first to appreciate the existence of genuine anti-socialist forces, which had increased, particularly during the last years of Novotný's office, because of his dogmatic policies and inability to solve the problems that had accumulated. Anti-socialist forces did not come into being after January 1968 in consequence of the renewal process: they merely floated to the surface from the holes and corners where they had existed for years, thanks chiefly to the Party's political mistakes. These opponents of socialism included, to be sure, certain former spokesmen of right-wing parties or natural antagonists such as members of families who had lost their property under socialism. But these were only a minority;

283

their ranks had been decimated after February 1948, while many had fled to the West, started new careers and given up any idea of returning. It is an awkward fact, on the other hand, that the anti-socialist ranks had been replenished by young people, both students and young workers, who mainly saw the negative sides of the socialist system: the curbing of freedom of travel and assembly, discrimination on the basis of parents' social origin, promotion of unqualified personnel by patronage, deliberate restriction of news, illegal arrests and trials, boorish handling of national feelings, economic incompetence, technical backwardness and, finally, the lack of prospects for the young themselves. Such critics were not, of course, class enemies, but merely opponents of the Stalin or Novotný models of socialism. All the same, they provided a certain basis for anti-socialist forces after January, when public meetings and discussions gave them an opportunity to come out into the open. At first, indeed, they gained a good deal of ground, because the communists were disoriented and unable to formulate a new programme while they were still preoccupied with rectifying their own past mistakes. Gradually, however, as the Party began to shake off those responsible for the old distortions, to acquire intelligent and respectable people with good records as its spokesmen and to formulate the new programme of 'socialism with a human face', and as the public for its part was able to satisfy itself that the Party was serious in criticizing its past errors and proposing to put them right, the wind was taken out of the sails of the anti-socialist and anti-communist elements. These accordingly lost their pull on the public and found themselves more and more isolated. Ironically enough, what gave their propaganda repeated reinforcement were acts of interference from the Soviet side and press attacks on the Czechoslovak reformers by some of the socialist countries, as well as various counter-offensives by native hard-liners who could always rely on support and publicity in the newspapers of the Five even where they did not actually draw their inspiration from that quarter.

Contrasting assessments of the importance and prospects of the anti-socialist camp produced two opposite reactions.

The Soviet leaders and their allies in the four other States regarded the existence of anti-socialist elements, and especially the opportunity such elements had to find spokesmen and to express themselves in print or at public meetings, as a lethal danger requiring radical counter-measures: the immediate proscription of the organizations involved and the silencing of their spokesmen by the use of 'instruments of State power'. *This reaction derives basically from a lack of confidence in the force of socialist ideas and in the ability of communists to win over the majority of the nation to their policies by persuasion and example.* It reflects first-hand experience of the dependence of the bureaucratic, police-state version of socialism upon these same 'instruments of State power' and hence on fear and repression. When the straitjacket is loosened, as it was in Hungary in 1956, such a system collapses in chaos through its lack of any real support among the masses.

The Czechoslovak communist leaders and the healthy forces in the Party, on the other hand, saw the anti-socialist forces primarily as the consequence of the preceding period. They were not afraid, then, of any public confrontation with such arguments, particularly after they had overcome their own initial hesitations and established the right political platform for a socialist renascence. In the course of countering anti-socialist views they sought to differentiate between dyed-in-the-wool enemies of socialism on the one hand, and on the other hand people who had merely come to identify socialism with its perverted form and were ready to acknowledge the new efforts to cleanse socialism of its impurities and give such efforts their tentative support– support which might one day, especially among the young, turn into active participation. *This second reaction arose from confidence in the strength and attractiveness of socialism, in its ability to win the support of the majority of the public without the use of bureaucratic police-state methods, and to compete with opposing opinions by purely political means.*

This dichotomy is very significant and will be found to recur in other socialist countries. For opposition elements exist in forms peculiar to each country and may either grow or decline according to the domestic and international situations. In Poland, for example, the authorities deal with them by means of deterrent trials and purges, in China by the 'cultural revolution' intended to give the masses, particularly the young, a chance to break up the bureaucratized machinery of Party and State. Almost all such devices, however, have so far been aimed at 'crushing' anti-socialist forces. This makes it impossible *a priori* to differentiate between such forces, to carry on an overt dialogue with them and to secure their defeat by political argument; it tends on the contrary to drive them into illegality underground, where they continue to be sources of sudden conflict and may really produce counter-revolutionary explosions.

Developments in Czechoslovakia after the military intervention of 20 August furnish a case in point. Whereas before that date no mass display of anti-Soviet or anti-socialist sentiments was feasible and isolated manifestations were mainly provoked by external pressure, once the occupation began anti-Soviet resentment grew rapidly as a result of the presence of Soviet troops in the country, which made people feel insulted and humiliated. The present leaders of the Czechoslovak Communist Party are trying to compel the public to pay tribute to that 'eternal friendship with the Soviet Union' which was genuine and popular enough after 1945 but now strikes most of the public as unacceptable and hypocritical. Accordingly, anti-Soviet and anti-socialist feelings now tend to reach heights unprecedented in the country's history. This development cannot be arrested unless the Party returns to the resolutions of the Fourteenth Congress and itself leads the struggle to end the occupation, renew the country's full sovereignty and continue the post-January course of socialist rebirth.

It follows from this that *those who gave most nourishment to anti-socialist trends and reactionary right-wing groups are the spokesmen of Great Power policies and bureaucratic police-state rule within the leadership of the communist parties of the Soviet Union and some other socialist States, particularly when they engage in such operations as the military occupation of Czechoslovakia.* Such policies and operations are capable in certain socialist countries of producing situations where popular anger explodes unpredictably and may convert otherwise negligible and uninfluential right-wing groups into a truly counter-revolutionary force. The suppression of such a force will necessarily involve the police and army, and their use will in turn be explained to the public by the presence of counter-revolutionary elements. In this way socialist countries are led by bureaucratic police-state methods into a vicious circle from which there is no escape.

The only solution is to eliminate this whole concept of socialism, which arose in the Soviet Union and other countries as a result of various objective and subjective factors, and to carry out – in several socialist countries at the same time, if possible – thoroughgoing reforms aimed at extending socialist democracy to the utmost. *A socialist system relying on the confidence of the broad masses and their active share in running the State and managing production in conditions of wide freedom of speech and assembly, a system such as the Czechoslovak Communist Party strove for between January and August 1968 and*

*which the Extraordinary Fourteenth Congress endorsed, is the best in-
surance against counter-revolutionary plots and putsches on the one
hand, and against the degeneration of a socialist society into a bureaucratic police-state and army dictatorship by élite groups. The two
dangers are basically the same: both lead to the enfeeblement and destruction of socialism.*

5. It has often been asserted by the instigators of military action
against Czechoslovakia, by native 'conservatives' and present-day
'realists' and '100 per cent internationalists', that the Czechoslovak
Communist Party could never have coped with the situation alone
because its leaders had no time to develop their policies and were
under continuous right-wing pressure.

It is true, as we have said before, that the Party was to a certain
extent on the defensive at the beginning of the renewal process,
especially between January and May 1968. It then reacted to stimuli
from below, from basic Party organizations and from the general
public. A sharp struggle was in progress within the Party as people
sought to wipe out the mistakes and injustices of the past and the new
Action Programme was being worked out in the midst of internal
differences. That the Party failed to exercise its leading role was its
own fault and above all the fault of die-hard elements among its
leaders and inside the Central Committee, who did all they could to
put a brake on the reforms and, by halting their application within the
leadership itself, to keep the rank-and-file ignorant and inert. An
additional factor was a certain hesitancy on the part of Dubček who,
in his creditable desire to offend no one and to introduce genuinely
comradely relationships into the Party, constantly sought compromises on both sides. Thus it came about that the Party was left unin-
formed for two months about what had actually happened at the
January plenum of the Central Committee, and that the drafting of the
Action Programme dragged on until most of its admirable principles
had already been published as demands from Party or other organizations, so that the leadership was not given credit for the initiative.
Then there was delay in convening the Extraordinary Fourteenth
Congress despite the expressed desire of most Party branches and despite the obvious fact that without personal changes in the Central
Committee the new line would never be accepted and the Committee's
own authority never reinforced or restored. Again, situation reports

were repeatedly postponed about the state of the economy, progress made on economic reform and the work of rehabilitation.

This situation lasted until around May 1968, when a breakthrough occurred with the decision to summon a Congress. District and regional conferences were held in a spirit of Party mobilization and consolidation. Most reform proposals now originated from communists. The Party's hold on the public increased and after the Presidium's reply to the Warsaw Letter in July the Party became the recognized spokesman of the overwhelming majority of both peoples, Czech and Slovak.

In its 25 July resolution the Presidium summed up the situation as follows:

The conclusion of [district and regional] conferences has shown that the Party is strong enough to solve the problems associated with the current process of rebirth by political means, especially after the impressive shift of support toward progressive elements and progressive ideas.

Even the Information Collating Unit's report, submitted to the Presidium actually on 20 August, and certainly not publicized in the following July to provide arguments for the reformists, makes this admission:

The trend within the Party is on the contrary characterized by a decline of fringe tendencies, the gradual consolidation of a firm Party core and, to a great extent, growing self-confidence among active members . . . The district and regional conferences testify to the whole Party's conviction that it is equipped to cope with the problems before it and to find a way out of the situation which faces the Party and the whole country.

The Party, then, was on the way to calm and stability; the Fourteenth Congress and the election of a fresh Central Committee and other Party bodies would doubtless have completed the process. What were those forces which, it is often now claimed, were preventing the Party from developing a positive course of action? *These forces were nothing other than the continual attempts by the Soviet leaders, together with Ulbricht and Gomulka, to interfere in Czechoslovak developments by exerting brute pressure on Dubček and the other Czechoslovak leaders in a way without precedent among allies even in the imperialist world.* In the six months or so prior to August 1968 the leaders of the

Czechoslovak Communist Party were obliged to make more journeys to Moscow than during the preceding four or five years.

The endless invitations to consult at meetings – Sofia, Dresden, Warsaw, Moscow, Čierná, Bratislava – where they had to explain their intentions and declare their loyalty to the Warsaw Pact; the constant visits and telephone calls from the Soviet ambassador, Chervonenko, who behaved like a provincial governor in Tsarist days; the arrival of 'friendly' delegations, especially military ones; the obligation to accept manoeuvres on Czechoslovak soil without any clear date being agreed for their conclusion, which was then artificially delayed; the repeated letters from fraternal parties expressing their anxieties and culminating in the notorious Warsaw Letter from the Five – all these things amounted to a single series of operations calculated to provoke nervousness and disagreement within the Czechoslovak Party, and above all to deny its leaders the time they needed – time to carry out a 'positive policy', to apply their minds to new measures and to make preparations for the Congress.

In its answer to the Five the Presidium put it clearly enough: 'We therefore regard all those pressures upon the Party to adopt a different procedure, i.e. to settle basic questions of Party policy at any other time or place than at the Fourteenth Congress, as constituting the chief threat to our success in strengthening the Party's leading role in Czechoslovakia.' From this it follows that *the principal pressures that hampered the Party in developing a constructive policy of socialist renewal were not those exerted by domestic right-wing forces* (these existed, it is true, but had no great impact): *they were those exerted by the Soviet leadership* par excellence, *with support from Ulbricht and Gomulka.*

6. Advocates of the bureaucratic police-state version of socialism delight in boasting that they pursue their policies 'from class positions', i.e. from a working-class standpoint. The post-January policies of the Czechoslovak Party, they complain, represented a retreat from class positions to 'cosmopolitan politics'. It is in fact stated in the conclusion to the Warsaw Letter that 'faced by the threat of counter-revolution, the voice of the working class must ring out powerfully at the Communist Party's call'. The working class of Czechoslovakia did indeed raise its voice powerfully in answer to the Five: in thousands of resolutions and at meetings with record attendance it expressed its full

289

support for the Party leadership around Dubček and for the post-January line. And when, on the night of 20 August, tanks and troops of the five countries burst into Czechoslovakia in the name of our 'class brethren', *it was the workers who stood up most resolutely and bravely against the occupation. It was the workers under whose protection in a Prague factory the Extraordinary Fourteenth Congress was held* – that Congress which it was the occupation armies' task to prevent.

The part played by the working class in Czechoslovakia after January 1968 conveys an invaluable lesson for the international movement. Its workers have an old revolutionary tradition. Even under the pre-war bourgeois Republic their Communist Party was one of the largest parties in the country. Despite its losses under the German occupation, it was one of the main bastions of the Resistance; after the liberation it grew rapidly and led the struggle to convert the national-democratic revolution into a socialist one. At that time, and during the subsequent laying of the foundations of a socialist State, the working class was undoubtedly the mainspring of progress and produced from its own ranks able politicians and organizers as well as a new intelligentsia. Since, however, the authorities rapidly adapted themselves to the bureaucratic Stalinist model, the role of the working class was steadily reduced to that of fulfilling production targets, joining voluntary labour brigades and – as its only political activity – loudly approving whatever the ruling group did. The majority of senior Party officials were of working-class origin. But their privileges, their power and their way of life quickly alienated them from their own class and turned them into a kind of independent force, running things 'in the name of the workers' but really without regard for what the workers thought or felt. For twenty years the Czechoslovak working class under this system was steadily purged of its revolutionary outlook and diluted with new workers from the middle class, sent into the factories as 'punishment' by the ruling clique, and cut off from political activity except for being occasionally set against the intelligentsia or the farmers in this or that demagogic campaign. The men who gradually emerged as the workers' representatives were a group of officials who had once been workers but had long since forgotten their trades, had acquired no skill to suit them for their new functions and merely battened upon their working-class origin. Such people became the chief buttress in society of Novotný's system of personal power;

they opposed change of any kind, seeing it primarily as a threat to their privileged position.

This state of affairs produced an understandable, though erroneous, reaction in other social groups, particularly among the students and intellectuals who had tried to rebel against the bureaucratic police-state system and been persecuted for their pains. These people had the impression that the workers were not merely failing to support them, but even denouncing them through the mouths of their officials. This led many progressive theorists to conclude that the working class had fulfilled its revolutionary mission and was handing over the torch, as befitted the age of the technico-scientific revolution, to the intelligentsia. The publicity given to this theory in the Czechoslovak press during 1966 and 1967, even in periodicals regarded as the mouthpieces of progressive forces, was naturally not calculated to assist understanding between the workers and the discontented intellectuals.

For this very reason, in the initial phase of the renewal process from January to March 1968, it was the journalists, writers, students and some of the scientific and technical intelligentsia, quicker than others to realize what was at stake at the January plenum and better prepared for the changes to come through their ideological tussle with the dogmatists in the preceding period, who now played the most active part. The stand taken by these intellectuals was naturally affected by what they had been through: they concentrated on demanding freedom of speech and information and on criticizing the distortions of the past. This in turn aroused suspicions among the workers – which their officials were eager to confirm – that the intelligentsia was now arrogating the right to lead the Party and the State, underestimating the workers and completely ignoring the aspects of most concern to them, namely how to solve the economic crisis, how to secure for the workers a share in the management of enterprises and how to pursue policies that made sense to the working man.

It was not until April 1968 that there was an impressive degree of participation in the reform movement by working men identifying themselves with the struggle and carrying it into their own factories. A new type of working-class spokesman now made its appearance – wise, intelligent officials miles removed from the old Party and union bosses, who were obliged to keep quiet and in many cases to resign. In this period workers developed an insatiable appetite for speeches and articles by progressive politicians; they would ask journalists such awkward questions as 'Where were you before this happened? Why did you not protest?'; they debated amongst themselves and gradually acquired a new self-confidence and revolutionary *élan*; they sent their own delegations to attend Party conferences and Central Committee sessions; they passed resolutions and demanded the right to share in drafting Party policy. It was a time of incipient *rapprochement* between workers and intellectuals, particularly journalists, writers and radio and TV personnel, but also scientists and technicians. It is sheer casuistry for the dogmatists to claim, as they still do, that the Fourteenth Congress was not a workers' Congress because only 18 per cent of the delegates were working men. Even this figure is higher than for the previous Congresses, when moreover it had been based on the delegates' original class affiliation. (If this method were applied to the 1968 Congress the figure of 18 per cent would have to be increased to include the many delegates of proletarian origin listed among 'technical and economic workers' – 32 per cent – and 'political workers' – 23 per cent.) Moreover, the identification of interests as between workers and the technical intelligentsia had reached the point where working-class Party branches were often choosing popular and progressive technicians to speak for them.

We have already mentioned how the working class in fact behaved on 20 August 1968. What is more important, it became clear that their reaction was no flash in the pan. *Even during the harsh repression that followed the invasion it was the workers who most consistently defended the January line.* They made agreements with artists, journalists and students, supported the massive student strike of November 1968, backed the progressive core of the Party against the attempted dogmatist *putsch* in December, opposed any disrespect for the student Palach's tragic deed in January 1969, pressed for legislation to approve the system of workers' councils and took the lead in setting them up in a number of factories without even waiting for the Party leaders' agreement. Through strikes and demonstrations they gave daily proof of their hostility to the occupation and to the new policy embraced by Husák, which was to bow before Soviet pressure and that of the native hard-liners.

Those, by contrast, who occupied Czechoslovakia in the name of the working class and claim to rule on its behalf have proved themselves the chief grave-diggers of the working man's rights. They refuse to listen to his views or print his resolutions; they have revived extreme pressure on the working class, taking charge of the unions and announcing the 'conquest of the factories' as their main platform at the May 1969 plenum. By rejecting workers' councils, by refusing to hold a Congress or general elections and by tightening the central direction of the economy they are proving how little they trust the workers and how remote from their interests they feel themselves to be. The occupation and the anti-national policies followed since then have led the country into an economic crisis unparalleled in Czechoslovakia and perhaps in all Europe. The new men cannot guarantee the workers even their basic foodstuffs and other essential requirements; they cannot halt the continuous rise in living costs which bears hardest on the working class; and working conditions are worse than in many capitalist countries.

The Czechoslovak working class has confirmed that in a socialist society the workers do not cease to represent a powerful revolutionary force, preventing degeneration into a bureaucratic police-state system. To perform this role they need a democratically run Party, adequate sources of information, trade union autonomy, co-operation with the intelligentsia and peasantry, industrial self-management and a share in running industry and the State machine. *Sponsors of the bureaucratic, police-state version of socialism, by contrast, have shown in Czechoslovakia how they distrust and fear the working class, how they strive to debar it from political activity,* to restrict it to production tasks and make it the passive subject of their own policies. *The revolutionary character of the working class and its alliance with other social groups, above all the students and creative intelligentsia, represents the greatest hope for the people in the socialist countries.*

This is why the Stalinists are trying, and will go on trying, to make the working class as unmilitant and unpolitical as possible – witness their campaign against the unions, the workers' councils and many factory branches of the Communist Party. For a time this pressure may weaken the revolutionary urges of the workers, but it is already clear that they cannot be drugged into the state of obedient lethargy which afflicted them before January 1968.

7. The Soviet leaders and their allies in Poland, East Germany, Bulgaria and Hungary have evolved a theory of '*limited sovereignty*' and '*common defence of socialism*'. They invaded Czechoslovakia

under the banner of 'saving socialism' and protecting the country from the 'imperialist menace'. True, they deny the existence of the 'limited sovereignty' doctrine and use every opportunity to assert their respect for sovereignty, independence, equality and the principle of non-interference in other countries' internal affairs. However, it is enough to read the Warsaw Letter, that explanatory prologue to the military occupation, to see the basic attitude of the Five. 'We cannot agree', says the Letter, 'to hostile forces edging your country off the socialist path and threatening to tear Czechoslovakia out of the socialist community. This is not a matter for you alone!' And again: 'The borders of the socialist world have moved forward to the centre of Europe, to the Elbe and the Šumava Hills . . . We shall never consent to seeing imperialism, with or without violence, from within or from without, make a breach in the socialist system and change the European balance of power in its own favour.'

We may leave aside the writers' concept of 'paths to socialism': they accept only the Soviet path and regard this as obligatory for all other countries too. What can be inferred from the Warsaw Letter, however, is that its authors consider intervention, political or military, to be justified in the following cases:

(a) It would be justified if any socialist country wished to leave the socialist community, by which they clearly mean the Warsaw Pact. In effect, then, they believe themselves entitled to occupy any country which either intended to leave the Pact or was unwilling to join it. This gives them an excuse at any time to occupy Romania, Yugoslavia, Albania, or even China. For a socialist country's choice of foreign policy, or its right to conclude treaties, is 'not a matter for that country alone'. On the contrary, it is apparently a matter for those who claim the right to decide who belongs to the socialist community and who does not!

(b) The borders of the socialist community have moved forward, we are told, to the Šumava Hills. This is no longer, then, the border of a sovereign Czechoslovakia entitled to decide on its own how to defend it, but a 'common frontier'. If the self-styled guarantors of socialism should at any time take it into their heads that this frontier is ill-defended they are entitled to occupy it. For it is their frontier too.

This, clearly, is an idea quite irrelevant to the defence of socialism or to internationalism. It is the purely militaristic,

Great Power concept of defending frontiers and interests by means of a *cordon sanitaire.*

(c) 'We shall never consent to seeing imperialism . . . change the European balance of power.' Since the invasion, and again recently, Soviet propaganda has frequently reverted to the thesis of an 'immutable balance of power' as established at Yalta by the outcome of the Second World War. Everyone will certainly concede that the Soviet Union, after its bitter wartime experiences and great sacrifices, has a claim to see its security guaranteed against further aggression. But what has the defence of the *status quo* and the allocation of spheres of influence between the two superpowers to do with world socialism and the revolutionary movement? *Would not the same doctrine give the United States a moral right, and a practical capacity, to intervene anywhere to the west of the Elbe and the Šumava Hills where an attempt was being made to change the social system, e.g. by a socialist revolution?* Where is it laid down, and how can it be claimed by anyone who professes a doctrine of revolution, that an agreement made in 1945, when many present-day States had not even come into existence, should be binding upon all and be regarded as 'permanent'?

In actual fact *this theory vividly illustrates the complete divorce between today's leaders in the Soviet Union, and Marxist internationalism. If the borders of the socialist world run along the Elbe and the Šumava Hills, this means that everything to the west of them is a hostile world, complete with its working class, students, socialists and communists.* If we add the smug assertion, often repeated at the time of the armed clashes on the Ussuri, that Soviet troops ranged along that river frontier are defending 'the whole of European civilization against the Chinese' (see M. Dedianc's reports in *Le Monde*), we have *a picture of the complete collapse of Marxist thought among contemporary Soviet leaders, a picture even more dismal than that provided by the failure of the Second International at the beginning of the First World War and the consequent break-up of that organization.*

So much for the theoretical implications. The practical effects are even more disturbing. The facts already quoted show that:

- Czechoslovakia never left the socialist path, but on the contrary reinforced its own approach to socialism;
- far from intending to leave the Warsaw Pact, Czechoslovakia never even entertained the thought of changing to a policy of non-alignment like Yugoslavia, or of independent initiative like Romania. She played a full part in the Warsaw Pact and merely took the liberty of proposing measures to ensure its better functioning;
- the Czechoslovak army was one of the most efficient in the Warsaw Pact countries and was quite capable of effecting the defence of the western frontiers by conventional means;
- in the summer of 1968 neither American nor West German imperialism constituted a direct threat to Czechoslovakia's safety, nor did they seek the overthrow of socialism in that country. The Soviet leaders are well aware of this. Indeed, *American ruling circles were informed by the Soviet leaders in advance of their intention to occupy Czechoslovakia and raised no objection to it (whatever their public attitude after 20 August); they were evidently relieved when the attractive model of 'socialism with a human face' was smothered.*

The effect of the military occupation of Czechoslovakia was to reverse all these factors, for

- it demoralized the Czechoslovak army and ruled it out as a fighting force;
- it changed Czechoslovakia from a reliable into an unfriendly hinterland, whose inhabitants have considered the Warsaw Pact troops an occupying force ever since 20 August 1968 and in the event of conflict would behave accordingly;
- it strengthened NATO at a time when that organization had been badly eroded and played into the hands of those who wished to see it given 'more teeth';
- it hamstrung the international workers' and communist movement, and progressive forces everywhere.

One consequence of the invasion was that Czechoslovakia became one of the weakest links in the Warsaw Pact, while the Pact itself was discredited and undermined as a defence community. Albania used the opportunity (plus its favourable geographical position) to leave the Pact officially; Romania, though a member, was not even informed of the invasion plan, which can hardly have enhanced her interest in further co-operation; Yugoslavia, a non-member, drew still further away from the Pact and even started defence preparations against a possible attack by its members, thus further dissipating their military resources.

The occupation of Czechoslovakia against the will of Party and State leaders was a slap in the face to all rules of behaviour between socialist countries and nullified what had been thought a great achievement of socialism, namely the prevention of war between nations, hitherto considered to be a product of capitalism. If Czechoslovakia had not refrained from armed resistance, the occupation would have led to the first open warfare between two socialist countries. As it was, we witnessed the first case of one socialist country being overrun by the armed forces of other socialist countries – which in international law has always been termed aggression. At the same time a dangerous precedent has been created. What will the rulers of the Soviet Union say if the Chinese copy her example and march on Moscow under the banner of protecting socialism in that country? Or do the Soviet leaders propose to use the same pretext for a blow against socialist China, declaring a crusade against the yellow peril and attempting to succeed where the imperialists of England, Japan and America all failed?

8. The occupation has lent new point to the problem of recognizing each socialist country's 'specific road to socialism'. When the excommunication of Yugoslavia in 1948–9 and the campaign against national deviations were followed by the dissolution of the Cominform and the annulment of numerous statements put out by the Soviet Communist Party and the international gatherings of communist and workers' parties, it might have seemed that the right to specific roads to socialism, long since asserted by Lenin, had attained universal recognition. Moreover, the Soviet leaders have several times proclaimed the equality of parties within the international movement and denied the existence of a 'leading Party'.

The measures taken against Czechoslovakia expose the hollowness of these statements. The Soviet leadership continues to maintain its sole right to decide what form of socialism is 'good', and what form is 'revisionist' or even no longer socialist at all. The Soviet leadership has continued to send the Czechoslovak Party letters 'analysing' the inter-

nal situation in Czechoslovakia and criticizing speeches by this or that
official; to summon senior Czechoslovak Party officials and dress them
down; to dispatch plenipotentiaries on inspection trips as if the
Czechoslovak Party were some provincial committee of the Soviet
Party. In Czechoslovakia's case the Soviets rejected the views of a
socialist country's own Party leaders, assembled armies behind their
backs, occupied the country overnight, had those leaders carried off
as 'enemies' and forced them to sign a humiliating agreement – all to
be followed up with hypocritical hugs and kisses!

If to all this one adds the gross and undisguised interference by
Soviet leaders after the Moscow agreement, the appointment of
advisers to key positions, the reservation of all personnel matters for
decision in Moscow, the prior discussion of all Central Committee
resolution drafts, the duty journeys to Czechoslovakia undertaken by
Soviet Ministers and plenipotentiaries without even informing the
Czechoslovak government or party of their arrival, the maintenance
of an army of occupation and a secret-police force on Czechoslovak
soil, then *it is clear how little has changed since Cominform days. The
Soviet leaders still maintain and exercise their right to act as supreme
arbiters, as the 'centre of international communism', determining what is
authentic and what false socialism, which country deserves to be protected
and which country to be excommunicated, punished or even – if it refuses
to kowtow – occupied by force.*

The occupation of Czechoslovakia has thrown the international
communist movement back into the Cominform phase of 1948–9,
except that Brezhnev has gone further than Stalin. For Stalin hoped
to starve Yugoslavia out, to isolate her and break her resistance. He
never dared to send an army into the land.

*The step taken against Czechoslovakia was intended to warn every
socialist country against trying to formulate its own specific road to
socialism.* By forcing other socialist countries to join in a punitive
expedition against 'socialism with a human face', even though the
Soviet army could easily have performed this task on its own, the
Soviet leaders hoped to restore iron discipline in the socialist camp and
to frighten not only Romania and Yugoslavia but also domestic opposition forces in the other countries, including the Soviet Union itself.
But the attempt miscarried. Romania re-emphasized her independent
position by the line she took at the Moscow Conference and by staging
the Nixon visit; Yugoslavia still stands pat on her jealously guarded

sovereignty; Albania, with Chinese and Yugoslav assistance, has widened her breach with the USSR; Vietnam, her energies absorbed by war, has shown no interest in backing Soviet claims to hegemony, and therefore maintains equally correct relations with China; China herself is mustering her resources for an historic confrontation, both political and military, with the Soviet Union.

The socialist community, then, is creaking in all its joints and not even the straitjacket of 'limited sovereignty' can hold it together. This situation can improve only if the Soviet leaders agree genuinely to respect each country's right to its own specific path to socialism; to respect each country's sovereignty; and to respect the principles of equality and of non-interference in domestic matters, whatever solidarity is preserved on a voluntary basis.

It is necessary at this point to refute an argument used not only by the Soviet leaders, but by many Czech communists too. 'Nothing can be done about it,' they say. 'The world is divided into two camps and socialism cannot be built without the Soviet Union.' To accept this thesis is to surrender before one of two alternatives: either the inevitability of the Soviet Party's leading role and its right to judge, punish and occupy other Parties and countries, or an obligation to oppose the Soviet hegemony and so fall into the lap of capitalism. There is, alas, no third way, say the expositors of this hopeless 'reality', adding that life is the same the whole world over. The argument has an apparent logic and the Czech 'little man' is ready to accept it.

The truth, however, is quite different. The frontier in the struggle for socialism and progress no longer, these days, runs along the line between the Warsaw Pact and NATO territories; it lies inside the various countries, where forces are being born that seek to change the *status quo*. Quite a few countries are constructing socialism without being in the Warsaw Pact and without the blessing of the Soviet Party – often indeed in sharp conflict with it, as in Yugoslavia, Albania, China and Cuba. The Italian Communist Party has defended Czechoslovak socialism against Soviet Great Power politics; it has not thereby become an agent of capitalism but is, on the contrary, one of the sturdiest components in the communist movement.

From this it follows that *it is today possible, and indeed necessary, to construct socialism where need be against the wishes of the Soviet leadership, outside the Warsaw Pact and even in temporary conflict with both if they try to impose their own brute authority and their own political platform.* Czechoslovakia could perfectly well follow other countries in building a real socialist society without, for the moment, Soviet approval, and would still not run any risk of that instant attack from neighbouring imperialist countries which the 'limited sovereignty' theorists pretend to fear.

The whole idea of a world divided into 'imperialist' and 'socialist' areas is un-Marxist. It is intended to justify the hegemony of the USA in one half and the USSR in the other, and so to give each the right to punish any country seeking to go its own way. Marxists in every land must therefore fight against this theory, for it hampers the progress of the revolutionary movement.

The suggestion that socialism can or must be constructed against the will, if necessary, of the Soviet leadership arises only from today's abnormal situation, where that leadership has itself deviated from Marxism. All sincere socialists and communists trust that the deviation is a temporary one. In Czechoslovakia, above all, communists feel no hostility at all towards the nations of the Soviet Union. On the contrary we are ever mindful that the Soviet Union was the first socialist country, that it grew under infinitely complex domestic and international conditions and that the Soviet people made boundless sacrifices to fight Fascism in the last war (sacrifices made all the greater, it is true, by the unforgivable blunders of the leaders of the country, Stalin foremost). We shall not forget that the Soviet people contributed in large degree to the defeat of Fascism and hence to the liberation of Czechoslovakia, and that the Soviet Union represents an important component in the world-wide progressive movement, thanks to an enormous economic potential which even today, unfortunately, remains largely unexploited. For all their bitter experience of Soviet occupation, then, anti-Sovietism remains alien both to communists and to the general public in Czechoslovakia. All the more urgently do they feel it their duty to criticize the present Soviet leaders, whose policies are directed against the advancement of socialism in the world, offend the national feelings of other people, inspire distrust and hatred, and so offend the interests of the Soviets themselves.

Attempts by the Soviet leaders and their Czechoslovak accomplices to brand anyone who refuses to endorse their policy as 'anti-Soviet' are quite preposterous. To criticize the mistakes of today's leaders in the USSR is far from being anti-Soviet behaviour. On the contrary, it represents the duty of every true Marxist and can only help both communists and the general public in the Soviet Union.

*

Such are a few of the issues which stand out when one reads the records of the Fourteenth Congress and considers the whole train of events in Czechoslovakia. Clearly, a Congress held under such abnormal circumstances could not provide all the answers. Indeed, it added to the number of questions.

One cardinal question will obviously never be answered, even by historians of the future. *Could the occupation have been prevented?* Some hold that it could have been, if the Czechoslovak Communist Party had been more modest, cautious and submissive. Certain extreme reactions and needless acts of bravado might have been avoided. But it is clear from what we have already seen that forcible suppression of the Czechoslovak experiment was an inevitable consequence of the authoritarian political attitudes of the group in charge of the Soviet Union.

Was the occupation, then, inevitable? It appears to the present writer that the only way in which it could have been avoided was for the Czechoslovak Party leaders to have relied resolutely on the working masses and on the international solidarity of progressive forces; and to have stated unambiguously before the Soviet Party and the whole world that any attempt to strangle political developments in Czechoslovakia by armed intervention would be resisted with all possible means. If the Czechoslovak Party leaders had adopted such a clear attitude at the beginning of that series of conversations and minatory encounters that culminated at Čierná nad Tisou in the meeting with the Soviet *Politburo*, and had taken practical measures at the same time for the defence of the country, the Soviet Party leaders would in all probability never have dared to undertake military action.

It may be objected that any armed resistance would have been crushed by the Soviets' overwhelming superiority, at the cost of irreplaceable losses of life and property such as a small nation like Czechoslovakia cannot afford, and that her position was all the less tenable because of her thousands of miles of joint frontier with Warsaw Pact countries.

However, the history of nations – including the recent experience of

Czechoslovakia herself – teaches us the bitter lesson that those who abandon their right and duty to defend their independence and freedom on the pretext of saving life and property end up by paying a far higher price. The real outcome of all such compromises is national demoralization, the decay of both material and spiritual existence and, in the end, far greater expense of life and values than would have resulted from fighting – even from defeat. After losing a battle a nation can muster its strength again, for its dignity and morale are intact. A nation that surrenders without a fight cannot so easily recover.

The paradox of Czechoslovakia's capitulation in August 1968, as distinct from the Munich surrender of 1938, is that she was talked into it by the communists themselves with the slogan, 'Reality must be accepted'. They seemed to have forgotten that it was their Party that had always proclaimed the need to change reality rather than accept it. Here again the action of the Fourteenth Congress in denouncing the occupation is a moral asset which will in future redound to the honour of the Party, whereas those who call upon the public to reconcile itself 'realistically' to the occupation will be rightly condemned by history as traitors to the nation and as the source of all that suffering and humiliation which the Czechoslovak people must now endure under an alien heel.

It is probable to the point of certainty that *the Soviet leaders would have thought twice if they had known they would come up against real resistance. For the Soviets could not afford a new Vietnam in the middle of Europe.* To be sure, Czechoslovakia does not offer the same scope for prolonged partisan warfare as the jungles or mountains of Vietnam, Yugoslavia and Cuba. But the Czechs and Slovaks have in the course of history acquired skill in the use of other effective weapons: sabotage; the practice of ignoring or ridiculing the enemy; inventiveness and perseverance in resistance. And just as Czechoslovakia can never defeat the Soviet Union (and never tried to) so on the other hand the *Soviet Union can never acquire permanent control over our country, for its inhabitants will never abandon their right to freedom, independence and their own path to socialism.* Even today there is abundant evidence for these truths.

The leaders of the Czechoslovak Communist Party, then, despite their positive achievements, have a great deal to answer for to the two nations of Czechoslovakia. Having failed to show enough resolution to prevent the occupation, they should have put up at least a token

302

resistance when the invasion actually occurred. Subsequent events only confirmed what history had taught us after Munich, that surrender demoralizes even the best men in the country; even a short fight is better than none at all.

The foremost men in the Party, from Dubček down, proved themselves honourable and brave individuals but bad revolutionaries and bad politicians. For on the night of the attack they were content to issue a statement; they made no attempt to evade arrest or go underground among the Prague factories, whence they could have directed the struggle by the Party and the whole people against the occupation. This task was taken over instead by middle-rank officials and workers, hand-in-hand with the delegates to *the Fourteenth Congress, which saved the Party's good name by meeting under the noses of the invader's tanks, denouncing the occupation and declaring a struggle against it.* Only the future will show whether the Fourteenth Congress will prove a sufficient asset to enable the Party to recover from the rot that set in following the Moscow Protocols – and more especially after the April and May (1969) plenary sessions of its Central Committee – and to reassert its authority and its role.

The way of escape from the Party's crisis, and that of Czechoslovak society in general, can only be through a return to the conclusions and the spirit of the Fourteenth Congress. This, in effect, means refusing to submit to the occupation and to the dictates of the Soviet leaders; refusing obedience to the new 'leaders' of the Czechoslovak Communist Party who have betrayed the ideals of 'socialism with a human face' and submitted to the Soviet Party's hegemony; unwavering insistence on the departure of Soviet troops, the complete restoration of sovereignty to our socialist State and the disappearance from political office of those who stooped to collaboration. It means returning to the post-January political programme, after objectively analysing all mistakes and shortcomings and evaluating the lessons of 20 August and of what came after.

If Husák and his followers repeat that there is no alternative to capitulation and that the opposition has no positive programme to offer, one can only reply that *there most certainly is another way out of the crisis. And that is to continue along the lines of the Fourteenth Extraordinary Congress, to return to the Action Programme and fully implement its principles*: freedom of expression; abolition of censorship; execution of the economic reforms and establishment of industrial self-management; respect for the autonomy of the trade unions and other National Front organizations; equal rights for Czechs and Slovaks in a common State; acceptance of the new Party Statutes and extension of socialist democracy; strict adherence to the law, rehabilitation of all those wrongly sentenced (including people dismissed from their posts after 20 August) and, finally, development of an independent foreign policy. This would be a policy based on the socialist character of the Republic, consistent with our national interests and favouring co-operation with all socialist countries on the basis of equality, non-interference, respect for sovereignty and refusal to recognize any one 'leading State' or 'leading Party'.

Such are the principles which the story of the unfinished Fourteenth Congress must bring to mind, not only for communists in Czechoslovakia but all over the world. For the issue is not merely a domestic one; it concerns the whole international progressive movement. Just as the Second International failed in its moment of trial during the First World War because it subordinated international solidarity to the interests of power politics, so the whole future of socialism and world progress is jeopardized if the sovereignty and freedom of a small socialist country is allowed to be trodden underfoot by a stronger one, with more tanks, more rockets and more soldiers. To redeem the crime of 20 August 1968 is essential in the interest of Czechoslovak socialism and in the interest of socialism everywhere. And that includes the Soviet Union, whose revolutionary prestige was badly scarred by an act of aggression that only damaged her own cause. To redeem the crime is, moreover, the only way of preventing it from being persisted in, and repeated.

The record of the Extraordinary Fourteenth Congress, and of the inchoate Czechoslovak experiment in 'socialism with a human face', bids us attempt the task. Just as the experience of the Paris Commune was a topic of study and a source of inspiration throughout the half-century leading up to the October Revolution, so the Czechoslovak Spring of January to August 1968 will remain, for the international progressive moment, a treasury of instruction and bitter lessons, and a revolutionary spur for the next battle in the struggle to achieve true socialism.

Jiří Pelikán
7 November 1969